TABLE OF CONT...

2018 SUPPLEMENT TO

STATUTES, REGULATION, AND INTERPRETATION

LEGISLATION AND ADMINISTRATION IN THE REPUBLIC OF STATUTES

■ ■ ■

William N. Eskridge Jr.
John A. Garver Professor of Jurisprudence
Yale Law School

Abbe R. Gluck
Professor of Law
Yale Law School

Victoria F. Nourse
Professor of Law
Georgetown University Law School

AMERICAN CASEBOOK SERIES®

444 Cedar Street, Suite 700
St. Paul, MN 55101
1-877-888-1330

Printed in the United States of America

ISBN: 978-1-63460-642-4

TABLE OF CASES

The principal cases are in bold type.

2018 SUPPLEMENT TO

STATUTES, REGULATION, AND INTERPRETATION

LEGISLATION AND ADMINISTRATION IN THE REPUBLIC OF STATUTES

PART 1

INTRODUCTION TO CONGRESS, AGENCIES, AND COURTS

▪ ▪ ▪

CHAPTER 1

THE CONGRESS

■ ■ ■

Some courses will discuss **King v. Burwell**, the 2015 challenge to the Affordable Care Act, at the end of Chapter 1 as an introduction to basic statutory interpretation. Other courses may read *King* later, at the end of Chapter 6, as the most recent culmination of the Court's interpretive evolution over the course of the Roberts Court. For purposes of the topics covered in Chapter 1, *King* is most significant for what it tells us about the "new normal" in *congressional lawmaking.* Whatever one thinks of the *King* opinion, it is extremely significant both for the fact that the *King* court, for the first time in recent memory, at least tried to take into account the circumstances of a statute's legislative process in interpreting it but, at the same time, the Court failed to fully understand the modern legislative context in our highly charged, politically polarized environment. We explain some of the process in a note at the end of this chapter on the Legislative Process and the ACA, and offer more on these points in Chapter 6.

DAVID KING ET AL. V. SYLVIA BURWELL, SECRETARY OF HEALTH AND HUMAN SERVICES, ET AL.

United States Supreme Court, 2015.
___ U.S. ___, 135 S.Ct. 2480, 192 L.Ed.2d 483.

CHIEF JUSTICE ROBERTS delivered the opinion of the Court.

The Patient Protection and Affordable Care Act adopts a series of interlocking reforms designed to expand coverage in the individual health insurance market. First, the Act bars insurers from taking a person's health into account when deciding whether to sell health insurance or how much to charge. Second, the Act generally requires each person to maintain insurance coverage or make a payment to the Internal Revenue Service. And third, the Act gives tax credits to certain people to make insurance more affordable.

In addition to those reforms, the Act requires the creation of an "Exchange" in each State—basically, a marketplace that allows people to compare and purchase insurance plans. The Act gives each State the opportunity to establish its own Exchange, but provides that the Federal Government will establish the Exchange if the State does not.

This case is about whether the Act's interlocking reforms apply equally in each State no matter who establishes the State's Exchange. Specifically, the question presented is whether the Act's tax credits are available in States that have a Federal Exchange.

[I.A] The Patient Protection and Affordable Care Act, 124 Stat. 119, grew out of a long history of failed health insurance reform. [We have omitted several detailed pages of discussion about policy history and the Massachusetts model on which the ACA was based.] The Affordable Care Act adopts a version of the three key reforms that made the Massachusetts system successful: First, the Act adopts the guaranteed issue and community rating requirements [which requires insurers to accept all customers and charge them the essentially the same rates.] Second, the Act generally requires individuals to maintain health insurance coverage. * * * In Congress's view, that coverage requirement was "essential to creating effective health insurance markets." * * * Third, the Act seeks to make insurance more affordable by giving refundable tax credits to individuals with household incomes between 100 percent and 400 percent of the federal poverty line. * * *

These three reforms are closely intertwined. As noted, Congress found that the guaranteed issue and community rating requirements would not work without the coverage requirement. § 18091(2)(I). And the coverage requirement would not work without the tax credits. The reason is that, without the tax credits, the cost of buying insurance would exceed eight percent of income for a large number of individuals, which would exempt them from the coverage requirement. * * *

[I.C] In addition to those three reforms, the Act requires the creation of an "Exchange" in each State where people can shop for insurance, usually online. 42 U.S.C. § 18031(b)(1). An Exchange may be created in one of two ways. First, the Act provides that "[e]ach State shall . . . establish an American Health Benefit Exchange . . . for the State." *Ibid.* Second, if a State nonetheless chooses not to establish its own Exchange, the Act provides that the Secretary of Health and Human Services "shall . . . establish and operate such Exchange within the State." § 18041(c)(1). The issue in this case is whether the Act's tax credits are available in States that have a Federal Exchange rather than a State Exchange. The Act initially provides that tax credits "shall be allowed" for any "applicable taxpayer." 26 U.S.C. § 36B(a). The Act then provides that the amount of the tax credit depends in part on whether the taxpayer has enrolled in an insurance plan through "an Exchange *established by the State* under section 1311 of the Patient Protection and Affordable Care Act [hereinafter 42 U.S.C. § 18031]." 26 U.S.C. §§ 36B(b)–(c) (emphasis added).

The IRS addressed the availability of tax credits by promulgating a rule that made them available on both State and Federal Exchanges. 77

Fed. Reg. 30378 (2012). * * * At this point, 16 States and the District of Columbia have established their own Exchanges; the other 34States have elected to have HHS do so. * * *

[II] When analyzing an agency's interpretation of a statute, we often apply the two-step framework announced in *Chevron*, 467 U.S. 837. Under that framework, we ask whether the statute is ambiguous and, if so, whether the agency's interpretation is reasonable. *Id.*, at 842–843. This approach "is premised on the theory that a statute's ambiguity constitutes an implicit delegation from Congress to the agency to fill in the statutory gaps." *FDA v. Brown & Williamson Tobacco Corp.*, 529 U.S. 120, 159 (2000). "In extraordinary cases, however, there may be reason to hesitate before concluding that Congress has intended such an implicit delegation." *Ibid.*

This is one of those cases. The tax credits are among the Act's key reforms, involving billions of dollars in spending each year and affecting the price of health insurance for millions of people. Whether those credits are available on Federal Exchanges is thus a question of deep "economic and political significance" that is central to this statutory scheme; had Congress wished to assign that question to an agency, it surely would have done so expressly. *Utility Air Regulatory Group v. EPA*, 573 U.S. ___, ___ (2014) (slip op., at 19) (quoting *Brown & Williamson*, 529 U.S., at 160). It is especially unlikely that Congress would have delegated this decision to the *IRS*, which has no expertise in crafting health insurance policy of this sort. See *Gonzales v. Oregon*, 546 U.S. 243, 266–267 (2006). This is not a case for the IRS.

It is instead our task to determine the correct reading of Section 36B. If the statutory language is plain, we must enforce it according to its terms. *Hardt v. Reliance Standard Life Ins. Co.*, 560 U.S. 242, 251 (2010). But oftentimes the "meaning—or ambiguity—of certain words or phrases may only become evident when placed in context." *Brown & Williamson*, 529 U.S., at 132.

[II.A] We begin with the text of Section 36B. * * * Section 18031 provides that "[e]ach State shall . . . establish an American Health Benefit Exchange . . . for the State." § 18031(b)(1). Although phrased as a requirement, the Act gives the States "flexibility" by allowing them to "elect" whether they want to establish an Exchange. § 18041(b). If the State chooses not to do so, Section 18041 provides that the Secretary "shall . . . establish and operate *such Exchange* within the State." § 18041(c)(1) (emphasis added).

By using the phrase "such Exchange," Section 18041 instructs the Secretary to establish and operate the *same* Exchange that the State was directed to establish under Section 18031. See Black's Law Dictionary 1661

(10th ed. 2014) (defining "such" as "That or those; having just been mentioned").

* * * At the outset, it might seem that a Federal Exchange cannot fulfill this requirement. After all, the Act defines "State" to mean "each of the 50 States and the District of Columbia"—a definition that does not include the Federal Government. 42 U.S.C. § 18024(d). But when read in context, "with a view to [its] place in the overall statutory scheme," the meaning of the phrase "established by the State" is not so clear. *Brown & Williamson*, 529 U.S., at 133 (internal quotation marks omitted).

After telling each State to establish an Exchange, Section 18031 provides that all Exchanges "shall make available qualified health plans to qualified individuals." 42 U.S.C. § 18031(d)(2)(A). Section 18032 then defines the term "qualified individual" in part as an individual who "resides in the State that established the Exchange." § 18032(f)(1)(A). And that's a problem: If we give the phrase "the State that established the Exchange" its most natural meaning, there would be *no* "qualified individuals "on Federal Exchanges. But the Act clearly contemplates that there will be qualified individuals on *every* Exchange. * * * This problem arises repeatedly throughout the Act. See, *e.g.*, § 18031(b)(2)(allowing a State to create "one Exchange . . . for providing . . . services to both qualified individuals and qualified small employers," rather than creating separate Exchanges for those two groups).

These provisions suggest that the Act may not always use the phrase "established by the State" in its most natural sense. Thus, the meaning of that phrase may not be as clear as it appears when read out of context. The Act defines the term "Exchange" to mean "an American Health Benefit Exchange established under section 18031." § 300gg–91(d)(21). If we import that definition into Section 18041, the Act tells the Secretary to "establish and operate such 'American Health Benefit Exchange established under section 18031.' " That suggests that Section 18041 authorizes the Secretary to establish an Exchange under Section 18031, not (or not only) under Section 18041. Otherwise, the Federal Exchange, by definition, would not be an "Exchange" at all. See *Halbig*, 758 F. 3d, at 399–400 (acknowledging that the Secretary establishes Federal Exchanges under Section 18031).

This interpretation of "under [42 U.S.C. § 18031]" fits best with the statutory context. * * * If Federal Exchanges were not established under Section 18031, therefore, literally none of the Act's requirements would apply to them. Finally, the Act repeatedly uses the phrase "established under [42 U.S.C. § 18031]" in situations where it would make no sense to distinguish between State and Federal Exchanges. See, *e.g.*, 26 U.S.C. § 125(f)(3)(A) (2012 ed., Supp. I) ("The term 'qualified benefit' shall not include any qualified health plan . . . offered through an Exchange established under [42 U.S.C. § 18031]"). . . . 26 U.S.C. § 6055(b)(1)(B)(iii)(I) (2012 ed.) (requiring insurers to report whether each insurance plan they provided "is a qualified health plan offered through an Exchange" established by the State). * * *

The upshot of all this is that the phrase "an Exchange established by the State under [42 U.S.C. § 18031]" is properly viewed as ambiguous. * * * The conclusion that Section 36B is ambiguous is further supported by several provisions that assume tax credits will be available on both State and Federal Exchanges. For example, the Act requires all Exchanges to create outreach programs that must "distribute fair and impartial information concerning . . . the availability of premium tax credits under section 36B." § 18031(i)(3)(B). * * * And the Act requires all Exchanges to report to the Treasury Secretary information about each health plan they sell.

* * * Petitioners and the dissent respond that the words "established by the State" would be unnecessary if Congress meant to extend tax credits to both State and Federal Exchanges. Brief for Petitioners 20. But "our preference for avoiding surplusage constructions is not absolute." *Lamie v. United States Trustee*, 540 U.S. 526, 536 (2004); see also *Marx v. General Revenue Corp.*, 568 U.S. ___, ___ (2013) (slip op., at 13) ("The canon against surplusage is not an absolute rule"). And specifically with respect to this Act, rigorous application of the canon does not seem a particularly useful guide to a fair construction of the statute.

The Affordable Care Act contains more than a few examples of inartful drafting. (To cite just one, the Act creates three separate Section 1563s. See 124 Stat. 270, 911, 912.) Several features of the Act's passage contributed to that unfortunate reality. Congress wrote key parts of the Act behind closed doors, rather than through "the traditional legislative process." Cannan, A Legislative History of the Affordable Care Act: How Legislative Procedure Shapes Legislative History, 105 L. Lib. J. 131, 163 (2013). And Congress passed much of the Act using a complicated budgetary procedure known as "reconciliation," which limited opportunities for debate and amendment, and bypassed the Senate's normal 60-vote filibuster requirement. *Id.,* at 159–167. As a result, the Act does not reflect the type of care and deliberation that one might expect of such significant legislation. Cf. Frankfurter, Some Reflections on the Reading of Statutes, 47 Colum. L.Rev. 527, 545 (1947) (describing a cartoon "in which a senator tells his colleagues 'I admit this new bill is too complicated to understand. We'll just have to pass it to find out what it means.' ").

Anyway, we "must do our best, bearing in mind the fundamental canon of statutory construction that the words of a statute must be read in their context and with a view to their place in the overall statutory scheme." *Utility Air Regulatory Group*, 573 U.S., at ___ (slip op., at 15) (internal quotation marks omitted). After reading Section 36B along with other related provisions in the Act, we cannot conclude that the phrase "an Exchange established by the State under [Section 18031]" is unambiguous.

[II.B] Given that the text is ambiguous, we must turn to the broader structure of the Act to determine the meaning of Section 36B. "A provision that may seem ambiguous in isolation is often clarified by the remainder of the statutory scheme . . . because only one of the permissible meanings produces a substantive effect that is compatible with the rest of the law." * * * Here, the statutory scheme compels us to reject petitioners' interpretation because it would destabilize the individual insurance market in any State with a Federal Exchange, and likely create the very "death spirals" that Congress designed the Act to avoid. See *New York State Dept. of Social Servs. v. Dublino*, 413 U.S. 405, 419–420 (1973) ("We cannot interpret federal statutes to negate their own stated purposes.").[3] * * *

It is implausible that Congress meant the Act to operate in this manner. See *National Federation of Independent Business v. Sebelius*, 567 U.S. ___, ___ (2012) (Scalia, Kennedy, Thomas, and Alito, JJ., dissenting) (slip op., at 60) ("Without the federal subsidies . . . the exchange would not operate as Congress intended and may not operate at all."). Congress made the guaranteed issue and community rating requirements applicable in every State in the Nation. But those requirements only work when combined with the coverage requirement and the tax credits. So it stands to reason that Congress meant for those provisions to apply in every State as well.

* * * Section 18041 refutes the argument that Congress believed it was offering the States a deal they would not refuse—it expressly addressed what would happen if a State *did* refuse the deal.

[II.C] Finally, the structure of Section 36B itself suggests that tax credits are not limited to State Exchanges. Section 36B(a) initially provides that tax credits "shall be allowed" for any "applicable taxpayer." Section 36B(c)(1) then defines an "applicable taxpayer" as someone who (among other things) has a household income between 100 percent and 400 percent of the federal poverty line. Together, these two provisions appear to make anyone in the specified income range eligible to receive a tax credit. * * *

We have held that Congress "does not alter the fundamental details of a regulatory scheme in vague terms or ancillary provisions." *Whitman v. American Trucking Assns., Inc.*, 531 U.S. 457, 468 (2001). But in

---

[3] The dissent notes that several other provisions in the Act use the phrase "established by the State," and argues that our holding applies to each of those provisions. But "the presumption of consistent usage readily yields to context," and a statutory term may mean different things in different places. *Utility Air Regulatory Group v. EPA*, 573 U.S. ___, ___ (2014) (slip op., at 15) (internal quotation marks omitted). That is particularly true when, as here, "the Act is far from a *chef d'oeuvre* of legislative draftsmanship." *Ibid.*

petitioners' view, Congress made the viability of the entire Affordable Care Act turn on the ultimate ancillary provision: a sub-sub-sub section of the Tax Code. We doubt that is what Congress meant to do. Had Congress meant to limit tax credits to State Exchanges, it likely would have done so in the definition of "applicable taxpayer" or in some other prominent manner. It would not have used such a winding path of connect-the-dots provisions about the amount of the credit.

[II.D] Petitioners' arguments about the plain meaning of Section 36B are strong. But while the meaning of the phrase "an Exchange established by the State under [42 U.S.C. § 18031]" may seem plain "when viewed in isolation," such a reading turns out to be "untenable in light of [the statute] as a whole." *Department of Revenue of Ore. v. ACF Industries, Inc.*, 510 U.S. 332, 343 (1994). In this instance, the context and structure of the Act compel us to depart from what would otherwise be the most natural reading of the pertinent statutory phrase. * * *

In a democracy, the power to make the law rests with those chosen by the people. Our role is more confined—"to say what the law is." *Marbury v. Madison*, 1 Cranch 137, 177 (1803). That is easier in some cases than in others. But in every case we must respect the role of the Legislature, and take care not to undo what it has done. A fair reading of legislation demands a fair understanding of the legislative plan. Congress passed the Affordable Care Act to improve health insurance markets, not to destroy them. If at all possible, we must interpret the Act in a way that is consistent with the former, and avoids the latter. Section 36B can fairly be read consistent with what we see as Congress's plan, and that is the reading we adopt.

JUSTICE SCALIA, with whom JUSTICE THOMAS and JUSTICE ALITO join, dissenting.

* * * Words no longer have meaning if an Exchange that is *not* established by a State is "established by the State." It is hard to come up with a clearer way to limit tax credits to state Exchanges than to use the words "established by the State." And it is hard to come up with a reason to include the words "by the State" other than the purpose of limiting credits to state Exchanges. "[T]he plain, obvious, and rational meaning of a statute is always to be preferred to any curious, narrow, hidden sense that nothing but the exigency of a hard case and the ingenuity and study of an acute and powerful intellect would discover." *Lynch v. Alworth-Stephens Co.,* 267 U.S. 364, 370 (1925) (internal quotation marks omitted). Under all the usual rules of interpretation, in short, the Government should lose this case. But normal rules of interpretation seem always to yield to the overriding principle of the present Court: The Affordable Care Act must be saved.

* * * I wholeheartedly agree with the Court that sound interpretation requires paying attention to the whole law, not homing in on isolated words or even isolated sections. Context always matters. Let us not forget, however, *why* context matters: It is a tool for understanding the terms of the law, not an excuse for rewriting them.

* * * Reading the rest of the Act also confirms that, as relevant here, there are *only* two ways to set up an Exchange in a State: establishment by a State and establishment by the Secretary. §§ 18031(b), 18041(c). So saying that an Exchange established by the Federal Government is "established by the State" goes beyond giving words bizarre meanings; it leaves the limiting phrase "by the State" with no operative effect at all. That is a stark violation of the elementary principle that requires an interpreter "to give effect, if possible, to every clause and word of a statute." *Montclair v. Ramsdell*, 107 U.S. 147, 152 (1883). In weighing this argument, it is well to remember the difference between giving a term a meaning that duplicates another part of the law, and giving a term no meaning at all. Lawmakers sometimes repeat themselves—whether out of a desire to add emphasis, a sense of belt-and-suspenders caution, or a lawyerly penchant for doublets (aid and abet, cease and desist, null and void). Lawmakers do not, however, tend to use terms that "have no operation at all." *Marbury v. Madison*, 1 Cranch 137, 174 (1803). So while the rule against treating a term as a redundancy is far from categorical, the rule against treating it as a nullity is as close to absolute as interpretive principles get. The Court's reading does not merely give "by the State" a duplicative effect; it causes the phrase to have no effect whatever.

Making matters worse, the reader of the whole Act will come across a number of provisions beyond § 36B that refer to the establishment of Exchanges by States. Adopting the Court's interpretation means nullifying the term "by the State" not just once, but again and again throughout the Act. * * *

Equating establishment "by the State" with establishment by the Federal Government makes nonsense of other parts of the Act. The Act requires States to ensure (on pain of losing Medicaid funding) that any "Exchange established by the State" uses a "secure electronic inter face" to determine an individual's eligibility for various benefits (including tax credits). 42 U.S.C. § 1396w–3(b)(1)(D). How could a State control the type of electronic interface used by a federal Exchange? The Act allows a State to control contracting decisions made by "an Exchange established by the State." § 18031(f)(3). Why would a State get to control the contracting decisions of a federal Exchange? The Act also provides "Assistance to States to establish American Health Benefit Exchanges" and directs the Secretary to renew this funding "if the State . . . is making progress . . . toward . . . establishing an Exchange." § 18031(a). Does a State that refuses to set up an Exchange still receive this funding, on the premise that Exchanges established by the Federal Government are really established by States? It is presumably in order to avoid these questions that the Court concludes that federal Exchanges count as state Exchanges only "for purposes of the tax credits." *Ante,* at 13. (Contrivance, thy name is an opinion on the Affordable Care Act!)

It is probably piling on to add that the Congress that wrote the Affordable Care Act knew how to equate two different types of Exchanges when it wanted to do so. The Act includes a clause providing that "[a] *territory* that . . . establishes . . . an Exchange . . . shall be treated as a State" for certain purposes. § 18043(a) (emphasis added). Tellingly, it does not include a comparable clause providing that the *Secretary* shall be treated as a State for purposes of § 36B when *she* establishes an Exchange.

* * * The Court persists that these provisions "would make little sense" if no tax credits were available on federal Exchanges. Even if that observation were true, it would show only oddity, not ambiguity. Laws often include unusual or mismatched provisions. The Affordable Care Act spans 900 pages; it would be amazing if its provisions all lined up perfectly with each other. This Court "does not revise legislation . . . just because the text as written creates an apparent anomaly." *Michigan v. Bay Mills Indian Community*, 572 U.S. ___, ___ (2014) (slip op., at 10). At any rate, the provisions cited by the Court are not particularly unusual. Each requires an Exchange to perform a standardized series of tasks, some aspects of which relate in some way to tax credits. It is entirely natural for slight mismatches to occur when, as here, lawmakers draft "a single statutory provision" to cover "different kinds" of situations.

* * * Least convincing of all, however, is the Court's attempt to uncover support for its interpretation in "the structure of Section 36B itself." The Court finds it strange that Congress limited the tax credit to state Exchanges in the formula for calculating the *amount* of the credit, rather than in the provision defining the range of taxpayers *eligible* for the credit. Had the Court bothered to look at the rest of the Tax Code, it would have seen that the structure it finds strange is in fact quite common. Consider, for example, the many provisions that initially make taxpayers of all incomes eligible for a tax credit, only to provide later that the amount of the credit is zero if the taxpayer's income exceeds a specified threshold. See, *e.g.,* 26 U.S.C. § 24 (child tax credit); § 32 (earned-income tax credit); § 36 (first-time-homebuyer tax credit). * * * For what it is worth, lawmakers usually draft tax-credit provisions the way they do—*i.e.*, the way they drafted § 36B—because the mechanics of the credit require it. Many Americans move to new States in the middle of the year. Mentioning state Exchanges in the definition of "coverage month"—rather than (as the Court proposes) in the provisions concerning taxpayers' eligibility for the credit—accounts for taxpayers who live in a State with a state Exchange for a part of the year, but a State with a federal Exchange for the rest of the year.

[III] For its next defense of the indefensible, the Court turns to the Affordable Care Act's design and purposes. * * *

This reasoning suffers from no shortage of flaws. To begin with, "even the most formidable argument concerning the statute's purposes could not overcome the clarity [of] the statute's text." Statutory design and purpose matter only to the extent they help clarify an otherwise ambiguous provision. Could anyone maintain with a straight face that § 36B is unclear? To mention just the highlights, the Court's interpretation clashes with a statutory definition, renders words inoperative in at least seven separate provisions of the Act, overlooks the contrast between provisions that say "Exchange" and those that say "Exchange established by the State," gives the same phrase one meaning for purposes of tax credits but an entirely different meaning for other purposes, and (let us not forget) contradicts the ordinary meaning of the words Congress used. On the other side of the ledger, the Court has come up with nothing more than a general provision that turns out to be controlled by a specific one, a handful of clauses that are consistent with either understanding of establishment by the State, and a resemblance between the tax-credit provision and the rest of the Tax Code. If that is all it takes to make something ambiguous, everything is ambiguous. * * *

[IV] Perhaps sensing the dismal failure of its efforts to show that "established by the State" means "established by the State or the Federal Government," the Court tries to palm off the pertinent statutory phrase as "inartful drafting." This Court, however, has no free-floating power "to rescue Congress from its drafting errors." *Lamie v. United States Trustee*, 540 U.S. 526, 542 (2004). Only when it is patently obvious to a reasonable reader that a drafting mistake has occurred may a court correct the mistake. The occurrence of a misprint may be apparent from the face of the law, as it is where the Affordable Care Act "creates three separate Section 1563s." But the Court does not pretend that there is any such indication of a drafting error on the face of § 36B. The occurrence of a misprint may also be apparent because a provision decrees an absurd result—a consequence "so monstrous, that all mankind would, without hesitation, unite in rejecting the application." *Sturges*, 4 Wheat., at 203. But § 36B does not come remotely close to satisfying that demanding standard. It is entirely plausible that tax credits were restricted to state Exchanges deliberately—for example, in order to encourage States to establish their own Exchanges. We therefore have no authority to dismiss the terms of the law as a drafting fumble. Let us not forget that the term "Exchange established by the State" appears twice in § 36B and five more times in other parts of the Act that mention tax credits. What are the odds, do you think, that the same slip of the pen occurred in seven separate places? No provision of the Act—none at all—contradicts the limitation of tax credits to state Exchanges. And as I have already explained, uses the term "Exchange established by the

State" beyond the context of tax credits look anything but accidental. If there was a mistake here, context suggests it was a substantive mistake in designing this part of the law, not a technical mistake in transcribing it.

[V] The Court's decision reflects the philosophy that judges should endure whatever interpretive distortions it takes in order to correct a supposed flaw in the statutory machinery. That philosophy ignores the American people's decision to give *Congress* "[a]ll legislative Powers" enumerated in the Constitution. Art. I, § 1. * * * We lack the prerogative to repair laws that do not work out in practice, just as the people lack the ability to throw us out of office if they dislike the solutions we concoct. We must always remember, therefore, that "[o]ur task is to apply the text, not to improve upon it." * * *

Trying to make its judge-empowering approach seem respectful of congressional authority, the Court asserts that its decision merely ensures that the Affordable Care Act operates the way Congress "meant [it] to operate." First of all, what makes the Court so sure that Congress "meant" tax credits to be available everywhere? Our only evidence of what Congress meant comes from the terms of the law, and those terms show beyond all question that tax credits are available only on state Exchanges. More importantly, the Court forgets that ours is a government of laws and not of men. * * *

Even less defensible, if possible, is the Court's claim that its interpretive approach is justified because this Act "does not reflect the type of care and deliberation that one might expect of such significant legislation." It is not our place to judge the quality of the care and deliberation that went into this or any other law. A law enacted by voice vote with no deliberation whatever is fully as binding upon us as one enacted after years of study, months of committee hearings, and weeks of debate. Much less is it our place to make everything come out right when Congress does not do its job properly. It is up to Congress to design its laws with care, and it is up to the people to hold them to account if they fail to carry out that responsibility.

Rather than rewriting the law under the pretense of interpreting it, the Court should have left it to Congress to decide what to do about the Act's limitation of tax credits to state Exchanges. If Congress values above everything else the Act's applicability across the country, it could make tax credits available in every Exchange. * * * And if Congress thinks that the present design of the Act works well enough, it could do nothing.

* * * Perhaps the Patient Protection and Affordable Care Act will attain the enduring status of the Social Security Act or the Taft-Hartley Act; perhaps not. But this Court's two decisions on the Act will surely be remembered through the years. The somersaults of statutory interpretation they have performed ("penalty" means tax, "further

[Medicaid] payments to the State" means only incremental Medicaid payments to the State, "established by the State "means not established by the State) will be cited by litigants endlessly, to the confusion of honest jurisprudence. And the cases will publish forever the discouraging truth that the Supreme Court of the United States favors some laws over others, and is prepared to do whatever it takes to uphold and assist its favorites.

NOTES ON KING

1. *What Does* King *Tell Us About the Status of the Textualism vs. Purposivism Debate?* Much of this coursebook covers the interpretive battles that have raged over the past several decades between the Court's textualists, led by Justice Scalia, and the Court's purposivists, led by Justices Breyer and Stevens. Whether you read *King* in Chapter 1 or in Chapter 6, it should be evident that the Chief Justice seems to be trying to walk the line between the two camps, perhaps even charting a third way. What does he mean when he says "A fair reading of legislation demands a fair understanding of the legislative plan"? Why does he not use the word "purpose"? From where does the Chief Justice derive his understanding of the ACA's "plan" (*hint:* not from legislative history!). For those of you who have already read further into this book, you will also find *King* oddly free of most of the canons of statutory interpretation that make up the doctrines of the course. What to make of that?

One of us has suggested that *King* marks something of a middle way: a return to the Legal-Process-era sensibility (which not coincidentally had its heyday during the Chief's own years at Harvard Law). Congress tries to be rational and the Court is a competent partner able to understanding Congress's complex work. "Plans" are the work of rational people. "Plans" are meant to be understood by others. This is a 180-degree turn from textualism's view of Congress as impenetrable. But textualism and Justice Scalia's enormous influence on the Court's interpretive approach also is evident in *King*. The Chief Justice's opinion focuses exclusively on the ACA's enacted text (including its *enacted* statements of purpose) and structure. The difference is that, unlike some other Roberts Court statutory interpretation opinions, the *King* opinion takes a macro, not micro, view of the text. It is big-picture textualism and includes a functional understanding of how the different parts of a mega-statute work together. For more, see Abbe R. Gluck, *Imperfect Statutes, Imperfect Courts: Understanding Congress's Plan in the Era of Unorthodox Lawmaking*, 129 Harv. L. Rev. 62 (2015).

Is *King* a watershed moment? Might it mark a new direction in the Court's interpretive jurisprudence? It is too soon to tell. Some more recent cases also included in this Supplement—including *Yates* and *Lockhart*, both in Chapter 5—cast some doubt on this proposition.

2. *The Importance of the Whole Act: The Textual Argument for the Court's Result.* Query whether a textualist, uninterested in the notion of a "plan," could have resolved the case quite easily based on the whole text of the statute, in the government's favor. Political opponents of the health care law

relied on a single word in a 900-plus-page statute, isolating that word, and proclaiming that its meaning was plain, and plainly contrary to the Act's survival. The opponents' chosen word "state" appears in a tax provision providing the law's tax credits to health care exchanges "established by the State," when in fact many exchanges had been established by the federal government because states had failed to create such exchanges. The Court acknowledged the "strong" textualist claim of the law's opponents.

Opponents of the health care law were trying to persuade the Supreme Court that the health care tax credits only applied to state, not federal, exchanges, but their method creates that interpretation. *The isolation of the text,* its displacement from the rest of the statute, implicates exclusivity—that "only" states may create exchanges. Neo-Gricean linguistic theory supports this claim. When one says "some of the students did well," the implicature is that not "all" the students did well, the background unstated contrast set being "some" as eliminating the possibility of "all." In *King v. Burwell,* the unexpressed contrast set is "state versus federal." The phrase "established by the State," taken in isolation, rejects the federal exchange reading by implication from the choice of text. Implications are cheap, they are silent, inviting the interpreter to add meaning, to read "established by the State," as "established *only* by the State." On neo-Gricean theory, see John Mikhail, *The Constitution and the Philosophy of Language: Entailment, Implicature, and Implied Powers*, 101 Va. L. Rev. 1063 (2015).

This might be particularly unwise in complex statutes where one is trying to make sense of the *relationship between several provisions in a law.* In isolating a few words from the tax section ("established by the State"), the interpreter risks changing the meaning of the whole text, as we have seen above (to mean "*only* by the state"). Moreover, the very fact of isolation may defeat relationships created in other parts of the statute. The federal exchange provision directed that the federal exchange *substituted* for the state exchange "within the State" when the state failed to create its own exchange. By focusing on the tax provision's language, without regard to the exchange provisions, the "substitute relationship" text—that providing that the federal government may substitute for a state—is eliminated. See generally Victoria F. Nourse, *Misreading Law, Misreading Democracy*, ch. 4 (Harvard Press 2016).

3. *"Superstatute" Theory in* King. Chapter 9 introduces the concept of "superstatutes"—major legislative enactments that introduce new normative and institutional frameworks that fundamentally change whole fields of law. Eskridge and Ferejohn have argued that superstatutes deserve special interpretive treatment. See William N. Eskridge, Jr. and John Ferejohn, *Super-Statutes*, 50 Duke L. Rev. 1215 (2001). Look at the end of Justice Scalia's dissent in *King* in light of superstatute theory. Did the ACA get special treatment because the Court saw it as a superstatute? Should it have?

NOTES ON THE LEGISLATIVE PROCESS AND THE ACA

Here is the Supreme Court's account of how Congress drafted and passed the Affordable Care Act (punctuated by a cartoon!):

> The Affordable Care Act contains more than a few examples of inartful drafting. (To cite just one, the Act creates three separate Section 1563s. See 124 Stat. 270, 911, 912.) Several features of the Act's passage contributed to that unfortunate reality. Congress wrote key parts of the Act behind closed doors, rather than through "the traditional legislative process." Cannan, A Legislative History of the Affordable Care Act: How Legislative Procedure Shapes Legislative History, 105 L. Lib. J. 131, 163 (2013). And Congress passed much of the Act using a complicated budgetary procedure known as "reconciliation," which limited opportunities for debate and amendment, and bypassed the Senate's normal 60-vote filibuster requirement. Id., at 159–167. As a result, the Act does not reflect the type of care and deliberation that one might expect of such significant legislation. *Cf.* Frankfurter, Opinion of the Court Some Reflections on the Reading of Statutes, 47 Colum. L. Rev. 527, 545 (1947) (describing a cartoon "in which a senator tells his colleagues 'I admit this new bill is too complicated to understand. We'll just have to pass it to find out what it means.' ")

As noted, *King* is significant for being a rare modern instance in which the Court at least attempts to consider a statute's legislative-process realities in its interpretation but, even so, the Court's account has some important inaccuracies: (1) the Affordable Care Act (ACA) was not passed in the dark without debate—there were two years of debate; (2) the ACA did not bypass all filibuster or amendment—there were multiple filibusters, just not one for the reconciliation bill; and (3) it is not true that "much" of the bill was passed by reconciliation; the reconciliation bill, which was a separate bill, affected only a small minority of provisions, almost all of which were irrelevant to the question in *King*. Regardless, the opinion implies there was something illegitimate about the ACA's process, but every President since Reagan has used reconciliation for major tax cuts, health reform and similar matters; there is nothing new or sneaky about it.[1]

The Supreme Court's account in *King* begins to, but does not fully acknowledge, the modern congressional lawmaking context. The Court incorrectly implies that the ACA's process was uniquely unorthodox. One must throw away the *Schoolhouse Rock!* view of legislative procedure and replace it with the "new normal": Lengthy, omnibus bills are inevitable; committee avoidance for highly salient issues is the norm; filibusters are launched multiple times on a single bill; and, finally, as we see in *King*, questions about reconciliation and fast track rules muddy the waters. The Gluck-Bressman survey of congressional drafters, teeing off Barbara Sinclair's pioneering work

1 Megan Suzanne Lynch, Cong. Research Serv., R40480, *Budget Reconciliation Measures Enacted into Law: 1980–2010* (Sept. 2, 2010) (listing 20 major uses of reconciliation).

in this area, documents both the rise of these deviations from the "textbook process" and also the fact that such deviations are universally recognized as the new normal in Congress.[2] *See also* Gluck, O'Connell and Po, *Unorthodox Lawmaking, Unorthodox Rulemaking*, 115 Colum. L. Rev. 1789 (2015) (detailing the wide array of unorthodox procedures, their links across legislation and administrative law, and their implications for doctrine). This landscape of unorthodox lawmaking plays a part of the story of how the Affordable Care Act was passed.

1. *"Three Separate Section 1563s" or Sloppy Drafting*. In *King*, the Chief Justice begins by noting that the ACA's "inartful drafting" was reflected in "3 section 1563s." The fact that the bill might have had 3 section 1563s most likely has nothing to do with a failure of deliberation, but of drafting by Senate and House professional scriveners. Senators do not number the bill; the legislative counsels' offices dot the "i"s and cross the "t"s. They have no substantive authority to "inartfully" craft policy.[3] See Gluck, *Imperfect Statutes, Imperfect Courts*, 129 Harv. L. Rev. 62 (2015) (arguing that real issue in the case was not that the statute was not deliberated but that it was not properly cleaned up).

The new orthodoxy means that "normal" bills will be complex and, as complexity increases, so will errors. The new filibuster-normal means that bills will be longer. Getting sixty votes is likely to increase the chances for subject matter different from the main bill (germaneness only kicks in once cloture is voted). If the bill is headed toward cloture, those with unrelated bills are encouraged to add their own bills to avoid filibuster on their favored project, further lengthening the overall, now omnibus, bill. As political controversy increases, filibusters increase, warring parties may choose not to share the latest bill drafts with expert drafters, and this in turn increases the likelihood of scrivener's errors.[4]

2. *Multiple Filibusters*. The *King* opinion states that the ACA "bypassed" the traditional legislative process, including deliberation, filibuster and amendment. This is wrong. The bill went through at least five congressional committees and was filibustered several times and debated for hundreds of pages in the Congressional Record. The Hein company has published a legislative history in 9 volumes, each volume about 2 and a half inches thick.[5] Senators from both sides of the aisle agreed that there had been lengthy committee deliberations over two years. Indeed, after the Senate committees failed to reach agreement, a bipartisan Senate Gang of Six met for months to hammer out a solution, but they failed to reach consensus.[6] When

---

[2] Abbe R. Gluck & Lisa Schultz Bressman, Statutory Interpretation from the Inside: An Empirical Study of Congressional Drafting, Delegation and the Canons—Parts I and II, 65 & 66 Stan. Law Rev. 901 & 726 (2013 & 2014).

[3] Victoria F. Nourse & Jane S. Schacter, *The Politics of Legislative Drafting: A Congressional Case Study*, 77 N.Y.U. L. REV. 575, 588–89 (2002).

[4] *Id.*

[5] Health Care Reform: A Legislative History of the Patient Protection and Affordable Care Act, Public Law No. 111–148 (2010) (Bernard D. Reams & Michael P. Forrest eds, 2011).

[6] 155 Cong. Rec. 28,701 (statement of Sen. Snowe) (Nov. 20, 2009); *id.* at 28,811 (statement of Sen. Grassley) (Nov. 30, 2009); *id.* at 28,809 (statement of Sen. Baucus) (Nov. 30, 2009).

the bill was brought to the floor, there was a lengthy, intense and contentious—even dramatic—Senate debate.[7]

Using the method of reverse engineering,[8] we focus on the final, crucial, filibuster phase. The Senate dominates this discussion because, under the "new normal," the difficulty of reaching 60 votes in the Senate makes it the more powerful chamber. Large numerical majorities in the House can effectuate nothing if the Senate cannot reach 60 votes. And if obtaining 60 votes proves extremely difficult, the House is left with a *fait accompli*, whether to accept or reject the bill as written in the Senate where the 60th vote for cloture might not remain available to agree to possible House changes. Conferences have dried up because the Senate's procedures allow for the filibustering of the three motions necessary to convene a conference, disagreeing to any House amendment, agreeing to a request for conference, and the naming of conferees.

According to Professor Nourse's research, and review by the Senate Parliamentarian at the time, on November 19, 2009, the Senate Majority Leader made a motion to proceed to H.R. 3590, and facing unified minority opposition to the motion, filed a cloture motion on it. On November 21, cloture was invoked on that motion to proceed, and the bill was only then before the Senate for debate and amendment. At that time, the Majority Leader proposed the Senate leadership amendment to H.R. 3590, merging the bills from two Senate committees. Opponents objected to the motion to proceed.[9] By November 21, cloture had been invoked on the motion to proceed on that bill. The Majority Leader revealed that a letter had been circulated among opposition Senators instructing them in how "to bring the Senate to a screeching halt," including the forced reading of amendments, the manipulation of points of order, and how to stop a conference.[10] Over a period of two weeks, motions were made to recommit the bill to committee (a motion that kills the bill); opposing Senators demanded the reading of lengthy amendments, and filibustered a defense appropriations bill set to expire in days. The Majority Leader held the Senate in after midnight to vote on the defense bill, with the Minority Leader stating "We are, of course, prepared to talk around the clock."[11]

On Friday, December 19, the Senate adjourned until 6:45 am on Saturday morning to vote on the defense bill. That day, the Majority Leader introduced and posted on the internet the final "managers' amendment" to the health care bill. Almost every major bill has a managers' amendment (typically, managers'

[7] *See id.* at 32,906 (Dec. 21, 2009) (Senate meeting at midnight).

[8] Chapter 6 of this coursebook.

[9] 155 Cong. Rec. 28,350 (Nov. 19, 2009) (unanimous consent agreement governing debate on the motion to proceed).

[10] *Id.* at 29,295–96 (Dec. 3, 2009) (reprinting letter).

[11] *Id.* at 32, 617 (statement of Sen. McConnell) (Dec. 17, 2009); *see id.* at 31,974 (statement of Sen. Sanders on withdrawing his amendment because opponents were requiring that it be read) (Dec. 16, 2009); *id.* at 31,979 (vote on motion to commit); *id.* at 32,661–32,664 (debate about the defense bill) (Dec. 16, 2009); *id.* at 32,664 (Dec. 16, 2009) (cloture vote on defense bill).

agreements involve technical corrections to the bill). When the managers' amendment was brought up, the Minority Leader objected to a motion to dispense with the reading of the amendment. The clerks began to read each line of the managers' amendment, and did so for 7 to 8 hours.[12] That day, the Majority Leader then sent three cloture motions to the desk, one for the managers' amendment to the Reid substitute, one for the Reid substitute, and one for the amended bill, H.R. 3590. The cloture process, however, takes time: upon a single objection from a single Senator, hours and hours of Senate time may be required. On Sunday, December 20, debate continued until 11:30 pm. On Monday, the Senate reconvened at 12:01 am in the middle of a snowstorm. Cloture was invoked on the managers' amendment. But the bill would take four more days to pass, several votes, and another cloture motion, as Senators made points of order under the Senate Rules, the Budget Act, and the Constitution, each requiring a vote.[13]

On December 23, the Majority Leader filed a cloture motion on H.R. 3590 to defeat a filibuster on the underlying bill, H.R. 3590. At 6:45 am the next morning, the Senate reconvened on Christmas Eve, December 24, 2009, with the Vice President of the United States in the chair as presiding officer, for the final vote in favor of the ACA, H.R. 3590, the bill now known as the Patient Protection and Affordable Care Act.[14] On March 21, the House concurred in the Senate's amendment to H.R. 3590, thereby passing that bill, and it was enacted into law when the President signed it on March 23, 2010, becoming Public Law 111–148. The Reconciliation bill, as discussed below, was passed one week later.

3. *"Behind Closed Doors" and Leadership Drafting*. The *King* Court's version of the ACA debate states that the bill was drafted "behind closed doors," in some uniquely secret way. As we have seen, the implication of this claim—that there was no debate on the bill—is untrue. It is true that the bill's opponents repeated the "closed door" claim over and over again.[15] From November 17 until December 24, Senators used this phrase over one hundred times.[16]

---

[12] *Id.* at 32,739 (Dec. 19, 2009) (statement of Sen. McConnell) ("I know it has been a challenging experience to have to read for the last 7 or 8 hours.").

[13] *Id.* at 32,905 (Senate recesses at 11:30 pm) (Dec. 20, 2009); *id.* at 32,906 (Senate called to session at 12:01 am) (Dec. 21, 2009); *id.* at 32,912 (cloture vote) (Dec. 21, 2009); *id.* at 32,906 (snowstorm) (statement of Sen. Alexander) (Dec. 21, 2009); *id.* at 33,077 (point of order under the Budget Act) (Dec. 23, 2009); *id.* at 33, 084 (point of order under the Senate rules) (Dec. 23, 2009); *id.* at 33,100 (point of order based on constitutional liberty) (Dec. 23, 2009); *id.* at 33,105 (point of order under the Tenth Amendment) (Dec. 23, 2009); *id.* at 33,109 (cloture vote) (Dec. 23, 2009).

[14] *Id.* at 33,109 (cloture vote) (Dec. 23, 2009); *id.* at 33,168 (6:45 am start of day; Vice President presiding) (Dec. 24, 2009); id. at 33,169–70 (final vote) (Dec. 24, 2009).

[15] *See, e.g.*, *id.* at 28,286 (Sen. McConnell, twice); *id.* at 28,291–92 (Sen. Barrasso, twice); *id.* at 28,305 (Sen. Hutchison); *id.* at 28,345–46 (Sen. Grassley, three times); *id.* at 28,357 (Sen. Thune); *id.* at 28,602 (Sen. Hatch, twice) (all Nov. 19, 2009).

[16] This research is based on a search for the specific phrase "closed doors" in each of the four parts of Volume 155 of the Congressional Record in the Hein on Line database, parts 21 through 24, covering the debate from Nov. 17, 2009 until Dec. 24, 2009. One must search each of the 4 parts under the "full volume" tab, then open the page results to find the number of times the word is actually used. As noted above, in some cases, a single Senator used these particular words more

What were these Senators talking about? They were talking about the "new normal"—leadership drafting. There is no secret about how this works, because similar practices have occurred in Congress for the past five decades. When consensus fails on a particularly controversial matter, the Majority Leader and the committee chairs sit down and work to create a bill that will garner 60 votes. They work from bills that have passed and bills that have emerged from committee. This leadership group cannot create an entirely new bill out of whole cloth. Why? Any resulting bill will lose the votes of those who had worked on the bill (in this case some for months and years) and so, as a practical matter, would not yield 60 votes. Precedent, both substantive and procedural, is important in the Senate: after staking out a claim on a particular issue, Senators will be unlikely to change their votes.

This process is no secret to the members of the Senate and has been no secret since the passage of the Civil Rights Act of 1964. Bypassing committee consideration is often a mark of too much, not too little, debate. The ACA did not bypass committee in any event; its text comes from the merged drafts of the work of two Senate committees, Finance and Health, Education, Labor and Pensions (HELP). But there are many examples of legislation that bypassed committee procedure because it was too difficult to reach consensus within the committee process. Take the federal death penalty or the Brady gun-check bill—neither of these bills were drafted in committee. Why? Such controversial measures would have died in committee, not by virtue of the Chairman's ire, but because of endless committee debate.

4. *The Role of Reconciliation.* Finally, let us move to the crux of the argument that Congress did something sneaky or unconventional in passing the law through reconciliation. As a technical matter, this claim confuses two different laws. The ACA itself, Public Law 111–148, became law on March 23, 2010. Although the Supreme Court says "much" of the law was passed by reconciliation, in fact, Public Law 111–148 was not passed by reconciliation. Seven days later, the President signed a different, much smaller law, running about 55 pages of bill text (44 pages of which dealt with health care[17]), the Health Care and Education *Reconciliation* Act, Public Law 111–152. As its title reveals, it was that law, not the ACA, that was enacted using the *reconciliation* process under the Budget Act of 1974, procedures permitting passage by a simple majority vote in the Senate. It may well be that House members viewed the Reconciliation bill as central to their support for the ACA, because it amended the ACA in discrete places, but they had to trust that the Senate would pass the same bill.

At the outset, lest anyone think that there was something odd about using reconciliation in considering the second law, one must note this simple fact: almost *every major tax or health or budget bill with substantial budgetary effects that has passed the Senate, over the past thirty-four years, has gone*

---

than once in a speech. The total number of instances was over 140 based on a count performed on June 23, 2016. If one adds "closed door," the singular, the number increases.

[17] As reprinted in the Congressional Record, the text of the Reconciliation bill in its entirety was 156 Cong. Rec. 4445–4460, or 15 pages.

through reconciliation. Reconciliation is the process authorized by section 310 of the Budget Act. That law requires that Congress, by concurrent resolution, direct certain committees to report revenue and/or spending legislation to help achieve budgetary levels set out in that concurrent resolution. When it passes legislation, these budget targets must be "reconciled."[18]

Republican and Democratic congressional majorities alike have used the reconciliation process to help Presidents of their respective parties achieve their policy objectives. President Reagan was the first President to reap the benefits of the procedure, as it was used seven times during his time in office to pursue, among other things, deficit reduction and tax reform. Presidents Carter, George H.W. Bush, and Clinton all benefited from the use of reconciliation. President George W. Bush signed 4 reconciliation bills, including one enacting a ten year tax cut agenda. Indeed, where budget matters are concerned, it may well be that without reconciliation the government could not operate, given the kind of filibuster possibilities available in the Senate.[19]

More importantly, nothing in *King v. Burwell* depended upon the reconciliation law. The reconciliation measure did not change the central language at issue in *King v. Burwell*. Those provisions had been in the bill at least since November 19, 2009—requiring state exchanges and providing for a federal exchange in the event that the states did not create an exchange—and were in the ACA the President signed on March 23, 2010, Public Law 111–148. The Reconciliation bill, Public Law 111–152, signed by the President on March 30, 2010 did not affect that language. Nor did it change the language providing the taxpayer subsidy, only the formula for eligibility. In other words, even if the much smaller reconciliation bill had significantly changed the 906 page ACA,[20] reconciliation was irrelevant to the issue in *King*. That language was law in Public Law 111–148 days before the Senate passed the reconciliation bill.[21] (In fact, the only provision of the reconciliation bill that had any relevance to *King* at all was a provision requiring federal exchanges to report the tax subsidies they distributed to the government—a provision that clearly operated in the Government's favor because it made clear that the expectation was that the federal exchanges would indeed have subsidies, as the Court noted.)

---

[18] Lynch, *supra* note 1.

[19] *Id.* at 5–12.

[20] Throughout the health care debate, there were questions about the actual length of the bill. The Public Law 111–148 is 906 pages. As printed in the Congressional Record, when passed by the House, the ACA was 242 pages (smaller type). See 156 Cong. Rec. 4202 to 4444 (Mar. 21, 2010). Bill text uses bigger font and fewer lines per page; hence the fact that the *bill* as opposed to the *law* was over 2000 pages. The bill corresponding to Public Law 111–148 is about 2,400 pages on Congress.gov if one looks for H.R.3590 in the 111th Congress.

[21] Compare ACA, Public Law No. 111–148 sec. 1311(b), 1321(c), 124 Stat. 119, 173, 186 (2010), codified at 42 U.S.C. sec. 18031(b)(1), 18041(c)(1) with 155 Cong. Rec. 28,397 (sec. 1311(b)(1) ("Each State shall, . . . establish an American Health Benefit Exchange . . . "); *id.* at 28,400 (sec. 1321(c)(1)("Failure to Establish Exchange . . . (1) . . . the Secretary shall . . . establish and operate such Exchange within the State . . . ") (Nov. 19, 2009).

Of course, it would be disingenuous to believe that there was no reason for linking ACA passage to the later Reconciliation bill. House members wanted to amend the Senate amendment to the underlying bill, H.R. 3590. In the Rules committee, which sets the House agenda for floor debate, opponents sought mightily to offer amendments.[22] If the House wanted to amend the Senate amendment substantively, it would face an inevitable flurry of Senate filibusters to a conference, either against a Senate motion to agree to the house amendments, or on the three separate motions necessary to go to a conference. Then-Minority Leader McConnell was clear on the last day of Senate debate on December 24, 2009: he vowed to "stop this bill from becoming law."[23] Soon, the Democrats, who had exactly 60 votes for the ACA, would no longer have the votes to break a filibuster at that point: Senator Ted Kennedy died in November 2009 and was replaced two months later with Republican Scott Brown. Thus, the House was going to have to pass the Senate bill or there would be no ACA. The only way around that, for budgetary matters, was to introduce and pass a House reconciliation bill containing only provisions having a budgetary effect, and that bill would have to pass the Senate. Reconciliation was already authorized by the budget resolution, but to reassure members, the House leadership linked the votes in a single Rule.[24] First the House would have to pass the ACA, then if the ACA was passed, the House would vote on a much smaller reconciliation measure which made various fiscal amendments. That reconciliation bill would then have to go to the Senate. The House leadership had to convince its members to trust that the Senate would pass that reconciliation bill without significant amendment.[25]

This explains why Public Law 111–148 was signed into law on March 23, and the Reconciliation law, Public Law 111–152, was signed into law by the President seven days later. There was no guarantee, as leaders of the House explained, that the House would in fact pass the ACA, or if it did, that the Reconciliation bill would pass and then survive the Senate. In that sense, although the agenda was set, and some members may have voted in the hope that both would pass, there was no logical necessity that reconciliation was necessary to pass the ACA.[26] The ACA had already been signed into law when the Reconciliation bill passed the Senate.

Some have speculated that the use of reconciliation was motivated solely by the loss of a 60th Democratic vote in the Senate. The story may be more complex. There is some evidence that the leadership of the House and Senate agreed that there would be no conference regardless given the difficulties of passage, and the ease of blocking a conference committee. Like the Civil Rights Act of 1964, the House appeared to be faced with a *fait accompli*. Hopes for any

---

[22] See H.R. Rep. 111–448 at 2–21 (Mar. 21, 2010) (showing results of 64 committee votes).

[23] 155 Cong. Rec. 33,168 (Dec. 24, 2009).

[24] H. Con. Res. 1203 (Mar. 20, 2010).

[25] See 156 Cong. Rec. 4105 (statement of Rep. Issa) (Mar. 21, 2010).

[26] 156 Cong. Rec. 4105 (statement of Rep. Dreier) ("We have heard all about this reconciliation package. . . . But is it not true that this rule guarantees that the only thing that will be law is the Senate bill. . . ?") (Mar. 21, 2010).

kind of an unofficial conference or compromise House-Senate bill were scotched when Scott Brown took office in January 2010, with the Senate Democrats losing their 60th vote. At that point, the only option for House input was to focus on budget-related changes using reconciliation.

3. RETHINKING CONGRESS'S RULES

Pages 125–126: Delete the final paragraph on page 125 and the first paragraph on page 126.

CHAPTER 2

THE PRESIDENT AND AGENCIES

■ ■ ■

1. THE STRUCTURE OF THE EXECUTIVE BRANCH

Page 149: Insert the following new Problem and Case at the bottom of the page:

PROBLEM 2–0: IS THE STRUCTURE OF THE CONSUMER FINANCIAL PROTECTION BUREAU UNCONSTITUTIONAL?

The 2008 financial crisis destabilized the economy and left millions of Americans economically devastated. After hearings, Congress concluded that the financial services industry had pushed consumers into unsustainable forms of debt and that federal regulators had failed to prevent mounting risks to the economy, in part because those regulators were overly responsive to the industry they purported to police. Congress saw a need for an agency to help restore public confidence in markets: a regulator attentive to individuals and families. In the Dodd-Frank Wall Street Reform and Consumer Protection Act of 2010, P.L. 111–203, Congress established the Consumer Financial Protection Bureau (CFPB).

The CFPB is a financial regulator that applies a set of preexisting statutes to financial services marketed "primarily for personal, family, or household purposes." 12 U.S.C. § 5481(5)(A); *see also id.* §§ 5481(4), (6), (15). Congress has historically given a modicum of independence to financial regulators like the Federal Reserve, the FTC, and the Office of the Comptroller of the Currency. Rather than a multi-member commission, the CFPB's chief decision-maker is its Director, who is appointed by the President for a five-year term. The Director in 2017 would have seen his term expire in 2018; the next expiration date would be 2023, and so forth. The Director may be fired only for "inefficiency, neglect of duty, or malfeasance in office," 12 U.S.C. § 5491(c)(3)—the same language the Supreme Court approved for the independent commission in *Humphrey's*.

The Director has a considerable amount of authority. He or she sets the agency's general agenda; determines what proposed rules ought to be advanced for public comment; decides whether to issue a final rule, after notice and comment; manages the agency's budget; and accepts or rejects adjudicatory decisions rendered by administrative law judges (ALJs), who conduct the formal hearings and draft proposed orders and decisions.

You represent a company that has been sanctioned by the CFPB, based upon an agency adjudication presided over by an ALJ appointed by the Director and applying consumer-protective rules promulgated by the Director. Your main argument is that the order is inconsistent with the regulatory statute, but you are also considering an argument is that the decision-making structure of the agency violates the Constitution's separation of powers and/or Article II. Jot down the points you would make and the precedent(s) you would invoke. Would such arguments succeed in federal court? Why or why not? After you have jotted down your thoughts, read the following debate within the D.C. Circuit and a subsequent Supreme Court decision.

PHH Corp. v. Consumer Financial Protection Bureau

881 F.3d 75 (D.C. Cir. en banc, Jan. 31, 2018).

Sitting en banc, ten judges of the D.C. Circuit considered the constitutional issue posed by Problem 2–0. Speaking for a majority of six judges, **Judge Pillard** authored the opinion for the Court. The Court of Appeals was bound by *Humphrey's Executor*, and Judge Pillard found the CFPB constitutionally indistinguishable from the FTC, whose "for cause" removal provision was upheld in that case. The challengers claimed that decision-making by a single Director made the CFPB constitutionally vulnerable, but Judge Pillard found that agency structure "neither unprecedented nor constitutionally significant."

As historical precedents for "sole-headed financial regulators," Judge Pillard cited "the Comptroller of the Treasury, dating back to [1789]; and the Office of the Comptroller of the Currency, established in [1863]. Other examples of single-headed independent agencies include the Social Security Administration, which was placed under a single director in 1994, and the Office of Special Counsel established under a sole director in 1978, the same year as the Office of Independent Counsel upheld in *Morrison*. Congress established the sole-headed, for-cause-protected Federal Housing Finance Agency in 2008, in response to similar concerns as gave rise to the CFPB. This longstanding tradition provides historical pedigree to the CFPB, and refutes the contention that the CFPB's single director structure is anything new."

Judge Pillard distinguished cases like *Myers* on the ground that "the functions of the CFPB and its Director are not core executive functions, such as those entrusted to a Secretary of State or other Cabinet officer who we assume must directly answer to the President's will. Rather, the CFPB is one of a number of federal financial regulators—including the Federal Trade Commission, the Federal Reserve, the Federal Deposit Insurance Corporation, and others—that have long been permissibly afforded a degree of independence. The CFPB matches what the Supreme Court's removal-power cases have consistently approved. Accepting PHH's claim to the contrary would put the historically established independence of financial regulators and numerous other independent agencies at risk."

In short, Judge Pillard found "nothing constitutionally suspect about the CFPB's leadership structure. *Morrison* and *Humphrey's Executor* stand in the way of any holding to the contrary. And there is no reason to assume an agency headed by an individual will be less responsive to presidential supervision than one headed by a group. It is surely more difficult to fire and replace several people than one. And, if anything, the Bureau's consolidation of regulatory authority that had been shared among many separate independent agencies allows the President more efficiently to oversee the faithful execution of consumer protection laws. Decisional responsibility is clear now that there is one, publicly identifiable face of the CFPB who stands to account—to the President, the Congress, and the people—for all its consumer protection actions. The fact that the Director stands alone atop the agency means he cannot avoid scrutiny through finger-pointing, buck-passing, or sheer anonymity. What is more, in choosing a replacement, the President is unhampered by partisan balance or *ex-officio* requirements; the successor replaces the agency's leadership wholesale. Nothing about the CFPB stands out to give us pause that it—distinct from other financial regulators or independent agencies more generally—is constitutionally defective."

Judge Pillard also found unpersuasive PHH's reliance on the CFPB's independence from the ordinary budget process: the agency can claim funds from the Federal Reserve. There is nothing new about a federal agency reliant on fees, assessments, or investments, rather than congressional appropriations. To protect against interest group pressure, "Congress has consistently exempted financial regulators from appropriations: The Federal Reserve, the Federal Deposit Insurance Corporation, the Office of the Comptroller of the Currency, the National Credit Union Administration, and the Federal Housing Finance Agency all have complete, uncapped budgetary autonomy." Moreover, the CFPB's independent funding source has no constitutionally salient effect on the President's power. The Supreme Court has recently dismissed issues including "who controls the agency's budget requests and funding" as "bureaucratic minutiae"—questions of institutional design outside the ambit of the separation-of-powers inquiry. *Free Enterprise Fund*.

Writing also for Judge Rogers, **Judge Wilkins** wrote a concurring opinion, adding that "removal restrictions of officers performing adjudicatory functions intrude far less on the separation of powers than removal restrictions of officers who perform purely executive functions." Even as to its rulemaking authority, the CFPB was not the regulatory gorilla that PHH made it out to be. For one thing, Dodd-Frank imposed dozens of requirements that the CFPB coordinate its rulemaking and enforcement with other agencies. See generally Jody Freeman & Jim Rossi,

Agency Coordination in Shared Regulatory Space, 125 Harv. L. Rev. 1131 (2012). The Director's failure to abide by these many coordination requirements would, Judge Wilkins opined, surely constitute "neglect of duty" that would justify dismissal under the "for cause" provision.

Finally, "Congress created a new entity, the * * * Financial Stability Oversight Council, with veto power over any rule promulgated by the Director that the Council believes will "put the safety and soundness of the United States banking system or the stability of the financial system of the United States at risk." 12 U.S.C. § 5513. Any member of the Council can file a petition to stay or revoke a rule, which can be granted with a two-thirds majority vote. Thus, if the Director's decisionmaking goes awry on a critical rulemaking, a multi-member body of experts can step in. Significantly, a supermajority of persons on the Council are designated by the President."

Judge Griffith concurred in the judgment of the en banc Court. He opined that *Humphrey's* and *Morrison* are inconsistent with the text and original meaning of Article II, but that only the Supreme Court can overrule those precedents. In any event, he asked an antecedent question: "How difficult is it for the President to remove the Director? The President may remove the CFPB Director for 'inefficiency, neglect of duty, or malfeasance in office.' After reviewing these removal grounds, I conclude they provide only a minimal restriction on the President's removal power, even permitting him to remove the Director for ineffective policy choices. Therefore, I agree that the CFPB's structure does not impermissibly interfere with the President's ability to perform his constitutional duties."

Surveying dictionaries from the nineteenth century, Judge Griffith found that "inefficiency" can mean "ineffective or failing to produce some desired result." For example, one prominent turn-of-the-century dictionary defined "efficient" as "[a]cting or able to act with due effect; adequate in performance; bringing to bear the requisite knowledge, skill, and industry; capable; competent." 3 *The Century Dictionary and Cyclopedia*, 1849. The same dictionary also defined "inefficient" to mean "[n]ot efficient; not producing or not capable of producing the desired effect; incapable; incompetent; inadequate." 5 *id.* at 3072. If the President's removal authority can be exercised by a finding that the CFPB Director has not been producing the policy desired by the President and his supporters, then the constitutional conflict between the statute and Article II loses most if not all of its edge.

Writing also for Judge Randolph, **Judge Kavanaugh** wrote the principal dissenting opinion, based on the extensive opinion he had written for the earlier panel, 831 F.3d 1 (D.C. Cir. 2016): "This is a case about executive power and individual liberty," he opened, with a bang.

"To prevent tyranny and protect individual liberty, the Framers of the Constitution separated the legislative, executive, and judicial powers of the new national government. To further safeguard liberty, the Framers insisted upon accountability for the exercise of executive power. The Framers lodged full responsibility for the executive power in a President of the United States, who is elected by and accountable to the people. The first 15 words of Article II speak with unmistakable clarity about who controls the executive power: 'The executive Power shall be vested in a President of the United States of America.' U.S. Const. art. II, § 1. And Article II assigns the President alone the authority and responsibility to 'take Care that the Laws be faithfully executed.' *Id.* § 3. The purpose 'of the separation and equilibration of powers in general, and of the unitary Executive in particular, was not merely to assure effective government but to preserve individual freedom.' *Morrison v. Olson* (Scalia, J., dissenting).

"Of course, the President executes the laws with the assistance of subordinate executive officers who are appointed by the President, often with the advice and consent of the Senate. To carry out the executive power and be accountable for the exercise of that power, the President must be able to supervise and direct those subordinate officers. In its landmark decision in *Myers v. United States*, authored by Chief Justice and former President Taft, the Supreme Court recognized the President's Article II authority to supervise, direct, and remove at will subordinate officers in the Executive Branch.

"In 1935, however, the Supreme Court carved out an exception to *Myers* and Article II by permitting Congress to create *independent* agencies that exercise executive power. *See Humphrey's Executor*. An agency is 'independent' when the agency's commissioners or board members are removable by the President only for cause, not at will, and therefore are not supervised or directed by the President. Examples of independent agencies include well-known bodies such as the Federal Trade Commission, the Federal Communications Commission, the Securities and Exchange Commission, the National Labor Relations Board, and the Federal Energy Regulatory Commission. * * *

"The independent agencies collectively constitute, in effect, a headless fourth branch of the U.S. Government. They hold enormous power over the economic and social life of the United States. Because of their massive power and the absence of Presidential supervision and direction, independent agencies pose a significant threat to individual liberty and to the constitutional system of separation of powers and checks and balances.

"To mitigate the risk to individual liberty, the independent agencies historically have been headed by *multiple* commissioners or board members. In the Supreme Court's words, each independent agency has traditionally been established as a 'body of experts appointed by law and informed by experience.' *Humphrey's Executor*. Multi-member independent agencies do not concentrate all power in one unaccountable individual, but instead divide and disperse power across multiple commissioners or board members. The multi-member structure thereby reduces the risk of arbitrary decisionmaking and abuse of power, and helps protect individual liberty.

"In other words, the heads of *executive* agencies are accountable to and checked by the President; and the heads of *independent* agencies, although not accountable to or checked by the President, are at least accountable to and checked by their fellow commissioners or board members. No independent agency exercising substantial executive authority has ever been headed by *a single person*."

Judge Kavanaugh would draw the constitutional line in this case: "Because the CFPB is an independent agency headed by a single Director and not by a multi-member commission, the Director of the CFPB possesses more unilateral authority—that is, authority to take action on one's own, subject to no check—than any single commissioner or board member in any other independent agency in the U.S. Government. Indeed, other than the President, the Director enjoys more unilateral authority than any other official in any of the three branches of the U.S. Government." Because this structure is, according to Judge Kavanaugh, unprecedented, a direct threat to liberty, and inconsistent with Article II's baseline of agency accountability to the elected President, he would invalidate it.

"In traditional multi-member agencies, the President may designate the chair of the agency, and the President may remove a chair at will from the chair position. (Of course, the President may not remove that official from the commission or board altogether, only from the position as chair.) By contrast, the CFPB has only one Director, and the President may not designate a new Director until the former Director leaves office or the Director's term expires. That structure diminishes the President's power to influence the direction of the CFPB, as compared to the President's power to influence the direction of traditional multi-member independent agencies." Indeed, Judge Kavanaugh argued, the CFPB involves a greater invasion of presidential power than the structure invalidated in *Free Enterprise Fund*.

"[A]s the Supreme Court indicated in *Free Enterprise Fund*, an independent agency's structure violates Article II when it is not historically rooted and when it causes an *additional* diminution of Presidential control beyond that caused by a traditional independent agency. * * * The CFPB's single-Director structure contravenes that diminution principle. As a result of the CFPB's novel single-Director structure and the five-year fixed term for the Director, a President may be stuck for years—or even for his or her entire four-year term—with a single Director who was appointed by a prior President and who has different policy views.

"Nothing comparable happens in traditional multi-member independent agencies. Rather, the traditional multi-member structure ordinarily allows the current President to exercise some influence over the agency through Presidential appointment. That is because the President may designate agency chairs and may remove agency chairs at will from their positions as chairs." See Kirti Datla & Richard Revesz, *Deconstructing Independent Agencies (and Executive Agencies)*, 98 Cornell L. Rev. 769, 818 (2013); Rachel Barkow, *Insulating Agencies: Avoiding Capture Through Institutional Design*, 89 Tex. L. Rev. 15, 39 (2010). Both Presidents Obama and Trump replaced chairs of major multi-member agencies within a week of taking office in 2009 and 2017, respectively.

Disagreeing with Judge Griffith, Judge Kavanaugh did not believe that the statutory "for cause" standard for removal gave the President sufficient control over the CFPB. As the Supreme Court ruled in *Free Enterprise, Humphrey's Executor* refuted the idea that "simple disagreement" with an agency head's "policies or priorities could constitute 'good cause' for its removal." The Court expressly confirmed that *Humphrey's Executor* "rejected a removal premised on a lack of agreement on either the policies or the administering of the Federal Trade Commission."

Judge Kavanaugh reasoned that the Supreme Court's precedents did not authorize the CFPB structure, which is materially different than the structures allowed in *Humphrey's* and *Morrison v. Olson*. The multi-member FTC, with party balance required, is more deliberative than the single-director CFPB. Because his five-year term is separated from the presidential election cycle, the CFPB Director appointed by President Obama would occupy two years of President Trump's term—and anyone appointed by President Trump would serve until 2023, well into the next presidential term. This is a more direct assault on presidential control over the executive branch. And the Director is completely different from the Independent Counsel in *Morrison* because the Director is a Principal Officer, and so *Myers* controls, rather than *Morrison,* which turned on the Independent Counsel's being an Inferior Officer for purposes of the Appointments Clause of Article II.

In the wake of the CFPB's activities, Judge Kavanaugh found the question that the Supreme Court asked in *Free Enterprise* to be right on point: "Where, in all this, is the role for oversight by an elected President?" By disabling the President from supervising and directing the Director of the CFPB, the Dodd-Frank Act contravenes the Supreme Court's statement in *Free Enterprise*: "Congress cannot reduce the Chief Magistrate to a cajoler-in-chief."

Following the Chief Justice's lead in *Free Enterprise,* Judge Kavanaugh urged his colleagues to strike down the Dodd-Frank "for cause" limitation, but sever it from the remainder of Title X. Thus, the CFPB would continue to operate with a single Director, but he or she would be removable at will by the President.

Judge Henderson wrote a broader dissenting opinion. Because the CFPB is unique, and not controlled by the earlier precedents, Judge Henderson insisted that judges must hew to the "first principles" found in the Constitution, starting with Article II. Because "[o]ur Constitution was adopted to enable the people to govern themselves, through their elected leaders," the President "as a general matter" has power to remove the principal officers of an agency—based on "simple disagreement with the [agency's] policies or priorities"—as a means of ensuring that the agency does not "slip from the Executive's control, and thus from that of the people." *Free Enterprise.* The Supreme Court has carved out an ill-defined exception to that constitutional baseline in *Humphrey's*—and Judge Henderson would be disinclined to expand that exception one iota. "If forced to expand the *Humphrey's Executor* exception, I would limit it to an agency that answers in *some* meaningful way to the policy oversight of at least one political branch." The CFPB does not come close to such an agency, because of its budgetary autonomy (freeing it from congressional control) as well as its political autonomy (freeing it from presidential control).

In response to Judge Wilkins' argument that the Oversight Council would operate as a check on the CFPB, Judge Henderson noted that a similar argument had no bite in *Free Enterprise* and cited a "recent episode" of CFPB independence. In July 2017, the CFPB finalized a rule prohibiting certain providers from entering arbitration agreements with consumers to stave off class actions. CFPB, *Final Rule: Arbitration Agreements* (July 10, 2017). The acting Comptroller of the Currency, one of the Council's ten voting members, sought data so that he could determine the rule's "safety and soundness implications." Letter from Keith Noreika to Richard Cordray (July 17, 2017). In response, the CFPB Director asserted that, because the rule's projected impact is "less than $1 billion per year," it is "plainly frivolous" to suggest the rule "poses a safety and soundness issue." Letter from Richard Cordray to Keith Noreika (July 18, 2017). The rule was published in the Federal Register the next day. *Arbitration Agreements*, 82 Fed. Reg. 33210 (July 19, 2017). Judge Henderson: "The fact that anyone mentions the Council's narrow veto as a check is instead a testament to the CFPB's unaccountable policymaking power." [Eds. In 2017, Congress overrode the arbitration rule pursuant to its authority under the Congressional Review Act of 1995.]

Unlike Judge Kavanaugh, Judge Henderson would not sever that provision from the remainder of Title X, and so her constitutional ruling would abrogate the agency's authority altogether. "Above all else, the 111th Congress wanted the CFPB to be independent: free, that is, from industry influence and the changing political tides that come with accountability to the President. Severing section 5491(c)(3) would yield an executive agency entirely at odds with the legislative design. In my view, the Congress would not have enacted Title X in its current form absent for-cause removal protection. I believe, therefore, that the appropriate remedy for the CFPB's Article II problem is to invalidate Title X in its entirety."

Judge Randolph joined Judge Kavanaugh's dissenting opinion and penned an additional reason for rejecting the result here. After the CFPB's enforcement unit filed a Notice of Charges, an ALJ held a nine-day hearing and issued a recommended decision, concluding that PHH had violated the real estate settlement law. The Director affirmed the ALJ's recommended decision. "I believe the ALJ who presided over the hearing was an 'inferior Officer' within the meaning of Article II, section 2, clause 2 of the Constitution. That constitutional provision requires 'inferior Officers' to be appointed by the President, the 'Courts of Law,' or the 'Heads of Departments.' This ALJ was not so appointed. Pursuant to an agreement between the CFPB and the Securities and Exchange Commission, the SEC's Chief Administrative Law Judge assigned him to the case. In addition to the unconstitutional structure of the CFPB, this violation of the Appointments Clause rendered the proceedings against PHH unconstitutional." Judge Randolph found the case indistinguishable from *Freytag v. Commissioner of Internal Revenue*, 501 U.S. 868 (1991).

The en banc Court declined to take up Judge Randolph's issue. Is that defensible? If Judge Randolph is correct, there is another fundamental constitutional flaw in the process by which PHH's liberty was compromised. And he seems to have a more compelling case, based on Supreme Court precedent, right? Jot down your thoughts and read the next decision.

Raymond Lucia v. Securities and Exchange Commission

138 S.Ct. 2044 (June 21, 2018).

One way the SEC administers the nation's securities laws is by instituting an administrative proceeding against an alleged wrongdoer. Typically, the Commission delegates the task of presiding over such a proceeding to one of the agency's five ALJs, all selected by the agency's staff and not appointed by the Commission. An ALJ assigned to hear an SEC enforcement action has the "authority to do all things necessary and appropriate" to ensure a "fair and orderly" adversarial proceeding. 17 C.F.R. §§ 201.111, 200.14(a). After a hearing ends, the ALJ issues an initial decision. The Commission can review that decision, but if it opts against review, it issues an order that the initial decision has become final. See

§ 201.360(d). The initial decision is then "deemed the action of the Commission." 15 U.S.C. § 78d–1(c).

Raymond Lucia was charged with violating certain securities laws. ALJ Cameron Elliot conducted the hearing and issued an initial decision concluding that Lucia had violated the law and imposing sanctions. On appeal to the SEC, Lucia objected that the ALJ was an "Officer of the United States" who had not been properly appointed. The SEC disagreed and ruled that an ALJ is just an "employee" of the agency, not an "Officer." The Supreme Court agreed with Lucia. Under Supreme Court precedent, to qualify as an Officer, rather than an employee, an individual must occupy a "continuing" position established by law and must "exercis[e] significant authority pursuant to the laws of the United States."

In *Freytag v. Commissioner,* 501 U.S. 868 (1991), the Supreme Court applied this framework to "special trial judges" (STJs) of the United States Tax Court. STJs could issue the final decision of the Tax Court in "comparatively narrow and minor matters." In major matters, they could preside over the hearing but could not issue a final decision. Instead, they were to "prepare proposed findings and an opinion" for a regular Tax Court judge to consider. The proceeding challenged in *Freytag* was a major one. The losing parties argued on appeal that the STJ who presided over their hearing was not constitutionally appointed.

Freytag held that STJs are Officers for purposes of the Appointments Clause. Such persons occupy a "continuing office established by law" and exercised "significant" authority" pursuant to the laws of the United States. The Tax Court argued that STJs were employees in all cases in which they could not enter a final decision. But the focus on finality "ignore[d] the significance of the duties and discretion that [STJs] possess." STJs "take testimony, conduct trials, rule on the admissibility of evidence, and have the power to enforce compliance with discovery orders. * * * [I]n the course of carrying out these important functions," STJs "exercise significant discretion."

Justice Kagan's opinion for the Court followed *Freytag* and decide that the SEC's ALJs were "Officers" who had to be appointed by one of the bodies listed in the Appointments Clause. Like the Tax Court's STJs, the SEC's ALJs hold a continuing office established by law. SEC ALJs "receive[ ] a career appointment," 5 C.F.R. § 930.204(a), to a position created by statute, see 5 U.S.C. §§ 556–557, 5372, 3105. And they exercise the same "significant discretion" when carrying out the same "important functions" as STJs do. Both sets of officials have all the authority needed to ensure fair and orderly adversarial hearings—indeed, nearly all the tools of federal trial judges. The Commission's ALJs, like the Tax Court's STJs, "take testimony," "conduct trials," "rule on the admissibility of evidence," and "have the power to enforce compliance with discovery orders." So point for point from *Freytag*'s list, SEC ALJs have equivalent duties and powers as STJs in conducting adversarial inquiries.

Moreover, at the close of those proceedings, SEC ALJs issue decisions much like that in *Freytag*. STJs prepare proposed findings and an opinion adjudicating charges and assessing tax liabilities. Similarly, the Commission's ALJs issue initial decisions containing factual findings, legal conclusions, and appropriate remedies. And what happens next reveals that the ALJ can play the more autonomous role. In a major Tax Court case, a regular Tax Court judge must always review an STJ's opinion, and that opinion comes to nothing unless the regular judge adopts it. By contrast, the SEC can decide against reviewing an ALJ's decision, and when it does so the ALJ's decision itself "becomes final" and is "deemed the action of the Commission."

Writing also for Justices Ginsburg and Sotomayor, **Justice Breyer** would have resolved the case on statutory rather than constitutional grounds. Dissenting, **Justice Sotomayor** (joined by Justice Ginsburg) would interpret the "significant authority" requirement to exclude agency personnel (such as the SEC ALJs) who did not have the authority to issue final, binding decisions.

Query: The en banc judgment of the D.C. was to remand the case to the CFPB, in light of the Court's ruling that it had misinterpreted the relevant statute. In light of *Lucia,* should PHH seek an amendment of the mandate? What should the D.C. Circuit do in the event of such a petition?

2. THE PRESIDENT'S "TAKE CARE" DUTIES

Page 168: Replace Problem 2–2 with the following case:

NATIONAL LABOR RELATIONS BOARD V. NOEL CANNING

United States Supreme Court, 2014.
572 U.S. ___, 134 S.Ct. 2550, 189 L.Ed.2d 538.

JUSTICE BREYER delivered the opinion of the Court.

Ordinarily the President must obtain "the Advice and Consent of the Senate" before appointing an "Office[r] of the United States." U.S. Const., Art. II, § 2, cl. 2. But the Recess Appointments Clause creates an exception. It gives the President alone the power "to fill up all Vacancies that may happen during the Recess of the Senate, by granting Commissions which shall expire at the End of their next Session." Art. II, § 2, cl. 3. We here consider three questions about the application of this Clause.

The first concerns the scope of the words "recess of the Senate." Does that phrase refer only to an inter-session recess (*i.e.,* a break between formal sessions of Congress), or does it also include an intra-session recess, such as a summer recess in the midst of a session? We conclude that the Clause applies to both kinds of recess.

The second question concerns the scope of the words "vacancies that may happen." Does that phrase refer only to vacancies that first come into existence during a recess, or does it also include vacancies that arise prior to a recess but continue to exist during the recess? We conclude that the Clause applies to both kinds of vacancy.

The third question concerns calculation of the length of a "recess." The President made the appointments here at issue on January 4, 2012. At that time the Senate was in recess pursuant to a December 17, 2011, resolution providing for a series of brief recesses punctuated by "*pro forma* session[s]," with "no business . . . transacted," every Tuesday and Friday through January 20, 2012. S. J., 112th Cong., 1st Sess., 923 (2011) (hereinafter 2011 S. J.). In calculating the length of a recess are we to ignore the *pro forma* sessions, thereby treating the series of brief recesses as a single, month-long recess? We conclude that we cannot ignore these *pro forma* sessions.

Our answer to the third question means that, when the appointments before us took place, the Senate was in the midst of a 3-day recess. Three days is too short a time to bring a recess within the scope of the Clause. Thus we conclude that the President lacked the power to make the recess appointments here at issue. * * *

[II] Before turning to the specific questions presented, we shall mention two background considerations that we find relevant to all three. First, *the Recess Appointments Clause sets forth a subsidiary, not a primary, method for appointing officers of the United States.* The immediately preceding Clause—Article II, Section 2, Clause 2—provides the primary method of appointment. It says that the President "shall nominate, *and by and with the Advice and Consent of the Senate*, shall appoint Ambassadors, other public Ministers and Consuls, Judges of the supreme Court, and all other Officers of the United States" (emphasis added).

The Federalist Papers make clear that the Founders intended this method of appointment, requiring Senate approval, to be the norm (at least for principal officers). Alexander Hamilton wrote that the Constitution vests the power of *nomination* in the President alone because "one man of discernment is better fitted to analise and estimate the peculiar qualities adapted to particular offices, than a body of men of equal, or perhaps even of superior discernment." The Federalist No. 76, p. 510 (J. Cooke ed. 1961). At the same time, the need to secure Senate approval provides "an excellent check upon a spirit of favoritism in the President, and would tend greatly to preventing the appointment of unfit characters from State prejudice, from family connection, from personal attachment, or from a view to popularity." *Id.*, at 513. * * *

Thus the Recess Appointments Clause reflects the tension between, on the one hand, the President's continuous need for "the assistance of subordinates," *Myers v. United States*, 272 U.S. 52, 117 (1926), and, on the other, the Senate's practice, particularly during the Republic's early years, of meeting for a single brief session each year, see Art. I, § 4, cl. 2; Amdt. 20, § 2 (requiring the Senate to "assemble" only "once in every year"). We seek to interpret the Clause as granting the President the power to make appointments during a recess but not offering the President the authority routinely to avoid the need for Senate confirmation.

Second, *in interpreting the Clause, we put significant weight upon historical practice*. For one thing, the interpretive questions before us concern the allocation of power between two elected branches of Government. Long ago Chief Justice Marshall wrote that

> "a doubtful question, one on which human reason may pause, and the human judgment be suspended, in the decision of which the great principles of liberty are not concerned, but the respective powers of those who are equally the representatives of the people, are to be adjusted; if not put at rest by the practice of the government, ought to receive a considerable impression from that practice." *McCulloch v. Maryland*, 4 Wheat. 316, 401 (1819).

And we later confirmed that "[l]ong settled and established practice is a consideration of great weight in a proper interpretation of constitutional provisions" regulating the relationship between Congress and the President. *The Pocket Veto Case*, 279 U.S. 655, 689 (1929); see also *id.*, at 690 ("[A] practice of at least twenty years duration 'on the part of the executive department, acquiesced in by the legislative department, . . . is entitled to great regard in determining the true construction of a constitutional provision the phraseology of which is in any respect of doubtful meaning' " (quoting *State v. South Norwalk*, 77 Conn. 257, 264, 58 A. 759, 761 (1904))). * * *

There is a great deal of history to consider here. Presidents have made recess appointments since the beginning of the Republic. Their frequency suggests that the Senate and President have recognized that recess appointments can be both necessary and appropriate in certain circumstances. We have not previously interpreted the Clause, and, when doing so for the first time in more than 200 years, we must hesitate to upset the compromises and working arrangements that the elected branches of Government themselves have reached.

[III] The first question concerns the scope of the phrase *"the recess* of the Senate." Art. II, § 2, cl. 3 (emphasis added). The Constitution provides for congressional elections every two years. And the 2-year life of each elected Congress typically consists of two formal 1-year sessions, each separated from the next by an "inter-session recess." The Senate or the House of Representatives announces an inter-session recess by approving a resolution stating that it will "adjourn *sine die*," *i.e.*, without specifying a date to return (in which case Congress will reconvene when the next formal session is scheduled to begin).

The Senate and the House also take breaks in the midst of a session. The Senate or the House announces any such "intra-session recess" by adopting a resolution stating that it will "adjourn" to a fixed date, a few days or weeks or even months later. All agree that the phrase "the recess of the Senate" covers inter-session recesses. The question is whether it includes intra-session recesses as well.

In our view, the phrase "the recess" includes an intra-session recess of substantial length. Its words taken literally can refer to both types of recess. Founding-era dictionaries define the word "recess," much as we do today, simply as "a period of cessation from usual work." 13 The Oxford English Dictionary 322–323 (2d ed. 1989) (hereinafter OED) (citing 18th- and 19th-century sources for that definition of "recess"). The Founders themselves used the word to refer to intra-session, as well as to intersession, breaks. See, *e.g.*, 3 Records of the Federal Convention of 1787, p. 76 (M. Farrand rev. 1966) (hereinafter Farrand) (letter from George Washington to John Jay using "the recess" to refer to an intra-session break of the Constitutional Convention).

We recognize that the word "the" in "*the* recess" might suggest that the phrase refers to the single break separating formal sessions of Congress. * * * But the word can also refer "to a term used generically or universally." 17 OED 879. The Constitution, for example, directs the Senate to choose a President *pro tempore* "in *the* Absence of the Vice-President." Art. I, § 3, cl. 5 (emphasis added). And the Federalist Papers refer to the chief magistrate of an ancient Achaean league who "administered the government in *the* recess of the Senate." The Federalist No. 18, at 113 (J. Madison) (emphasis added). Reading "the" generically in this way, there is no linguistic problem applying the Clause's phrase to both kinds of recess. And, in fact, the phrase "the recess" was used to refer to intra-session recesses at the time of the founding. See, *e.g.*, 3 Farrand 76 (letter from Washington to Jay); New Jersey Legislative-Council Journal, 5th Sess., 1st Sitting 70, 2d Sitting 9 (1781) (twice referring to a 4-month, intra-session break as "the Recess").

The constitutional text is thus ambiguous. And we believe the Clause's purpose demands the broader interpretation. The Clause gives the President authority to make appointments during "the recess of the Senate" so that the President can ensure the continued functioning of the Federal Government when the Senate is away. The Senate is equally away during both an inter-session and an intra-session recess, and its capacity to participate in the appointments process has nothing to do with the words it uses to signal its departure.

History also offers strong support for the broad interpretation. We concede that pre-Civil War history is not helpful. But it shows only that Congress generally took long breaks between sessions, while taking no significant intra-session breaks at all (five times it took a break of a week or so at Christmas). * * * In 1867 and 1868, Congress for the first time took substantial, nonholiday intra-session breaks, and President Andrew Johnson made dozens of recess appointments. The Federal Court of Claims upheld one of those specific appointments, writing "[w]e have *no doubt* that a vacancy occurring while the Senate was thus temporarily adjourned" during the "first session of the Fortieth Congress" was "legally filled by appointment of the President alone." *Gould v. United States*, 19 Ct. Cl. 593, 595–596 (1884) (emphasis added). Attorney General Evarts also issued three opinions concerning the constitutionality of President Johnson's appointments, and it apparently did not occur to him that the distinction between intra-session and inter-session recesses was significant. See 12 Op. Atty. Gen. 449 (1868); 12 Op. Atty. Gen. 455 (1868); 12 Op. Atty. Gen. 469 (1868). Similarly, though the 40th Congress impeached President Johnson on charges relating to his appointment power, he was not accused of violating the Constitution by making intra-session recess appointments. Hartnett, Recess Appointments of Article III Judges: Three Constitutional Questions, 26 Cardozo L. Rev. 377, 409 (2005).

In all, between the founding and the Great Depression, Congress took substantial intra-session breaks (other than holiday breaks) in four years: 1867, 1868, 1921, and 1929. And in each of those years the President made intra-session recess appointments. [Justice Breyer included an Appendix to his opinion for the Court, with documentation of recess appointments.]

Since 1929, and particularly since the end of World War II, Congress has shortened its inter-session breaks as it has taken longer and more frequent intra-session breaks; Presidents have correspondingly made more intra-session recess appointments. Indeed, if we include military appointments, Presidents have made thousands of intra-session recess appointments. President Franklin Roosevelt, for example, commissioned Dwight Eisenhower as a permanent Major General during an intra-session recess; President Truman made Dean Acheson Under Secretary of State; and President George H. W. Bush reappointed Alan Greenspan as Chairman of the Federal Reserve Board.

Not surprisingly, the publicly available opinions of Presidential legal advisers that we have found are nearly unanimous in determining that the Clause authorizes these appointments. In 1921, for example, Attorney

General Daugherty advised President Harding that he could make intra-session recess appointments. He reasoned:

> "If the President's power of appointment is to be defeated because the Senate takes an adjournment to a specified date, the painful and inevitable result will be measurably to prevent the exercise of governmental functions. I can not bring myself to believe that the framers of the Constitution ever intended such a catastrophe to happen." 33 Op. Atty. Gen. 20, 23.

We have found memoranda offering similar advice to President Eisenhower and to every President from Carter to the present. * * *

Similarly, in 1940 the Senate helped to enact a law regulating the payment of recess appointees, and the Comptroller General of the United States has interpreted that law functionally. An earlier 1863 statute had denied pay to individuals appointed to fill up vacancies first arising prior to the beginning of a recess. The Senate Judiciary Committee then believed that those vacancies fell outside the scope of the Clause. In 1940, however, the Senate amended the law to permit many of those recess appointees to be paid. Act of July 11, 1940, 54 Stat. 751. Interpreting the amendments in 1948, the Comptroller General—who, unlike the Attorney General, is an "officer of the Legislative Branch," *Bowsher*—wrote:

> "I think it is clear that [the Pay Act amendments'] primary purpose was to relieve 'recess appointees' of the burden of serving without compensation during periods when the Senate is not actually sitting and is not available to give its advice and consent in respect to the appointment, irrespective of whether the recess of the Senate is attributable to a final adjournment *sine die* or to an adjournment to a specified date." 28 Comp. Gen. 30, 37.

[Justice Breyer concluded that historical practice supported presidential appointments during intra-session recesses but further ruled that the President could not act when the Senate is in recess for fewer than 3 days, as the Constitution (Article I, § 5, cl. 4) bars the Senate from adjourning for more than 3 days without the consent of the House. Additionally, the Court ruled,] in light of historical practice, that a recess of more than 3 days but less than 10 days is presumptively too short to fall within the Clause. We add the word "presumptively" to leave open the possibility that some very unusual circumstance—a national catastrophe, for instance, that renders the Senate unavailable but calls for an urgent response—could demand the exercise of the recess-appointment power during a shorter break. * * *

[IV] [The second issue was whether the "Vacancies that may *happen*" must be vacancies that arise during the recess, and not vacancies that persist during the recess. Justice Breyer favored the latter, broader interpretation.] We believe that the Clause's language, read literally, permits, though it does not naturally favor, our broader interpretation. We concede that the most natural meaning of "happens" as applied to a "vacancy" (at least to a modern ear) is that the vacancy "happens" when it initially occurs. But that is not the only possible way to use the word.

Thomas Jefferson wrote that the Clause is "certainly susceptible of [two] constructions." Letter to Wilson Cary Nicholas (Jan. 26, 1802), in 36 Papers of Thomas Jefferson 433 (B. Oberg ed., 2009). It "may mean 'vacancies that may happen to be' or 'may happen to fall' " during a recess. *Ibid.* Jefferson used the phrase in the first sense when he wrote to a job seeker that a particular position was unavailable, but that he (Jefferson) was "happy that *another vacancy happens* wherein I can . . . avail the public of your integrity & talents," for "the office of Treasurer of the US. *is vacant* by the resignation of mr Meredith." Letter to Thomas Tudor Tucker (Oct. 31, 1801), in 35 *id.*, at 530 (B. Oberg ed. 2008) (emphasis added).

Similarly, when Attorney General William Wirt advised President Monroe to follow the broader interpretation, he wrote that the "expression seems not perfectly clear. It may mean 'happen to take place:' that is, '*to originate,*' " or it "may mean, also, without violence to the sense, 'happen to exist.' " 1 Op. Atty. Gen. 631, 631–632 (1823). The broader interpretation, he added, is "most accordant with" the Constitution's "reason and spirit." Id., at 632. * * *

The Clause's purpose strongly supports the broader interpretation. That purpose is to permit the President to obtain the assistance of subordinate officers when the Senate, due to its recess, cannot confirm them. Attorney General Wirt clearly described how the narrower interpretation would undermine this purpose:

> "Put the case of a vacancy occurring in an office, held in a distant part of the country, on the last day of the Senate's session. Before the vacancy is made known to the President, the Senate rises. The office may be an important one; the vacancy may paralyze a whole line of action in some essential branch of our internal police; the public interests may imperiously demand that it shall be immediately filled. But the vacancy happened to occur during the session of the Senate; and if the President's power is to be limited to such vacancies only as happen to occur during the recess of the Senate, the vacancy in the case put must continue, however ruinous the consequences may be to the public." 1 Op. Atty. Gen., at 632.

[What does history have to teach us? Justice Breyer found little relevant practice from the Washington, Adams, and Jefferson Administrations.] But the evidence suggests that James Madison—as familiar as anyone with the workings of the Constitutional Convention—appointed Theodore Gaillard to replace a district judge who had left office before a recess began. It also appears that in 1815 Madison signed a bill that created two new offices prior to a recess which he then filled later during the recess. See Act of Mar. 3, ch. 95, 3 Stat. 235; S. J. 13th Cong., 3d Sess., 689–690 (1815); 3 S. Exec. J. 19 (1828) (for Monday, Jan. 8, 1816). He also made recess appointments to "territorial" United States attorney and marshal positions, both of which had been created when the Senate was in session more than two years before. Act of Feb. 27, 1813, ch. 35, 2 Stat. 806; 3 S. Exec. J. 19.

[Upon the advice of Attorney General Wirt, the Monroe Administration followed the same understanding, as did every other Attorney General to opine on this issue.] Indeed, as early as 1862, Attorney General Bates advised President Lincoln that his power to fill pre-recess vacancies was "settled . . . as far . . . as a constitutional question can be settled," 10 Op. Atty. Gen., at 356, and a century later Acting Attorney General Walsh gave President Eisenhower the same advice "without any doubt," 41 Op. Atty. Gen., at 466. * * *

* * * No one disputes that every President since James Buchanan has made recess appointments to preexisting vacancies.

[Did the Senate object? Not early on.] Then in 1863 the Senate Judiciary Committee disagreed with the broad interpretation. It issued a report concluding that a vacancy "must have its inceptive point after one session has closed and before another session has begun." S. Rep. No. 80, 37th Cong., 3d Sess., p. 3. And the Senate then passed the Pay Act, which provided that "no money shall be paid . . . as a salary, to any person appointed during the recess of the Senate, to fill a vacancy . . . which . . . existed while the Senate was in session." Act of Feb. 9, 1863, § 2, 12 Stat. 646. [Justice Breyer minimized the extent to which the 1863 Pay Act was a constitutional pushback from the Senate.]

In any event, the Senate subsequently abandoned its hostility. In the debate preceding the 1905 Senate Report regarding President Roosevelt's "constructive" recess appointments, Senator Tillman—who chaired the Committee that authored the 1905 Report—brought up the 1863 Report, and another Senator responded: "Whatever that report may have said in 1863, I do not think that has been the view the Senate has taken" of the issue. 38 Cong. Rec. 1606 (1904). Senator Tillman then agreed that "the Senate has acquiesced" in the President's "power to fill" pre-recess vacancies. *Ibid.* And Senator Tillman's 1905 Report described the Clause's purpose in terms closely echoing Attorney General Wirt. 1905 Senate Report, at 2 ("Its sole purpose was to render it *certain* that at all times there should be, whether the Senate was in session or not, an officer for every office" (emphasis added)).

[The President continued to make recess appointments for vacancies that arose before the recesses.] Then in 1940 Congress amended the Pay

Act to authorize salary payments (with some exceptions) where (1) the "vacancy arose within thirty days prior to the termination of the session," (2) "at the termination of the session" a nomination was "pending," or (3) a nominee was "rejected by the Senate within thirty days prior to the termination of the session." Act of July 11, 54 Stat. 751 (codified, as amended, at 5 U.S.C. § 5503). All three circumstances concern a vacancy that did not initially occur during a recess but happened to exist during that recess. By paying salaries to this kind of recess appointee, the 1940 Senate (and later Senates) in effect supported the President's interpretation of the Clause.

[V] The third question concerns the calculation of the length of the Senate's "recess." On December 17, 2011, the Senate by unanimous consent adopted a resolution to convene "*pro forma* session[s]" only, with "no business . . . transacted," on every Tuesday and Friday from December 20, 2011, through January 20, 2012. At the end of each *pro forma* session, the Senate would "adjourn until" the following *pro forma* session. *Ibid.* During that period, the Senate convened and adjourned as agreed. It held *pro forma* sessions on December 20, 23, 27, and 30, and on January 3, 6, 10, 13, 17, and 20; and at the end of each *pro forma* session, it adjourned until the time and date of the next.

The President made the recess appointments before us on January 4, 2012, in between the January 3 and the January 6 *pro forma* sessions. We must determine the significance of these sessions—that is, whether, for purposes of the Clause, we should treat them as periods when the Senate was in session or as periods when it was in recess. If the former, the period between January 3 and January 6 was a 3-day recess, which is too short to trigger the President's recess-appointment power. If the latter, however, then the 3-day period was part of a much longer recess during which the President did have the power to make recess appointments.

[The Court unanimously rejected the Solicitor General's argument that the *pro forma* sessions did not count as sessions, and hence did not break up the periods of recess.] We hold that, for purposes of the Recess Appointments Clause, the Senate is in session when it says it is, provided that, under its own rules, it retains the capacity to transact Senate business. The Senate met that standard here.

The standard we apply is consistent with the Constitution's broad delegation of authority to the Senate to determine how and when to conduct its business. The Constitution explicitly empowers the Senate to "determine the Rules of its Proceedings." Art. I, § 5, cl. 2. And we have held that "all matters of method are open to the determination" of the Senate, as long as there is "a reasonable relation between the mode or method of proceeding established by the rule and the result which is sought to be attained" and the rule does not "ignore constitutional restraints or violate fundamental rights." *United States v. Ballin*, 144 U.S. 1, 5 (1892).

In addition, the Constitution provides the Senate with extensive control over its schedule. There are only limited exceptions. See Amdt. 20, § 2 (Congress must meet once a year on January 3, unless it specifies another day by law); Art. II, § 3 (Senate must meet if the President calls it into special session); Art. I, § 5, cl. 4 (neither House may adjourn for more than three days without consent of the other). See also Art. II, § 3 ("[I]n Case of Disagreement between [the Houses], with Respect to the Time of Adjournment, [the President] may adjourn them to such Time as he shall think proper"). The Constitution thus gives the Senate wide latitude to determine whether and when to have a session, as well as how to conduct the session. This suggests that the Senate's determination about what constitutes a session should merit great respect. [Accordingly, Justice Breyer ruled that the Senate was in session during the *pro forma* sessions and, hence, that the short breaks between *pro forma* sessions could not trigger the Recess Appointments Clause.]

[VI] The Recess Appointments Clause responds to a structural difference between the Executive and Legislative Branches: The Executive Branch is perpetually in operation, while the Legislature only acts in intervals separated by recesses. The purpose of the Clause is to allow the Executive to continue operating while the Senate is unavailable. We believe that the Clause's text, standing alone, is ambiguous. It does not resolve whether the President may make appointments during intra-session recesses, or whether he may fill pre-recess vacancies. But the broader reading better serves the Clause's structural function. Moreover, that broader reading is reinforced by centuries of history, which we are hesitant to disturb. We thus hold that the Constitution empowers the President to fill any existing vacancy during any recess—intra-session or inter-session—of sufficient length.

[Joined by CHIEF JUSTICE ROBERTS and JUSTICES THOMAS and ALITO, JUSTICE SCALIA's concurring opinion rejected the Court's analysis and maintained that the Recess Appointments Clause allowed presidential appointments *only* for vacancies that *arise* during *inter-session* recesses. Because these Justices agreed that the Obama appointments in this case violated the Constitution, they concurred in the Court's judgment. We discuss many of Justice Scalia's arguments in the Notes that follow.]

NOTES ON THE RECESS APPOINTMENTS CASE: CONSTITUTIONAL ADVERSE POSSESSION

Noel Canning is a dramatic showdown between the Obama Presidency and a filibuster-happy Senate. Does Justice Breyer's opinion, on its face, persuade you that the President's recess appointments power is in Justice

Jackson's "zone of twilight," and that the case is not clearly resolved against the Administration? Does the Steel Seizure framework constrain the President's power? Or is it a funnel through which presidential power is increasing, at the expense of a broken Congress?

1. *The Text.* As to the first issue, one historian has opined that "in government practice the phrase 'the Recess' *always* referred to the gap between sessions." Robert Natelson, *The Origins and Meaning of "Vacancies that May Happen During the Recess" in the Constitution's Recess Appointments Clause*, 37 Harv. J. L. & Pub. Pol'y 199, 213 (2014). Indeed, the Constitution uses the verb "adjourn" rather than "recess" to refer to the commencement of breaks *during* a formal legislative session. U.S. Const. art. I, § 5, cl. 1 and 4. In *Federalist* No. 67, Publius explained to the ratifying audience that appointments would require Senate consent "during the *session* of the Senate" but would be made by the President alone "*in their recess*," apparently using the term as a break between sessions.

As to the second issue, even Justice Breyer conceded that the narrow reading of "happens" is the "most natural" one. In dissent, Justice Scalia maintained that it is the only "plausible" one, a view he felt was confirmed by early practice. "In 1792, Attorney General Edmund Randolph, who had been a leading member of the Constitutional Convention, provided the Executive Branch's first formal interpretation of the Clause. He advised President Washington that the Constitution did not authorize a recess appointment to fill the office of Chief Coiner of the United States Mint, which had been created by Congress on April 2, 1792, during the Senate's session. Randolph wrote: '[I]s it a vacancy which has *happened* during the recess of the Senate? It is now the same and no other vacancy, than that, which existed on the 2nd. of April 1792. It commenced therefore on that day or may be said to have *happened* on that day.' Opinion on Recess Appointments (July 7, 1792), in 24 Papers of Thomas Jefferson 165–166 (J. Catanzariti ed. 1990). Randolph added that his interpretation was the most congruent with the Constitution's structure, which made the recess-appointment power "an exception to the general participation of the Senate." *Ibid.* President Adams's Attorney General, Charles Lee, came to the same conclusion. Even Attorney General Wirt in 1823 admitted that the letter of the Constitution did not support his broad reading.

2. *Constitutional Purposes.* Another way that history figures into the Justices' debate in *Noel Canning* is in determining the purpose of the Recess Appointments Clause. Indeed, because he finds the text ambiguous, Justice Breyer's opinion for the Court relies mainly on the historical purpose of the Clause. But is he any more persuasive on that front than in his treatment of original meaning?

Justice Breyer said the purpose of the Clause is to keep the government running efficiently when the Senate is not prepared to do business (and confirm appointees)—but his main evidence for that proposition is the opinion of Attorney General Wirt and other executive branch officers far removed from the founding era. Justice Scalia responded: "The majority disregards another self-evident purpose of the Clause: to preserve the Senate's role in the appointment process—which the founding generation regarded as a critical protection against 'despotism'—by clearly delineating the times when the President can appoint officers without the Senate's consent. Today's decision seriously undercuts *that* purpose."

Indeed, viewed structurally, the Constitution protects the liberty of citizens and corporations by making it harder for potentially tyrannical officials to act without the cooperation of officials in other branches. See *Federalist* No. 51 (Madison) (the Constitution's system of checks and balances provides a "double security" for citizens). Thus, the obvious purpose of the Appointments Clauses is to check the President's ability to make appointments without considering the views of the Senate. That purpose is liberty-protecting and democracy-enhancing, as it assures the country that persons acceptable to both the nationally elected President and the state-representing Senate will serve in high office. Under this framework, the Recess Appointments Clause is an *exception*, to accommodate practical problems when the Senate is unavailable to participate. Exceptions are supposed to be narrowly construed, not broadly, as Justice Breyer urged. And the Court's broad interpretation of the Recess Appointments Clause opens the way for the already imperial President to secure even more power in relation to Congress.

Justice Scalia made another point about purposive interpretation: "The rise of intra-session adjournments has occurred in tandem with the development of modern forms of communication and transportation that mean the Senate 'is always available' to consider nominations, even when its Members are temporarily dispersed for an intra-session break. Tr. of Oral Arg. 21 (Ginsburg, J.). The Recess Appointments Clause therefore is, or rather, should be, an anachronism—'essentially an historic relic, something whose original purpose has disappeared.' *Id.*, at 19 (Kagan, J.). The need it was designed to fill no longer exists, and its only remaining use is the ignoble one of enabling the President to circumvent the Senate's role in the appointment process." Justice Breyer responded that Justice Scalia was trying to read the Recess Appointments Clause out of the Constitution—which is not correct. Justice Scalia was merely responding to the purpose argument with the observation that the *original* purpose is no longer so pressing and, hence, provides even less reason to read the Clause broadly.

Consider Justice Scalia's analysis in light of what has transpired in Washington, D.C. in the last several years. Congress has shut down. Due to hyperpartisan bickering between the parties and to the fractured GOP caucus in the House (which the Republicans have controlled since 2011), not only does Congress fail to enact substantive legislation, but even routine legislative activities such as budgets, debt ceiling adjustments, and confirmations have slowed or stalled. Like the Bush-Cheney Administration, the Obama Administration has responded to an exacerbated congressional gridlock with aggressive executive action—including more recess appointments to positions that were once routine matters. Can you blame the Court majority for giving the President some slack, given his efforts to press onward with governance and given the contrast with an obstructionist and deeply unpopular Congress?

3. *Practice as Constitutional Adverse Possession.* As in the Steel Seizure Case itself, the Justices in the Recess Appointments Case took a variety of positions regarding the relevance of executive practice when judges set the meaning of constitutional provisions. Justice Breyer posited that constitutional ambiguities may be resolved by consulting a longstanding presidential practice which Congress has not decisively resisted. Like Chief Justice Vinson in the Steel Seizure Case, Justice Breyer applied the practice-as-adverse-possession standard fairly liberally. Following Justice Frankfurter's formulation of adverse possession, Justice Scalia opined that "where a governmental practice has been open, widespread, and unchallenged since the early days of the Republic, the practice should guide our interpretation of an ambiguous constitutional provision."

Even if the constitutional text were in any way ambiguous, and even if the Breyer/Vinson standard were the proper one, Justice Scalia argued that the majority did not make its case. "Intra-session recess appointments were virtually unheard of for the first 130 years of the Republic, were deemed unconstitutional by the first Attorney General to address them [Attorney General Philander Knox in 1901], were not openly defended by the Executive until 1921 [Attorney General Harry Daughtery], were not made in significant numbers until after World War II, and have been repeatedly criticized as unconstitutional by Senators of both parties."

On the availability of recess appointments arising beforehand, Justice Scalia had an even stronger historical response. Few Presidents made such appointments in the first century of the republic—and when they did, there was sometimes pushback. After President Lincoln appointed David Davis to the Supreme Court through a recess appointment to a preexisting vacancy, a number of Senators strenuously objected. And in 1863 Congress enacted the Pay Act, which provided that "no money shall be paid . . . out of the Treasury, as salary, to any person appointed during the recess of the Senate, to fill a vacancy . . . which . . . existed while the Senate was in session." Act of Feb. 9, 1863, § 2, 12 Stat. 646. Between 1863 and 1940, there were few recess appointments to fill preexisting vacancies.

As Justice Breyer observed, Congress amended the Pay Act in 1940. "Under the current version of the Act, '[p]ayment for services may not be made from the Treasury of the United States to an individual appointed during a recess of the Senate to fill a vacancy' that 'existed while the Senate was in session' *unless* either the vacancy arose, or a different individual's nomination to fill the vacancy was rejected, 'within 30 days before the end of the session'; or a nomination was pending before the Senate at the end of the session, and the individual nominated was not himself a recess appointee. § 5503(a)(1)–(3). And if the President fills a pre-recess vacancy under one of the circumstances specified in the Act, the law requires that he submit a nomination for that office to the Senate 'not later than 40 days after the beginning of the next session.' § 5503(b)."

Since the 1940 Amendment to the Pay Act, Presidents have made several dozen recess appointments to fill preexisting vacancies. Even as amended, the Pay Act seems disapproving of the practice generally, and certainly regulates it stringently. (If the President has the constitutional authority described by the Court, isn't the Pay Act unconstitutional because it burdens officials validly appointed by the President?) Senators, including the GOP Senators who participated in *Noel Canning,* have continued to object to the practice. Concluded Justice Scalia: "I can conceive of no sane constitutional theory under which this evidence of 'historical practice'—which is actually evidence of a long-simmering inter-branch conflict—would require us to defer to the views of the Executive Branch." Can you disagree with this assertion?

Return to first principles, and the Steel Seizure Case. Why should executive practice be relevant to the meaning of the Constitution? Understood thus, executive practice can easily bootstrap an institutionally biased viewpoint into the law of the land. Is that not disturbing—especially in light of the first-mover advantage the President already has and the imperial power the office has accumulated? The contrast between the President and the Senate is quite stark: the Presidency can mobilize quickly because one man or woman makes ultimate decisions, whereas the Senate cannot act on most matters (including adjournment!) without the cooperation of the House and is internally hamstrung by the filibuster and other vetogates that block legislative initiatives.

In light of these concerns, has the *Noel Canning* majority stacked the deck in its adverse possession analysis? If so, perhaps that is defensible because adverse possession itself is defensible. After all, property law, the home to rule-of-law values and bright line directives, originated the idea of adverse possession, where it has served a useful role in protecting reliance interests and providing incentives for property owners to assert their rights. The big problem for adverse possession in constitutional law, however, is that it is vastly easier for the President to assert executive authority than it is for a diffused and often disorganized Congress to assert its prerogatives.

Page 181: Add the following Problem 2–3A right after the Postscript on the Libyan Bombing Controversy:

PROBLEM 2–3A: IS THE WAR POWERS RESOLUTION UNCONSTITUTIONAL, AS APPLIED?

Although the Obama Administration did not denounce the War Powers Resolution as an unconstitutional infringement on the President's Commander-in-Chief authority, Presidents Nixon, Reagan, and Bush had done so. Assume that the Libyan Bombing Campaign had continued for several years and that Congress had more firmly stood up to the President and demanded that he cease American involvement in these "hostilities."

Would such an application of the WPR be an unconstitutional infringement on the President's Commander-in-Chief powers under Article II? Consider the text of the Constitution, as well as the following Supreme Court decision applying the Steel Seizure framework to a related issue. Based upon this new precedent and its analysis, what constitutional argument might Legal Adviser Koh have made in addressing the War Powers Resolution? How might the Counsel to the Senate or Counsel to the House of Representatives have responded? As you formulate your analysis, consider the Supreme Court's most recent application of the Steel Seizure framework.

Menachem Binyamin Zivotofsky, by His Parents and Guardians v. John Kerry, Secretary of State

___ U.S. ___, 135 S.Ct. 2076, 192 L.Ed.2d 83 (2015).

Since 1948, the United States, acting through the President, has recognized the state of Israel but has taken no position on the delicate issue of which state has sovereignty over Jerusalem. Consistent with this policy, the State Department will not identify Israel as the nation of citizenship for anyone born in Jerusalem; the passport will simply say "Jerusalem."

In 2002, Congress passed the Foreign Relations Authorization Act, Fiscal Year 2003, 116 Stat. 1350. Section 214 of the Act is titled "United States Policy with Respect to Jerusalem as the Capital of Israel." Section 214(d) allows citizens born in Jerusalem to list their place of birth as "Israel." "For purposes of the registration of birth, certification of nationality, or issuance of a passport of a United States citizen born in the city of Jerusalem, the Secretary shall, upon the request of the citizen or the citizen's legal guardian, record the place of birth as Israel." Did this statutory override of State Department and Presidential policy violate Article II?

Writing for the Court, **Justice Kennedy** applied the Steel Seizure framework and found that the President's assertion of authority fell under Category 3—"measures incompatible with the expressed or implied will of Congress," which can only be allowed when the President's own constitutional authority disables Congress from acting (Coursebook, p. 161). Unlike the Steel Seizure Case, where President Truman did not satisfy the stringent requirements of Category 3, the Court here upheld the President and ruled that the 2002 statute was invalid because Article II vested the President with exclusive authority to "recognize" foreign states.

The Constitution does not use the term "recognition," but Secretary Kerry relied on the Reception Clause, which directs that the President "shall receive Ambassadors and other public Ministers." Art. II, § 3. The Reception Clause received little attention at the Constitutional Convention, see Reinstein, Recognition: A Case Study on the Original

Understanding of Executive Power, 45 U. Rich. L. Rev. 801, 860–862 (2011), and during the ratification debates, Alexander Hamilton claimed that the power to receive ambassadors was "more a matter of dignity than of authority," a ministerial duty largely "without consequence." The Federalist No. 69, p. 420 (C. Rossiter ed. 1961).

"At the time of the founding, however, prominent international scholars suggested that receiving an ambassador was tantamount to recognizing the sovereignty of the sending state. See E. de Vattel, The Law of Nations § 78, p. 461 (1758) (J. Chitty ed. 1853) ('[E]very state, truly possessed of sovereignty, has a right to send ambassadors' and 'to contest their right in this instance' is equivalent to 'contesting their sovereign dignity'); [other sources]. It is a logical and proper inference, then, that a Clause directing the President alone to receive ambassadors would be understood to acknowledge his power to recognize other nations." "This in fact occurred early in the Nation's history when President Washington recognized the French Revolutionary Government by receiving its ambassador. After this incident the import of the Reception Clause became clear—causing Hamilton to change his earlier view. He wrote that the Reception Clause 'includes th[e power] of judging, in the case of a revolution of government in a foreign country, whether the new rulers are competent organs of the national will, and ought to be recognised, or not.' See A. Hamilton, Pacificus No. 1, in The Letters of Pacificus and Helvidius 5, 13–14 (1845) (reprint 1976) (President 'acknowledged the republic of France, by the reception of its minister'). [S]ee also 3 J. Story, Commentaries on the Constitution of the United States § 1560, p. 416 (1833) ('If the executive receives an ambassador, or other minister, as the representative of a new nation . . . it is an acknowledgment of the sovereign authority *de facto* of such new nation, or party'). As a result, the Reception Clause provides support, although not the sole authority, for the President's power to recognize other nations."

Justice Kennedy found the foregoing inference supported by the President's other Article II powers. The President, "by and with the Advice and Consent of the Senate," is to "make Treaties, provided two thirds of the Senators present concur." Art. II, § 2, cl. 2. Also, "he shall nominate, and by and with the Advice and Consent of the Senate, shall appoint Ambassadors" as well as "other public Ministers and Consuls." *Ibid.*

"As a matter of constitutional structure, these additional powers give the President control over recognition decisions. At international law, recognition may be effected by different means, but each means is dependent upon Presidential power. In addition to receiving an ambassador, recognition may occur on 'the conclusion of a bilateral treaty,' or the 'formal initiation of diplomatic relations,' including the dispatch of an ambassador. The President has the sole power to negotiate treaties, and the Senate may not conclude or ratify a treaty without Presidential action.

The President, too, nominates the Nation's ambassadors and dispatches other diplomatic agents. Congress may not send an ambassador without his involvement. Beyond that, the President himself has the power to open diplomatic channels simply by engaging in direct diplomacy with foreign heads of state and their ministers. The Constitution thus assigns the President means to effect recognition on his own initiative. Congress, by contrast, has no constitutional power that would enable it to initiate diplomatic relations with a foreign nation. Because these specific Clauses confer the recognition power on the President, the Court need not consider whether or to what extent the Vesting Clause, which provides that the 'executive Power' shall be vested in the President, provides further support for the President's action here. Art. II, § 1, cl. 1.

"The text and structure of the Constitution grant the President the power to recognize foreign nations and governments. The question then becomes whether that power is exclusive. The various ways in which the President may unilaterally effect recognition—and the lack of any similar power vested in Congress—suggest that it is. So, too, do functional considerations. Put simply, the Nation must have a single policy regarding which governments are legitimate in the eyes of the United States and which are not. Foreign countries need to know, before entering into diplomatic relations or commerce with the United States, whether their ambassadors will be received; whether their officials will be immune from suit in federal court; and whether they may initiate lawsuits here to vindicate their rights. These assurances cannot be equivocal."

Justice Kennedy also found it significant that "the President since the founding has exercised this unilateral power to recognize new states—and the Court has endorsed the practice. See *Banco Nacional de Cuba v. Sabbatino,* 376 U.S. 398, 410, 84 S.Ct. 923, 11 L.Ed.2d 804 (1964); [*United States v. Pink,* 315 U.S. 203, 229, 62 S.Ct. 552, 86 L.Ed.796 (1942)]; *Williams v. Suffolk Ins. Co.,* 13 Pet. 415, 420, 10 L.Ed.226 (1839). Texts and treatises on international law treat the President's word as the final word on recognition. See, *e.g.,* Restatement (Third) of Foreign Relations Law § 204, at 89 ('Under the Constitution of the United States the President has exclusive authority to recognize or not to recognize a foreign state or government'). In light of this authority all six judges who considered this case in the Court of Appeals agreed that the President holds the exclusive recognition power." Justice Kennedy found *Sabbatino* especially relevant, for the Court held that "[p]olitical recognition is exclusively a function of the Executive." 376 U.S., at 410, 84 S.Ct. 923.

Secretary Kerry urged the Court to define the executive power broadly, namely, "exclusive authority to conduct diplomatic relations," along with "the bulk of foreign-affairs powers." Brief for Respondent 18, 16. The Court refused to go that far. "In a world that is ever more compressed and interdependent, it is essential the congressional role in foreign affairs be understood and respected. For it is Congress that makes laws, and in countless ways its laws will and should shape the Nation's course. The Executive is not free from the ordinary controls and checks of Congress merely because foreign affairs are at issue."

Finally, Justice Kennedy considered the extensive historical record to discern whether there had been congressional acquiescence in the exclusive power claimed by the President and the Secretary of State. As Judge Tatel had remarked in the proceedings below, what is most remarkable is that, since the Washington Administration, the President had openly claimed the exclusive authority to recognize foreign states (or not) and had not been met with a congressional statute to the contrary—until the 2002 law at issue in this case.

Justice Breyer joined the opinion for the Court but noted his view, rejected by the Court in *Zivotofsky v. Clinton,* 132 S.Ct. 1421 (2012), that the controversy was a nonjusticiable political question. See Chapter 3, § 1 of the coursebook, as well as *Sabbatino*, where the Court ruled that the President's recognition of Cuba was not reviewable.

Justice Thomas concurred only in the Court's judgment and rejected the Court's constitutional analysis. Consistent with the unitary executive thesis, he argued that the Article II Vesting Clause ("executive power," without qualification) gives the President plenary authority to act in matters of foreign affairs or military deployment. Because Congress's Article I Vesting Clause only gives Congress "[a]ll legislative Powers herein granted," Congress can trump the President only where the Constitution has explicitly authorized congressional action, such as confirming ambassadors and providing funds for foreign affairs and military operations. See Saikrishna Prakash & Michael Ramsey, *The Executive Power Over Foreign Affairs*, 111 Yale L.J. 231, 298–346 (2001). Under his framework, Justice Thomas would invalidate § 214(d) as applied to passports (fully within the "executive Power" as understood in 1789) but would apply it to matters of naturalization, fully within Congress's enumerated powers. U.S. Const. art. I, § 8, cl. 4.

Chief Justice Roberts (joined by Justice Alito) noted that this was the first time the Supreme Court has allowed the President to defy an explicit congressional statute regulating foreign affairs. The Court's holding was not properly attentive to the "caution" urged by Justice Jackson in Steel Seizure Category 3 cases.

In a significant break from Justice Thomas's broad reading of the Article II Vesting Clause (a key feature of the unitary executive thesis advanced by Professor Calabresi, Coursebook, pp. 136–137), the dissenting opinion of **Justice Scalia** (joined by Chief Justice Roberts and Justice Alito) worked within the analytical structure of a balanced government, where both Congress and the President share foreign affairs authority.

"Congress's power to 'establish an uniform Rule of Naturalization,' Art. I, § 8, cl. 4, enables it to grant American citizenship to someone born abroad. The naturalization power also enables Congress to furnish the people it makes citizens with papers verifying their citizenship—say a consular report of birth abroad (which certifies citizenship of an American born outside the United States) or a passport (which certifies citizenship for purposes of international travel). As the Necessary and Proper Clause confirms, every congressional power 'carries with it all those incidental powers which are necessary to its complete and effectual execution.' *Cohens v. Virginia,* 6 Wheat. 264, 429, 5 L.Ed. 257 (1821). Even on a miserly understanding of Congress's incidental authority, Congress may make grants of citizenship 'effectual' by providing for the issuance of certificates authenticating them.

"One would think that if Congress may grant Zivotofsky a passport and a birth report, it may also require these papers to record his birthplace as 'Israel.' The birthplace specification promotes the document's citizenship-authenticating function by identifying the bearer, distinguishing people with similar names but different birthplaces from each other, helping authorities uncover identity fraud, and facilitating retrieval of the Government's citizenship records."

Having found that Congress possessed constitutional authority to enact § 214(d), Justice Scalia posed the question of whether Article II trumps that authority. Without resolving the thorny question of whether Article II trumps Article I, Justice Scalia found no conflict between the legislative and executive powers at issue, because "§ 214(d) has nothing to do with recognition," the core executive power the majority jealously protected. "Section 214(d) does not require the Secretary to make a formal declaration about Israel's sovereignty over Jerusalem. And nobody suggests that international custom infers acceptance of sovereignty from the birthplace designation on a passport or birth report, as it does from bilateral treaties or exchanges of ambassadors. Recognition would preclude the United States (as a matter of international law) from later contesting Israeli sovereignty over Jerusalem. But making a notation in a passport or birth report does not encumber the Republic with any international obligations. It leaves the Nation free (so far as international law is concerned) to change its mind in the future. That would be true even if the statute required *all* passports to list 'Israel.' But in fact it requires only those passports to list 'Israel' for which the citizen (or his guardian) *requests* 'Israel'; all the rest, under the Secretary's policy, list 'Jerusalem.' It is utterly impossible for this deference to private requests to constitute an act that unequivocally manifests an intention to grant recognition.

"Section 214(d) performs a more prosaic function than extending recognition. Just as foreign countries care about what our Government has to say about their borders, so too American citizens often care about what our Government has to say about their identities."

What of the Court's concern that the nation speak in one voice on matters of foreign relations? Nonsense, replied Justice Scalia. There is nothing in the Constitution that says Congress and the President must operate along exactly the same assumptions about foreign relations matters. Consider the President's power "to make Treaties," Art. II, § 2, cl. 2. "There is no question that Congress may, if it wishes, pass laws that openly flout treaties made by the President. Would anyone have dreamt that the President may refuse to carry out such laws—or, to bring the point closer to home, refuse to execute federal courts' judgments under such laws—so that the Executive may 'speak with one voice' about the country's international obligations? To ask is to answer. Today's holding puts the implied power to recognize territorial claims (which the Court infers from the power to recognize states, which it infers from the responsibility to receive ambassadors) on a higher footing than the express power to make treaties."

Justice Scalia concluded: "In the end, the Court's decision does not rest on text or history or precedent. It instead comes down to 'functional considerations'—principally the Court's perception that the Nation 'must speak with one voice' about the status of Jerusalem. The vices of this mode of analysis go beyond mere lack of footing in the Constitution. Functionalism of the sort the Court practices today will *systematically* favor the unitary President over the plural Congress in disputes involving foreign affairs. It is possible that this approach will make for more effective foreign policy, perhaps as effective as that of a monarchy. It is certain that, in the long run, it will erode the structure of separated powers that the People established for the protection of their liberty."

Query: Consider the cogency of Justice Scalia's critique of functionalism in light of the arguments made by the Obama Administration in the Libyan Bombing Problem. But also consider that Justice Scalia was in dissent in *Zivotofsky*. Does the majority opinion provide ammunition for Legal Adviser Koh's point of view? Explain.

Consider this: As a law professor, Harold Koh vigorously defended the constitutionality of the WPR—but as a State Department official he was open to the argument that Congress could not prevent or limit the President's core Commander-in-Chief authority to respond to international threats to our national security.

Would this line of argument have supported a unilateral decision by President George W. Bush to invade Iraq in 2003, upon the belief that its leader, Saddam Hussein, had weapons of mass destruction that posed an immediate threat to the United States and Israel? President Bush, unlike

President Obama, did secure congressional authorization. Although Bush acted upon an erroneous premise (because Hussein did not actually have the weapons attributed to him), isn't the same true of Obama? The premise of the Libyan bombing campaign was that the campaign would bring peace to Libya and rid the world of a troublemaking dictator—but the effect of the dictator's overthrow was chaos in the country, increased turmoil and suffering for its people, and the creation of terrorist nests that pose ever greater threats to our security.

If a justiciable controversy had brought the Libyan Bombing Campaign to the Supreme Court after *Zivotofsky,* how would the Justices have ruled?

PART 2

STATUTORY INTERPRETATION

■ ■ ■

CHAPTER 4

AN INTRODUCTION TO STATUTORY INTERPRETATION

■ ■ ■

3. TEXTUALIST THEORIES OF STATUTORY INTERPRETATION

B. THE NEW TEXTUALISM

Page 370: Insert the following Note after the Summary and Selected Quotations from Justice Scalia's *A Matter of Interpretation: Federal Courts and the Law* and before the "Statutory Preface" for *Green v. Bock Laundry*:

THE CURRENT SUPREME COURT AND JUSTICE GORSUCH'S NEW TEXTUALISM

Justice Scalia wrote *A Matter of Interpretation* twenty years ago, but his views appear alive and well with the nomination and confirmation of Justice Neil Gorsuch to take Justice Scalia's place. During his confirmation hearings, then-Judge Gorsuch declared, just as Justice Scalia has, that he was not a literalist or a strict constructionist, although he tried to consistently confine the law to its text. He testified, for example:

> The point of originalism, textualism, whatever label you want to put on it; what [a] good judge always strives to do, and I think we all do, is try to understand what the words on the page mean. Not import words that come from us. But apply what you, the people's representatives, the lawmakers have done.

Hearing on the Nomination of Neil Gorsuch to be an Associate Justice of the U.S. Supreme Court, March 22, 2017 Morning Session, Before the S. Comm. on the Judiciary, 115th Cong. 10 (2017) (statement of J. Neil Gorsuch).

In ways that are unthinkable without Justice Scalia's contributions, the Gorsuch confirmation hearings showcased the "new textualism." Supporters lauded the Judge's commitment to the text; Senator Cruz, for example, asserted that the people had voted for "originalism, textualism and rule of law," values the nominee symbolized. *Hearing on the Nomination of Neil Gorsuch to be an Associate Justice of the U.S. Supreme Court, March 20, 2017 Morning Session, Before the S. Comm. on the Judiciary*, 115th Cong. 27 (2017) (statement of Sen. Ted Cruz (R-Tex.)). Opponents, however, argued that commitments to abstract theories allowed Gorsuch to ignore the real world effects of his decisions. See *Hearing on the Nomination of Neil Gorsuch to be an Associate Justice of the U.S. Supreme Court, March 20, 2017 Afternoon Session, Before the S. Comm. on the Judiciary*, 115th Cong. 2–3 (2017) (statement of Sen. Chris Coons (D-Del.)). Senator Mazie Hirono contended that Gorsuch, while on the Tenth Circuit, had taken text "out of context," had gone to great lengths to disagree with his colleagues to "explain why some obscure or novel[ ] interpretation of a particular word in [a] statu[te] must result in finding for corporations instead of an individual who has suffered real life harm." *Id.* at 11 (statement of Sen. Mazie Hirono). Justice Gorsuch was confirmed in the Senate by a vote of 54 to 45.

In his first full opinion for a unanimous Court, Justice Gorsuch appeared to make good on his textualist promises. In *Henson v. Santander Consumer USA, Inc.*, 137 S.Ct. 1718 (2017), he rejected consumers' claims that a debt collection statute covered certain debt collectors. Phrasing the issue in home-spun fashion, Justice Gorsuch explained that the Fair Debt Collection Practices Act (FDCPA) covered the veritable "repo man," the prototypical abusive debt collector. The question was whether the FDCPA covered a consumer finance company that also collected debt. No one doubted that the company was a debt collector in the ordinary meaning sense of the term, but there was disagreement as to whether the company fell within the statute's definition of a "debt collector." Put differently, if a finance company agent came at you with a baseball bat to collect your debt, in violation of the FDCPA, would the law apply to the company? The Supreme Court (unanimously) said "no." Organizations which owned the debts they sought to collect, like Santander Consumer, were different.

Justice Gorsuch's opinion focuses on the precise words in the statute: collection of debts "owed . . . *another*." *Id.* at 1721. The repo man does not collect his own debts, but the debts of "another." Conversely, the financial services company in *Henson* was not collecting the debts of another, but its own debts (ones it bought from another company). There are some obvious consequentialist arguments supporting the Court's conclusion: to interpret the FDCPA to cover any debt collector might cover massive numbers of financial organizations, since banks as a regular matter buy, sell, and collect on debt in the contemporary marketplace. Rather than address these developments, however, Justice Gorsuch focused on arguments about grammar—whether "owed . . . another," was a past participle as opposed to an adjective (Justice Gorsuch adopted the adjective view, *id.* at 1722) and page long treatments about the meaning of the word "owed," and whether this meant previously or contemporaneously "owed." *Id.* at 1722–23.

Consistent with its textual analysis, the *Henson* opinion rejects what it dubs "policy" arguments. *Id.* at 1724. Justice Gorsuch refuses to credit the fact that, since the statute was passed, there had been a massive change in debt markets and how banks buy and collect debt. *Id.* In short, text triumphs over results or experience, a key tenet of the new textualism. Finally, Justice Gorsuch specifically embraced several of the subprinciples or assumptions of "new textualism": (1) recourse to the reasons for a statute amounts to "speculation"; (2) statutory purposes are not to be extended to meet new circumstances; and (3) statutes are inscrutable compromises whose limits should be respected. Here is Justice Gorsuch's conclusion in full, with citations omitted, *id.* at 1725:

> [W]hile it is of course our job to apply faithfully the law Congress has written, it is never our job to rewrite a constitutionally valid statutory text under the banner of speculation about what Congress might have done had it faced a question that, on everyone's account, it never faced. Indeed, it is quite mistaken to assume, as petitioners would have us, that "whatever" might appear to "further[ ] the statute's primary objective must be law." Legislation is, after all, the art of compromise, the limitations expressed in statutory terms often the price of passage, and no statute yet known "pursues its [stated] purpose[ ] at all costs." For these reasons and more besides we will not presume with petitioners that any result consistent with their account of the statute's overarching goal must be the law . . . ."

For a more recent example, in *Wisconsin Central, Ltd. v. United States,* 138 S.Ct. 2067 (June 21, 2018), District Judge Feinerman and Circuit Judge Posner *Chevron*-deferred to the IRS's interpretation that the Railroad Retirement Tax Act of 1937 includes stock options as taxable "compensation." Reversing, **Justice Gorsuch** found *Chevron* inapplicable, because the statutory text was clear: the Act defined compensation as "any form of money remuneration," and so the law could not plausibly include stock options that five Justices felt were not "monetary." Justice Gorsuch cited the agency's early construction of the law, soon after enactment, but rejected the views held by the lower courts and four Justices that there was sufficient ambiguity to justify *Chevron* deference.

PROBLEM ON NEW TEXTUALISM IN THE CURRENT COURT

In his first Term on the Court, Justice Gorsuch has proved that he aims to read statutes by intense parsing of text, a characteristic of the new textualism. Moreover, like new textualists, he has been willing to dissent to the use of legislative history, over the objections of Justice Sotomayor and Breyer. Compare *Digital Realty Trust v. Somers*, 138 S.Ct. 767, 782 (Sotomayor, J. and Breyer, J., concurring to defend the use of legislative history) with *id.* at 138 S.Ct. at 783–74 (2018) (Thomas, J, joined by Justices Alito and Gorsuch, concurring in part and concurring in judgment to reject legislative history). Continuing these themes, Justice Gorsuch wrote a significant dissent in a seemingly insignificant case involving a statute of limitations problem, *Artis v. District of Columbia*, 138 S.Ct. 594 (2018), a dissent joined by Justices Kennedy, Thomas, and Alito.

As the following problem suggests, Justice Gorsuch is following Justice Scalia's intense attention to statutory language. Also like Justice Scalia, he is ready to deploy canons of construction—strong substantive canons—to support such readings, here a federalism canon. Of course, canons are judicial canons, they are constructed by the judiciary. As you consider the following problem, ask yourself whether this intense parsing of text is faithful to the text as a whole or whether it amounts to a creative act of rewriting, and whether the federalism canon of construction—which is not textual—is doing the work. Read to the end and you will see Justice Ginsburg's rather mild chastisement that the dissenters were not in fact following the text.

The Supplemental Jurisdiction Statute, 28 U.S.C. 1367, involves cases filed in federal court that join state claims to federal claims (the state claims are called "pendent" or "supplemental" claims). The Supplemental Jurisdiction statute provides a direction to federal judges if the judge dismisses the federal claims, as to what will happen to the state claims:

> The period of limitations for any [state] claim [joined with a claim within federal-court competence] shall be tolled while the claim is pending [in federal court] and for a period of 30 days after it is dismissed unless State law provides a longer tolling period.

28 U.S.C. 1367.

The plaintiff, Stephanie Artis, brought her claims for employment discrimination against her employer, the District of Columbia. She added state law claims under the law of the District. The federal court dismissed her federal claim, and because there was no federal claim left in the case, dismissed her allied state claims. Artis then refiled her state claims in state court 59 days later. The state court dismissed her claims because they were not timely, having been filed more than 30 days after the dismissal of the federal claims. The D.C. court held that the statute quoted above, the Supplemental Jurisdiction Statute, 28 U.S.C. 1367, barred the state claims. Artis believed her claims were still good because the relevant state statute of limitations had been tolled during the federal case (she had filed in federal court with 23 months to run in the state court). But according to the state court, 28 U.S.C. 1367, the federal Supplemental Jurisdictional Statute, limited her to 30 days after federal dismissal.

Justice Ginsburg, writing for a majority, reversed. *Artis v. District of Columbia*, 138 S.Ct. 594 (2018). She interpreted the statute to be a "tolling rule," the "ordinary meaning" of "tolling" was to stop the clock on a statute of limitations. Therefore, Artis could pursue her claims in state court (call this the "stop the clock" interpretation). Justice Gorsuch, in dissent, argued that the statute should be read as giving only a "thirty day" grace period (call this the "grace period" interpretation).

Now reconsider the statute. It provides the word "tolled" first and then "tolling" later and, as the majority held, the ordinary meaning of "toll" means to "stop the clock." How, then, does the dissent get to the "grace period" conclusion? Answer: The word "tolled" is read to mean "grace period." And how is that accomplished? Well, "tolling period" is read to mean "grace period."

> So when a statute speaks of tolling a limitations period it can, naturally enough, mean *either* that the running of the limitations period is suspended *or* that the effect of the limitations period is defeated. The first understanding stops the limitations clock running until a specified event begins it running again: call it the stop clock approach. The second understanding allows the limitations clock to continue to run but defeats the effect of the clock's expiration for an additional specified period of time: call it the grace period approach.

138 S.Ct. at 609 (Gorsuch, J. dissenting) (emphasis in original).

> And the fact that Congress used a variant of the word "toll" in the second half of the sentence to refer to grace periods strongly suggests it did so in the first half of the sentence too. So that the first phrase "shall be tolled while the claim is pending and for a period of 30 days" should be understood to extend a grace period of 30 days after dismissal much as the second phrase "tolling period" is understood to refer the reader to parallel state law grace periods affording short periods for refiling after dismissal.

Id. at 610 (Gorsuch, J. dissenting). Summary: since "tolling period" in the back of the statute meant "grace period," the word "tolled" in the front part of the statute must mean "grace period."

After a lengthy discussion of the provenance of "grace period" statutes, including a seemingly erudite discourse on their historical origins in the notion of a "journey's account," Justice Gorsuch concluded with a rather dramatic statement about the importance of the case to questions of federalism.

> The Court today clears away a fence that once marked a *basic boundary between federal and state power*. Maybe it wasn't the most vital fence and maybe we've just simply forgotten why this particular fence was built in the first place. But maybe, too, we've forgotten because we've wandered so far from the idea of a federal government of limited and enumerated powers that we've begun to lose sight of what it looked like in the first place.

Id. at 617 (Gorsuch, J. dissenting).

Testing Textual Interpretations. One way to test a textual interpretation is to consider how it fares against the most parsimonious expression of that interpretation—the one using the fewest words. Think of how Congress might have written a "grace period" statute. The simplest of statutes would read: "litigants may have 30 days after the dismissal of pendant state claims to file in state court." One would not need to use the word "tolled" at all. This raises the question: Does the "new textualist" interpretation actually *eliminate* text—the word "tolled"—from the statute?

Now try this with Justice Ginsburg's interpretation. If Congress wanted to stop the clock and then provide a grace period of 30 days in addition to that tolling period, it would have written the following: "the clock on litigants' pendant state claims is stopped during the pendency of the federal claims and in addition for a grace period of thirty days, unless state law provides a longer grace period." Notice that this is similar to the actual statute but that, like Justice Gorsuch's ruling, it must read in language to make sense of the statute. The last reference to "tolling period" in the actual statute is read to be "grace period" just as the dissenters concluded. The difference in the interpretations is that the first reference to "tolled" is not eliminated from the statute.

Parsing and the Whole Act Rule. Linguists generally believe that it is impossible to know the meaning of a sentence by pulling each word from a sentence and gazing at it in isolation. In statutory interpretation, this wisdom is enshrined in the "whole act rule" which requires that the interpreter make sense of the "whole statute." In practice, this means that the interpreter toggles between a sharp focus on a particular word, and then puts that word back into the larger context to find the best meaning of the entire statute. This explains why we call "New Texualism" by the name "New" Textualism. Courts have always started with the text, they have not always engaged in this intense parsing of text, however.

Canons and Textualism. As we note in the chapter on Canons, Chapter 5, there is a tension between textualism and canons of construction. The text is provided by Congress; the canons come from judicial practice. One of the most interesting aspects of *Artis* is its strong insistence on the use of a federalism canon. In Chapter Five, we discuss the concept of the "federalism" canon first adopted by Justice O'Connor in *Gregory v. Ashcroft* (Chapter 5, § 2C). In the *Artis* dissent, Gorsuch read the statute in light of the principles of federalism, where "favoring the states" meant favoring state governments seeking to dismiss litigants' claims.

This raises two important questions about the consistency of intense textual focus and reliance on canons. Early in his career, Justice Scalia wrote that canons of construction were simply devices that tipped the scale in favor of a particular result, suggesting that they were tools of judicial activism. Later in his career, he became an enthusiast for a variety of substantive canons. Assuming that Justice Gorsuch's use of canons continues, should his critics on the court push harder on the tensions between using the text—which is created by Congress—and relying upon judge-made rules? If new textualism aims at restraint, should it be using canons at all? See Amy Coney Barrett, *Substantive Canons and Faithful Agency*, 90 B. U. L. Rev. 109 (2010) (questioning whether canons are consistent with textualism). Note that Professor Barrett, a former clerk for Justice Scalia, now sits on the Seventh Circuit and was under serious consideration for nomination to the Supreme Court in Summer of 2018.

Consequences and Textualism. The dissenters, like the twenty-four states filing amicus briefs, were concerned that a stale claim could be filed in federal court and gain new life through the federal supplemental statute. So, let us imagine a case where a plaintiff files a federal claim and appends state law claims that are about to expire in a month. Under 28 U.S.C. 1367, the state law claims are tolled, meaning the clock is stopped. If the federal claim is dismissed after four years, the plaintiff would have added four years to the state statute of limitations during the pendency of the federal claim. On the other hand, there were many cases in which the dissent's approach, like the *Artis* case itself, would appear to shorten the state statute of limitations or at least cause unfair surprise for litigants who were not sitting on their claims. Artis filed in federal court with 23 months to go on her state law claims, but under the dissent's approach, she was out of luck (in the future, such claimants would have to file simultaneously in federal and state court). Even odder claimed Justice Ginsburg, the dissenters' own interpretation could add "time" to some litigants' clocks, as for example, if the time on the state claim had already expired when the federal claim was filed. Whatever the actual practical effects, the theoretical question is whether textualism is consistent with looking at the "consequences" of an interpretation. In its early instantiations, new textualism claimed that it would not look to the "consequences" of a particular approach. Is that consistent with the dissent's focus on consequences in this case?

Consider in this light, Justice Ginsburg's rather mild chastisement that the dissent was relying not upon text but policy:

> Nor has the dissent, for all its mighty strivings, identified even one federal statute that fits its bill, i.e., a federal statute that says "tolled" but means something other than "suspended," or "paused," or "stopped." From what statutory text, then, does the dissent start?

Artis, 138 S.Ct. at 602. The footnote to this sentence states that the dissent relies upon "reasons of history, context, and policy," to argue that Congress should have written a "grace period" statute. *Id.* at 602 n. 8. Implicitly, of course, the majority is saying that the dissenters are not in fact relying upon the text.

Page 409: Insert after Notes and Questions on *Chisholm* and *Casey*, the following:

NOTE ON FALSE PRECISION: DO TEXTUALISTS ADD MEANING TO THE TEXT?

One of the most alluring aspects of textualism is its ability to appear precise and neutral as between interpretations. Query whether this is possible. As most linguists warn, when text is ambiguous, interpreters often add meaning to the text by "pragmatic enrichment," which is a linguistic term of art meaning that the interpreter is adding the interpreter's view to resolve ambiguities. A homely example comes from years of giving law school exams. Every year for the past twenty or so, one of us has told students not to "add facts" or "add law," to the exam hypothetical. Invariably they do. This is frustrating but natural—language is economical. We learn to read context into text to make sense of economical phrasing. If the context is shared, then communication is highly efficient. But what if the context is not shared? Any sophisticated consumer of interpretation must beware that the interpreter is simply "adding" their own ideas about the proper interpretation. Just as Karl

Llewellyn once critiqued canons "from the inside," as leading to no particular outcome, see Chapter 5, § 3, the questions raised in this Note amount to an internal critique of textualism as unfaithful to the text.

The classic tale comes from the linguistic philosopher Paul Grice who posed the following hypothetical. A professor writes a recommendation letter saying, "X student attended all classes." The average reader will add meaning to this brief communication, that the student is not a particularly good student. In linguistic terms, the reader will "pragmatically enrich" the text. The text says nothing about the quality of the student, but given the conventions of recommendation letter writing, the reader will infer such content, enriching the text's meaning. Pragmatic enrichments—because they come from omissions—can be "cancelled," which is to say that the letter writer could add text making the inference untenable. If the writer states that the student was the best student in the class, the original "enrichment" is negated or cancelled, to use linguistic parlance. See John Mikhail, *The Constitution and the Philosophy of Language: Entailment, Implicature, and Implied Powers*, 101 Va. L. Rev. 1063, 1073–75 (2015) (using a similar example drawn from Grice).

Adding meaning happens regularly in Supreme Court opinions even if judges fail to acknowledge it. It happens in constitutional and statutory cases. For example, consider Justice Scalia's rather famous dissent in *Morrison v. Olson,* Chapter 2, § 1. Here are his precise words: "To repeat, Article II, § 1, cl. 1, of the Constitution provides: 'The executive Power shall be vested in a President of the United States.' As I described at the outset of this opinion, this does not mean *some of* the executive power, *but all of the executive power.*" *Morrison*, 487 U.S. 654, 705 (1988) (Scalia, J., dissenting). Note the pragmatic enrichment: "*all* of the executive power." "All" executive power is *not in the text of the Constitution.* If this is correct, Scalia's textualist analysis is dependent on the interpreter's *addition of meaning, not the actual text.* Of course, some may agree with that addition in the context of the particular case—the President's control over executive officers—but no one should think the addition accurately reflects the constitutional text.

Statutory cases are full of such enrichments. Consider *West Virginia Hospitals v. Casey*, 499 U.S. 83 (1991). The statute provides for "a reasonable attorney's fee as part of the costs." Cut down to its essential textual analysis, Justice Scalia, for the majority, isolates the term "attorney," and concludes, from this isolation, that witness fees are excluded. An "attorney" is not a witness, ergo, no witness fees. But notice what happens if, like Justice Stevens in dissent, we switch our attention away from isolating the term "attorney" to isolating a different statutory term—"costs" (as did Justice Stevens in dissent). The result seems to change: if witnesses' costs are "costs," they are covered. Focus on attorneys' fees, and the claimants fail; focus on costs and the claimants win. Lesson: isolating particular texts reduces the information economy and invites interpreters to add meaning to the text.

Notice that this method—the choice of text—not only predetermines winners and losers, it excludes language in the statutory text. The statute says that an "attorney's fee" is to be provided as "part of the costs." *Id.* at 85 n.1. Isolation reduces the full statute by asking the interpreter to disregard the rest of the text. Taken literally, the words "as part of" mean that "costs" should be a larger category than fees, suggesting again that focusing on the term "attorney's" is not a proper reading of the statute—that the statute must cover more than attorneys' fees. Put differently, the choice of text has the capacity not only to focus the interpreter on particular terms but also to permit the interpreter to read out of the text important statutorily-prescribed relationships. "Attorney's fee," now isolated, thus becomes by implication *exclusive,* leading Justice Scalia to read the statute as if it said " '*only an attorney's fee*," even if the statute said no such thing.

From this humble example, we can posit three analytic stages: (1) textual *isolation* of particular terms, (2) isolation leading to statutory *reduction* of other terms, and (3) reading in additional meaning not found in the text—*addition.* As you read through the cases that follow, consider whether you can apply these analytic categories. Ask yourself whether textual interpreters are *adding* the very "hard edges"—*only, all*—of exclusivity or limitation that make the rule appear—emphasis on appear—precise and rule-like. If this is correct, however, the interpreter, not the text, is adding the hard edges. To see how this analysis applies to other statutory and constitutional cases, see Victoria Nourse, *Picking and Choosing Text: Lessons for Statutory Interpretation from the Philosophy of Language*, Fla. L. Rev. (forthcoming 2017); Victoria Nourse, *Executive Power, Reclaiming the Constitutional Text from Originalism*, Cal. L. Rev. (forthcoming 2017).

One of us adds another angle to this question. Even if one takes a textualist at her word that she "neutrally" applies linguistic canons on statutory language, isn't that itself not only a value choice but also its own form of activist legislation? Interpreting statutes using canons that impose perfection and consistency on statutes that were not drafted by Congress itself as perfect, consistent or coherent with other statutes across the U.S. Code can add and change statutory meaning as much as (if not more than) using purpose or policy norms. In the *Casey* case, detailed above, Justice Scalia looked at *forty-one* different statutes across the U.S. Code that contained the term "attorney's fee" and imposed a rule that they all must mean the same thing, even though Congress does not draft that way. Congressional committees are subject specific, and do not cohere statutes across topics. See Abbe R. Gluck & Lisa Schultz Bressman, *Statutory Interpretation from the Inside—An Empirical Study of Congressional Drafting, Delegation and the Canons—Part I,* 65 Stan. L. Rev. 901, 936–37 (2013). In *King v. Burwell*, the health care case discussed in Chapter 1, had the Chief Justice imposed drafting perfection on the Affordable Care Act, the result would have unquestionably been different from what Congress intended and indeed thought it had written. Textualists have been unwilling to admit this this kind of judicial activism lies within their doctrines, taking cover in claims of neutrality, as noted above. But there is just as much of a value choice here as there is when we impose policy canons. The values in play—consistency, notice, coherence, etc.—may be widely accepted judicial/legal system values, but they are still values superimposed on top of statutes, not derived from within them. For more on these points, see Abbe R. Gluck, *Congress, Statutory Interpretation, and the Failure of Formalism: The CBO Canon and Other Ways That Courts Can Improve on What They Are Already Trying to Do*, 84 U. Chi. L. Rev. 177, 186–87 (2017); Abbe R. Gluck, *Justice Scalia's Unfinished Business in Statutory Interpretation: Where Textualism's Formalism Gave Up*, 92 Notre Dame L. Rev. (2017).

C. PRAGMATIC APPROACHES

Page 445: End of Chapter. Insert the following case and notes at the end of the chapter:

STATUTORY PREFACE FOR *HIVELY*

TITLE VII OF THE CIVIL RIGHTS ACT OF 1964

Section 701, 42 U.S.C. § 2000e. Definitions * * *

(k) The terms "because of sex" or "on the basis of sex" include, but are not limited to, because of or on the basis of pregnancy, childbirth, or related medical conditions; and women affected by pregnancy, childbirth, or related medical conditions shall be treated the same for all employment-related purposes, including receipt of benefits under fringe benefit programs, as other persons not so affected but similar in their ability or inability to work * * *. This subsection shall not require an employer to pay for health insurance benefits for abortion, except where the life of the mother would be endangered if the fetus were carried to term, or except where medical complications have arisen from an abortion: Provided, That nothing herein shall preclude an employer from providing abortion benefits or otherwise affect bargaining agreements in regard to abortion. [Added 1978]

Section 703, 42 U.S.C. § 2000e–2. Unlawful Employment Practices.

(a) Employer Practices. It shall be an unlawful employment practice for an employer—

(1) to fail or refuse to hire or to discharge any individual, or otherwise to discriminate against any individual with respect to his compensation, terms, conditions, or privileges of employment, because of such individual's race, color, religion, sex, or national origin; or

(2) to limit, segregate, or classify his employees or applicants for employment in any way which would deprive or tend to deprive any individual of employment opportunities or otherwise adversely affect his status as an employee, because of such individual's race, color, religion, sex, or national origin. * * *

(e) Businesses or enterprises with personnel qualified on basis of religion, sex, or national origin; educational institutions with personnel of particular religion

Notwithstanding any other provision of this subchapter, (1) it shall not be an unlawful employment practice for an employer to hire and employ employees, for an employment agency to classify, or refer for employment any individual, for a labor organization to classify its membership or to classify or refer for employment any individual, or for an employer, labor organization, or joint labor-management committee controlling apprenticeship or other training or retraining programs to admit or employ any individual in any such program, on the basis of his religion, sex, or national origin in those certain instances where religion, sex, or national origin is a bona fide occupational qualification reasonably necessary to the normal operation of that particular business or enterprise * * *.

(m) Impermissible consideration of race, color, religion, sex, or national origin in employment practices

Except as otherwise provided in this subchapter, an unlawful employment practice is established when the complaining party demonstrates that race, color, religion, sex, or national origin was a motivating *factor* for any employment practice, even though other factors also motivated the practice. [Added 1991]

KIMBERLY HIVELY V. IVY TECH COMMUNITY COLLEGE

United States Court of Appeals for the Seventh Circuit (en banc), 2017.
853 F.3d 339.

WOOD, CHIEF JUDGE.

[Title VII of the Civil Rights Act of 1964 bars employment discrimination "because of * * * sex." A successful part-time teacher at Ivy Tech Community College, Kimberly Hively complained that the college refused to consider her for a permanent job because she is a lesbian. If true, does that constitute discrimination because of sex? Because Title VII does not bar discrimination "because of * * * sexual orientation," federal appeals courts have uniformly said "no" to this question—until the Seventh Circuit, sitting en banc, reconsidered the issue.]

Much ink has been spilled about the proper way to go about the task of statutory interpretation. One can stick, to the greatest extent possible, to the language enacted by the legislature; one could consult the legislative history that led up to the bill that became law; one could examine later actions of the legislature (*i.e.* efforts to amend the law and later enactments) for whatever light they may shed; and one could use a combination of these methods. See, *e.g.*, William Eskridge, Jr., & Philip Frickey, *Legislation and Statutory Interpretation* (2d ed. 2007); Antonin

Scalia & Bryan A. Garner, *Reading Law: The Interpretation of Legal Texts* (2012); Adrian Vermeule, *Judging Under Uncertainty: An Institutional Theory of Legal Interpretation* (2006); Victoria F. Nourse, *A Decision Theory of Statutory Interpretation: Legislative History by the Rules,* 122 Yale L.J. 70 (2012); Cass R. Sunstein, *Interpreting Statutes in the Regulatory State,* 103 Harv. L. Rev. 407 (1989).

Few people would insist that there is a need to delve into secondary sources if the statute is plain on its face. Even if it is not pellucid, the best source for disambiguation is the broader context of the statute that the legislature—in this case, Congress—passed. This is uncontroversial when the reading seems consistent with the conventional wisdom about the reach of the law. It becomes somewhat harder to swallow if the language reveals suspected or actual unintended consequences. It is then that some have thought that legislative history should be used to block a particular reading of a statute. Legislative history, however, is notoriously malleable. Even worse is the temptation to try to divine the significance of unsuccessful legislative efforts to change the law. Those failures can mean almost anything, ranging from the lack of necessity for a proposed change because the law already accomplishes the desired goal, to the undesirability of the change because a majority of the legislature is happy with the way the courts are currently interpreting the law, to the irrelevance of the non-enactment, when it is attributable to nothing more than legislative logrolling or gridlock that had nothing to do with its merits.

Ivy Tech sets great store on the fact that Congress has frequently considered amending Title VII to add the words "sexual orientation" to the list of prohibited characteristics, yet it has never done so. Many of our sister circuits have also noted this fact. In our view, however, it is simply too difficult to draw a reliable inference from these truncated legislative initiatives to rest our opinion on them. The goalposts have been moving over the years, as the Supreme Court has shed more light on the scope of the language that already is in the statute: no *sex* discrimination. * * *

Moreover, the agency most closely associated with this law, the Equal Employment Opportunity Commission, in 2015 announced that it now takes the position that Title VII's prohibition against sex discrimination encompasses discrimination on the basis of sexual orientation. See *Baldwin v. Foxx*, EEOC Appeal No. 0120133080, 2015 WL 4397641 (July 15, 2015). Our point here is not that we have a duty to defer to the EEOC's position. We assume for present purposes that no such duty exists. But the Commission's position may have caused some in Congress to think that legislation is needed to carve sexual orientation *out* of the statute, not to put it *in*. In the end, we have no idea what inference to draw from congressional inaction or later enactments, because there is no way of knowing what explains each individual member's votes, much less what explains the failure of the body as a whole to change this 1964 statute. * * *

Hively alleges that if she had been a man married to a woman (or living with a woman, or dating a woman) and everything else had stayed the same, Ivy Tech would not have refused to promote her and would not have fired her. This describes paradigmatic sex discrimination. * * * Ivy Tech is disadvantaging her *because she is a woman.* Nothing in the complaint hints that Ivy Tech has an anti-marriage policy that extends to heterosexual relationships, or for that matter even an anti-partnership policy that is gender-neutral.

Viewed through the lens of the gender non-conformity line of cases, Hively represents the ultimate case of failure to conform to the female stereotype (at least as understood in a place such as modern America, which views heterosexuality as the norm and other forms of sexuality as exceptional): she is not heterosexual. * * * Hively's claim is no different from the claims brought by women who were rejected for jobs in traditionally male workplaces, such as fire departments, construction, and policing. The employers in those cases were policing the boundaries of what jobs or behaviors they found acceptable for a woman (or in some cases, for a man).

This was the critical point that the Supreme Court was making in [*Price Waterhouse v. Hopkins*, 490 U.S. 228 (1989).] The four justices in the plurality and the two justices concurring in the judgment recognized that Hopkins had alleged that her employer was discriminating only against women who behaved in what the employer viewed as too "masculine" a way—no makeup, no jewelry, no fashion sense. And even before *Hopkins*, courts had found sex discrimination in situations where women were resisting stereotypical roles. As far back as 1971, the Supreme Court held that Title VII does not permit an employer to refuse to hire women with pre-school-age children, but not men. *Phillips v. Martin Marietta Corp.*, 400 U.S. 542 (1971). * * *

Hively also has argued that action based on sexual orientation is sex discrimination under the associational theory. It is now accepted that a person who is discriminated against because of the protected characteristic of one with whom she associates is actually being disadvantaged because of her own traits. This line of cases began with [*Loving v. Virginia,* 388 U.S. 1 (1967)], in which the Supreme Court held that "restricting the freedom to marry solely because of racial classifications violates the central meaning of the Equal Protection Clause. The Court rejected the argument that miscegenation statutes do not violate equal protection because they "punish equally both the white and the Negro participants in an interracial marriage." When dealing with a statute containing racial classifications, it wrote, "the fact of equal application does not immunize the statute from the very heavy burden of justification" required by the Fourteenth Amendment for lines drawn by race.

[Circuit courts have all but uniformly applied *Loving* to hold that an employer's discriminating against an employee because of the race of her partner or associates has discriminated "because of race" under Title VII. Chief Judge Wood applied the principle of those race discrimination cases to the sex discrimination claimed by Professor Hively.]

POSNER, CIRCUIT JUDGE, concurring.

* * * It is helpful to note at the outset that the interpretation of statutes comes in three flavors. The first and most conventional is the extraction of the original meaning of the statute—the meaning intended by the legislators—and corresponds to interpretation in ordinary discourse. Knowing English I can usually determine swiftly and straightforwardly the meaning of a statement, oral or written, made to me in English (not always, because the statement may be garbled, grammatically intricate or inaccurate, obtuse, or complex beyond my ability to understand).

The second form of interpretation, illustrated by the commonplace local ordinance which commands "no vehicles in the park," is interpretation by unexpressed intent, whereby we understand that although an ambulance is a vehicle, the ordinance was not intended to include ambulances among the "vehicles" forbidden to enter the park. * * *

Finally and most controversially, interpretation can mean giving a fresh meaning to a statement (which can be a statement found in a constitutional or statutory text)—a meaning that infuses the statement with vitality and significance today. An example of this last form of interpretation—the form that in my mind is most clearly applicable to the present case—is the Sherman Antitrust Act, enacted in 1890, long before there was a sophisticated understanding of the economics of monopoly and competition. Times have changed; and for more than thirty years the Act has been interpreted in conformity to the modern, not the nineteenth-century, understanding of the relevant economics. The Act has thus been updated by, or in the name of, judicial interpretation—the form of interpretation that consists of making old law satisfy modern needs and understandings. And a common form of interpretation it is, despite its flouting "original meaning." Statutes and constitutional provisions frequently are interpreted on the basis of present need and present understanding rather than original meaning—constitutional provisions even more frequently, because most of them are older than most statutes.

Title VII of the Civil Rights Act of 1964, now more than half a century old, invites an interpretation that will update it to the present, a present that differs markedly from the era in which the Act was enacted. But I need to emphasize that this third form of interpretation—call it judicial interpretive updating—presupposes a lengthy interval between enactment and (re)interpretation. A statute when passed has an understood meaning;

it takes years, often many years, for a shift in the political and cultural environment to change the understanding of the statute. * * *

We now understand that homosexual men and women (and also bisexuals, defined as having both homosexual and heterosexual orientations) are normal in the ways that count, and beyond that have made many outstanding intellectual and cultural contributions to society (think for example of Tchaikovsky, Oscar Wilde, Jane Addams, André Gide, Thomas Mann, Marlene Dietrich, Bayard Rustin, Alan Turing, Alec Guinness, Leonard Bernstein, Van Cliburn, and James Baldwin—a very partial list). We now understand that homosexuals, male and female, play an essential role, in this country at any rate, as adopters of children from foster homes * * *. The compelling social interest in protecting homosexuals (male and female) from discrimination justifies an admittedly loose "interpretation" of the word "sex" in Title VII to embrace homosexuality: an interpretation that cannot be imputed to the framers of the statute but that we are entitled to adopt in light of (to quote Holmes) "*what this country has become*," or, in Blackstonian terminology, to embrace as a sensible deviation from the literal or original meaning of the statutory language. * * *

The majority opinion states that Congress in 1964 "may not have realized or understood the full scope of the words it chose." This could be understood to imply that the statute forbade discrimination against homosexuals but the framers and ratifiers of the statute were not smart enough to realize that. I would prefer to say that theirs was the then-current understanding of the key word—sex. "Sex" in 1964 meant gender, not sexual orientation. What the framers and ratifiers understandably didn't understand was how attitudes toward homosexuals would change in the following half century. They shouldn't be blamed for that failure of foresight. *We* understand the words of Title VII differently not because we're smarter than the statute's framers and ratifiers but because we live in a different era, a different culture. Congress in the 1960s did not foresee the sexual revolution of the 2000s. What our court announced in *Doe v. City of Belleville*, 119 F.3d 563, 572 (7th Cir. 1997), is what Congress had declared in 1964: "the traditional notion of 'sex.' "

I would prefer to see us acknowledge openly that today we, who are judges rather than members of Congress, are imposing on a half-century-old statute a meaning of "sex discrimination" that the Congress that enacted it would not have accepted. This is something courts do fairly frequently to avoid statutory obsolescence and concomitantly to avoid placing the entire burden of updating old statutes on the legislative branch. We should not leave the impression that we are merely the obedient servants of the 88th Congress (1963–1965), carrying out their wishes. We are not. We are taking advantage of what the last half century has taught.

FLAUM, CIRCUIT JUDGE, joined by RIPPLE, CIRCUIT JUDGE, concurring.

* * * [D]iscrimination against an employee on the basis of their homosexuality is necessarily, in part, discrimination based on their sex. Fundamental to the definition of homosexuality is the sexual attraction to individuals of the "same sex." [Citing various dictionaries.] One cannot consider a person's homosexuality without also accounting for their sex: doing so would render "same" and "own" meaningless. As such, discriminating against that employee because they are homosexual constitutes discriminating against an employee because of (A) the employee's sex, *and* (B) their sexual attraction to individuals of the *same sex.* And "sex," under Title VII, is an enumerated trait.

This raises the question: Does Title VII's text require a plaintiff to show that an employer discriminated against them *solely* "because of" an enumerated trait? Again, I turn to the text, which clearly states:

> Except as otherwise provided in this subchapter, an unlawful employment practice is established when the complaining party demonstrates that . . . sex . . . was *a motivating factor for any employment practice, even though other factors also motivated the practice.*

42 U.S.C. § 2000e–2(m) (emphasis added). Congress added this amendment to Title VII partially in response to the Supreme Court's plurality decision in *Hopkins*, in which the Court stated:

> [S]ince we know that the words "because of" do not mean "*solely* because of," we also know that Title VII meant to condemn even those decisions based on a mixture of legitimate and illegitimate considerations. When, therefore, an employer considers both gender and legitimate factors at the time of making a decision, that decision was "because of" sex and the other, legitimate considerations. . . . We need not leave our common sense at the doorstep when we interpret a statute. It is difficult for us to imagine that, in the simple words "because of," Congress meant to obligate a plaintiff to identify the precise causal role played by legitimate and illegitimate motivations in the employment decision she challenges. We conclude, instead, that Congress meant to obligate her to prove that the employer relied upon sex-based considerations in coming to its decision.

The Court made clear that "[t]he critical inquiry . . . is whether gender was *a factor* in the employment decision" when it was made. So if discriminating against an employee because she is homosexual is equivalent to discriminating against her because she is (A) a woman who is (B) sexually attracted to women, then it is motivated, in part, by an enumerated trait: the employee's sex. That is all an employee must show to successfully allege a Title VII claim. * * *

SYKES, CIRCUIT JUDGE, with whom BAUER and KANNE, CIRCUIT JUDGES, join, dissenting.

* * * The majority deploys a judge-empowering, common-law decision method that leaves a great deal of room for judicial discretion. So does Judge Posner in his concurrence. Neither is faithful to the statutory text, read fairly, as a reasonable person would have understood it when it was adopted. The result is a statutory amendment courtesy of unelected judges. Judge Posner admits this; he embraces and argues for this conception of judicial power. The majority does not, preferring instead to smuggle in the statutory amendment under cover of an aggressive reading of loosely related Supreme Court precedents. Either way, the result is the same: the circumvention of the legislative process by which the people govern themselves.

Respect for the constraints imposed on the judiciary by a system of written law must begin with fidelity to the traditional first principle of statutory interpretation: When a statute supplies the rule of decision, our role is to give effect to the enacted text, interpreting the statutory language as a reasonable person would have understood it at the time of enactment. We are not authorized to infuse the text with a new or unconventional meaning or to update it to respond to changed social, economic, or political conditions. * * *

Judicial statutory updating, whether overt or covert, cannot be reconciled with the constitutional design. The Constitution establishes a procedure for enacting and amending statutes: bicameralism and presentment. *See* U.S. Const. art. I, § 7. Needless to say, statutory amendments brought to you by the judiciary do not pass through this process. That is why a textualist decision method matters: When we assume the power to alter the original public meaning of a statute through the process of interpretation, we assume a power that is not ours. The Constitution assigns the power to make and amend statutory law to the elected representatives of the people. However welcome today's decision might be as a policy matter, it comes at a great cost to representative self-government. * * *

* * * I agree with my colleagues that the proposed new interpretation is not necessarily incorrect simply because no one in the 1964 Congress that adopted Title VII intended or anticipated its application to sexual-orientation discrimination. The subjective intentions of the legislators do not matter. Statutory interpretation is an objective inquiry that looks for the meaning the statutory language conveyed to a reasonable person at the time of enactment. The objective meaning of the text is not delimited by what individual lawmakers specifically had in mind when they voted for the statute. The Supreme Court made this point clear in *Oncale* when it said that "statutory prohibitions often go beyond the principal evil to cover

reasonably comparable evils, and it is ultimately the provisions of our laws rather than the principal concerns of our legislators by which we are governed." *Oncale v. Sundowner Offshore Servs., Inc.*, 523 U.S. 75, 79 (1998). Broadly worded statutes are regularly applied to circumstances beyond the subjective contemplation of the lawmakers who adopted the text. * * *

Title VII does not define discrimination "because of sex." In common, ordinary usage in 1964—and now, for that matter—the word "sex" means biologically *male* or *female*; it does not also refer to sexual orientation. *See, e.g.*, *Sex*, The American Heritage Dictionary of the English Language (1st ed. 1969) (defining "sex" as "[t]he property or quality by which organisms are classified according to their reproductive functions[;] [e]ither of two divisions, designated *male* and *female*, of this classification") * * *.

To a fluent speaker of the English language—then and now—the ordinary meaning of the word "sex" does not fairly include the concept of "sexual orientation." The two terms are never used interchangeably, and the latter is not subsumed within the former; there is no overlap in meaning. * * * The words plainly describe different traits, and the separate and distinct meaning of each term is easily grasped. More specifically to the point here, discrimination "because of sex" is not reasonably understood to include discrimination based on sexual orientation, a different immutable characteristic. Classifying people by sexual orientation is different than classifying them by sex. The two traits are categorically distinct and widely recognized as such. There is no ambiguity or vagueness here. * * *

This commonsense understanding is confirmed by the language Congress uses when it *does* legislate against sexual-orientation discrimination. For example, the Violence Against Women Act prohibits funded programs and activities from discriminating "on the basis of actual or perceived race, color, religion, national origin, *sex*, gender identity, . . . *sexual orientation*, or disability." 42 U.S.C. § 13925(b)(13)(A) (emphases added). If sex discrimination is commonly understood to encompass sexual-orientation discrimination, then listing the two categories separately, as this statute does, is needless surplusage. The federal Hate Crimes Act is another example. It imposes a heightened punishment for causing or attempting to cause bodily injury "to any person, because of the actual or perceived religion, national origin, *gender*, *sexual orientation*, gender identity, or disability of any person." 18 U.S.C. § 249(a)(2)(A) (emphases added). * * *

The purpose of the comparative method is to isolate whether a statutorily forbidden motivation is at work *as a factual matter*—in a sex-discrimination case, to isolate whether the defendant employer took a particular adverse employment action against a particular female employee because she is a woman or against a particular male employee because he is a man. * * * The comparative method of proof is a useful technique for uncovering the employer's real motive for taking the challenged action. Comparing the plaintiff to a similarly situated employee of the opposite sex can help the fact finder determine whether the employer was actually motivated by the plaintiff's sex or acted for some other reason. It's a device for ferreting out a prohibited discriminatory motive as an actual cause of the adverse employment action; it does this by controlling for other possible motives. If a female plaintiff can point to a male employee who is identical to her in every material respect and was treated more favorably, then the fact finder can draw an inference that the unfavorable treatment was actually motivated by the plaintiff's sex. * * *

For the comparison to be valid as a test for the role of sex discrimination in this employment decision, the proper comparison is to ask how Ivy Tech treated qualified gay men. If an employer is willing to hire gay men but not lesbians, then the comparative method has exposed an actual case of sex discrimination. If, on the other hand, an employer hires only heterosexual men and women and rejects all homosexual applicants, then no inference of sex discrimination is possible, though we could perhaps draw an inference of sexual-orientation discrimination. * * *

The majority also draws on *Loving*, the Supreme Court's iconic decision invalidating Virginia's miscegenation statutes on equal-protection grounds. This case is not a variant of *Loving*. Miscegenation laws plainly employ invidious racial classifications; they are inherently racially discriminatory. In contrast, sexual-orientation discrimination springs from a wholly different kind of bias than sex discrimination. The two forms of discrimination classify people based on different traits and thus are not the same. * * *

This brings me to my last point, which concerns the principle of *stare decisis*. The general rule is that "*stare decisis* . . . has 'special force' " in the domain of statutory interpretation "for 'Congress remains free to alter what we have done.' " *John R. Sand & Gravel Co. v. United States*, 552 U.S. 130, 139 (2008) (quoting *Patterson v. McLean Credit Union*, 491 U.S. 164, 172–73 (1989)). Special force or no, the foundational assumptions of the rule of law and due regard for the prudential virtues of stability, reliability, and predictability should inspire some caution here. A decision to upend settled precedent "demands special justification." *Michigan v. Bay Mills Indian Cmty.*, 134 S.Ct. 2024, 2036 (2014) (quoting *Arizona v. Rumsey*, 467 U.S. 203, 212 (1984)). That "special justification" must *at least* begin with a convincing case that the challenged precedent is gravely wrong.

As I've explained, a convincing case has not been made. If more is needed, consider for a moment the next step in this litigation. When this case returns to the district court, it will not matter whether the evidence shows that Ivy Tech rejected Hively in favor of male applicants, female applicants, or a combination of men and women. If the facts show that Ivy Tech hired heterosexuals for the six full-time positions, then the community college may be found liable for discriminating against Hively *because of her sex*. That will be so even if *all six positions were filled by women*. Try explaining that to a jury. * * *

NOTES ON HIVELY *AND THEORIES OF STATUTORY INTERPRETATION*

Broadly speaking, the court of appeals judges started with different methodological approaches. Judges Sykes applied what she considered to be Title VII's *original meaning*: the original, objective meaning (to a reasonable speaker) entailed by the statutory text, namely, discrimination "because of * * * sex." Judge Flaum applied a *structural* approach: What does that language mean in light of the whole statute?[27] Judge Posner called for judicial *dynamic interpretation* of Title VII, whose original meaning, in his view, has been rendered obsolescent by changed social and workplace norms. Chief Judge Wood followed a *pragmatic approach* that considers statutory text, purpose, and precedents, as well as relevant constitutional norms and directives.

As you consider the cogency of each opinion in the case, consider, too, the cogency of the different theories of statutory interpretation. What follows are some materials not considered by these judges. For more detailed treatment of these additional materials, see William Eskridge Jr., *Title VII's Statutory History and the Sex Discrimination Argument for LGBT Workplace Protections*, 127 Yale L.J. 322 (2017).

1. *Original Meaning of "Discriminate Because of * * * Sex."* Start with *Webster's* definition of "sex" on the eve of the 1964 Act:

- "[o]ne of the two divisions of organisms formed on the distinction of male and female," or *sex as biology*;
- "[t]he sphere of behavior dominated by the relations between male and female," or *sex as gender* (man=masculine, woman=feminine);
- "the whole sphere of behavior related even indirectly to the sexual functions and embracing all affectionate and pleasure-seeking conduct," or *sex as sexuality*.

Webster's New International Dictionary of the English Language 2296 (2d unabridged ed. 1961). Can it be maintained (as the dissenters say) that "sex" had but one meaning in 1964? Many schools in the 1960s had "sex education" programs. What topics might have been covered in programs teaching about

[27] Judge Sykes did not believe Judge Flaum's whole act analysis was persuasive, because in her view there was zero discrimination because of sex. She did, however, consider the whole code—Congress's targeted terminology (barring discrimination because of "sexual orientation") in other statutes.

"sex"? As Judge Sykes would say, sex as biology would be covered: teach kids the morphological differences between men and women. But might a sex education course also teach about gender roles, either descriptively or prescriptively? And surely a sex education course might teach about human sexuality—including variation in sexual practices as well as reproductive sex.

Judge Sykes also maintained that "discriminate because of sex" has got to mean something different than "discriminate because of sexual orientation." If so, the question then becomes: Different in what way? Do the two types of discrimination have no overlapping application, as Judge Sykes assumed? Or might they overlap (Judge Flaum's view)? Or might one kind of discrimination be a subset of the other (Chief Judge Wood's perspective)? Overlapping or subsumed terms are common in antidiscrimination law. For an example of overlapping terms, Title VII bars discrimination because of skin color, national origin, and race, terms that overlap considerably. For an example of subsumed terms, many state and municipal laws prohibit discrimination both because of sex and because of pregnancy, even though the latter is a subset of the former.[28] Other state statutes, as well as Title VII, define discriminate because of pregnancy as a subset of discriminate because of sex.

2. *Original Meaning: Terms of Art and the* Loving *Analogy.* Handed down shortly after Congress enacted Title VII, *McLaughlin v. Florida,* 379 U.S. 184 (1964) (striking down a state law creating greater penalties for different-race cohabitation), was the leading Supreme Court case on this issue in 1964. *Loving* was the leading case when Congress significantly expanded Title VII in the 1972 Amendments. As a matter of original *legal* meaning, firing a white employee dating a black woman because of prejudice against "racial mixing" would have been discrimination "because of race" in 1964 and in 1972, as the circuit courts have held, almost uniformly. In parallel fashion, why (then) would it not be discrimination "because of sex" to fire a female employee because she is dating a woman?

The same Congress that enacted the expansive 1972 Amendments to Title VII also passed the Equal Rights Amendment, which would have barred state discrimination "on account of sex." Anticipating Chief Judge Wood's reasoning, Professor Paul Freund told the 1972 Congress that, by analogy to *Loving,* the ERA would bar states from discriminating against same-sex couples in their marriage laws. See Note, *The Legality of Homosexual Marriage*, 82 Yale L.J. 573, 574 (1973). This argument did not prevent Congress from passing the ERA, but it was persuasive to many state legislators and voters, who prevented the ratification of the ERA. Does this not suggest that Chief Judge Wood's argument is a plausible reading? That Title VII, as amended in 1972, was at least ambiguous?

---

[28] For statutes prohibiting employment actions based on both sex and pregnancy, see Utah Code Ann. § 34A–5–106; Va. Code Ann. § 2.2–3900; Wyo. Stat. § 27–9–105. For similar examples in housing discrimination law, see, e.g., Alaska Stat. § 18.80.200, 240. See also 775 ILCS 5/1–102 (general civil rights protection).

Judge Sykes resists the analogy: the different-race marriage bars rested upon racism, while same-sex employment bars rest upon antigay prejudice or stereotypes. There is a disconnect between the regulated classification and the class that benefits:

	Classification	**Class Harmed**	**Philosophy**
Loving	Race	Racial Minorities	Racism
ERA	Sex	Women	Sexism
Hively	Sex	Gay Men & Lesbians	Homophobia

One problem with this argument is that Title VII is not written just for the benefit of women (and racial minorities). It prohibits sex discrimination when men are the victims. Hence, there is no single beneficiary "class," there is just a regulated "classification."

So Judge Sykes has got to be relying on the purpose of Title VII. Parallel to constitutional equal protection, Title VII's sex discrimination bar has as its central purpose the entrenchment of a liberal workplace, where employees are hired and evaluated based upon their capabilities and not their race, sex, or religion. A corollary, emphasized in the congressional deliberations, was that sex-based stereotypes are banned from the workplace. See Vicki Schultz, *Taking Sex Discrimination Seriously,* 91 Denv. U. L. Rev. 995, 1108–09 (2015). Professor Koppelman has argued that antigay attitudes rest substantially on the same kind of gender stereotypes that underwrite sexism and patriarchy. See Andrew Koppelman, *Why Discrimination Against Lesbians and Gay Men Is Sex Discrimination,* 69 N.Y.U. L. Rev. 197, 219, 238–40 (1994). For example, few employers shun lesbians because they are disgusted by oral sex, which most Americans enjoy; instead, antilesbian policies are driven by disgust that a woman would choose another woman as her sexual partner.

Under such an analysis, *Hively* and Title VII look a lot like gay marriage and the ERA—and match up well with the *Loving* analogy.

	Classification	**Effective Policy**	**Philosophy**
Loving	Race	Racial Segregation	Racism
		No Racial Mixing	White Supremacy
ERA	Sex	Sex Segregation	Sexism
		Rigid Gender Roles	Patriarchy
Hively	Sex	Compulsory Heterosexuality	Sexism
		Rigid Gender Roles	Patriarchy

3. *Statutory History and Structure.* Judge Flaum argues from the whole act: it is very hard to say that an employer who objects to female employees because of the biological "sex" of their romantic partners is not discriminating at least in part "because of sex," even if "sex" has the one meaning conceded by Judge Sykes (i.e., sex as biology). As amended in 1991, Title VII provides that an employer can violate the law in "mixed motive" cases, so long as one significant "motivating factor" is sex, even if "other factors also motivated the practice." Does Judge Sykes have a persuasive answer to this structural argument?

The larger point raised by Judge Flaum is that the text of Title VII has evolved dramatically, rendering original meaning itself dynamic. The Supreme Court has repeatedly said that judges should impute knowledge about terms of art to Congress when it passes legislation, so when Congress expanded Title VII in the 1972 Amendments, is it fair to impute knowledge of *Loving*? The Freund argument about the ERA? Congress also amended Title VII in 1978, creating the current definition of "sex" in § 701(k). And Congress extensively expanded Title VII yet again in the 1991 Amendments, which added new § 703(m), invoked by Judge Flaum.

This is another example of how statutory interpretation is inevitably dynamic. Because of this and other amendments, Title VII means something different today than it did when it was enacted in 1964—based upon new statutory texts adopted by our democratically elected representatives. See William Eskridge Jr., *Dynamic Statutory Interpretation* (1994).

Do you agree with Judge Sykes that there is no ambiguity in Title VII as regards discrimination based upon the sex of the employee's intimate partners? What is her best argument for no ambiguity? One argument she makes is a whole code argument: Congress has repeatedly added "sexual orientation" to antidiscrimination statutes when it has sought to protect lesbian and gay people—so how can a court do the same thing in a statute just applicable to sex discrimination? Can an ambiguous text be rendered unambiguous by reference to the whole code?

4. *Statutory Purpose.* One way of understanding the central purpose of Title VII is to eliminate sex-based stereotypes and other bars to a liberal workplace for men as well as women. As § 701(k) puts it, Title VII demands that employers treat people who are "similar in their ability or inability to work" the same and bars dissimilar treatment partially motivated by the sex of the employee (or her spouse or associates, if you accept the *Loving* analogy). Is there a more narrow way to think about statutory purpose?

In thinking about sex stereotypes, a distinction is useful. *Descriptive* stereotypes are assumptions about the different capabilities and limitations supposedly linked with one's sex. If an employer believes most women are emotional and passive and do not have the same commitment to work as men do, this descriptive gender stereotype will disadvantage women applying for supervisory positions requiring initiative and long hours. *Prescriptive* stereotypes are preferences about what roles and attitudes ought to be associated with each sex. If an employer believes that women ought to be passive and compliant to men's initiatives, this prescriptive gender stereotype will disadvantage women applying for supervisory positions.

The original (1964) justifications for the sex discrimination provision in Title VII addressed both kinds of stereotyping. Women were disadvantaged in the workplace because employers believed that women's natural inclination was to be mothers and housekeepers (descriptive stereotyping) and that this was what a woman should be doing (prescriptive stereotyping). By its broad text and apparent legislative purpose, Title VII was supposed to make stereotype-based discrimination illegal. See Cary Franklin, *Inventing the "Traditional Concept" of Sex Discrimination*, 125 Harv. L. Rev. 1307 (2012).

During its deliberations in 1972, Congress's committees agreed with this understanding of the statutory purpose. Arguing for an expansion of Title VII to include local, state, and federal government employers and to empower the EEOC, committee reports understood that sex discrimination remained pervasive in the workplace, in large part because of traditional stereotypes that women's best role in life is as a wife and mother in the home. E.g., H.R. Rep. No. 92–238, at 4–5 (1971). In other words, the feminist understanding of Title VII was a building block upon which Congress constructed the 1972 Amendments, and was a central justification for exercising its Fourteenth Amendment power to abrogate state immunity from lawsuits for sex discrimination in government workplaces. *Fitzpatrick v. Bitzer*, 427 U.S. 445, 455 (1976).

A reason why *Hopkins* was an important precedent for Chief Judge Wood, and why Judge Sykes criticizes her reading, is that the Court in that case held that a purely prescriptive stereotype (this is what a woman should be like) could be the basis for a sex discrimination claim under Title VII. (Price Waterhouse assertedly denied Ann Hopkins partnership, in part because some partners considered her too butch; a friendly partner advised her to dress and act more "feminine," and go to "charm school.") Ivy Tech's discrimination against Professor Hively was, allegedly, grounded in a prescriptive stereotype that proper women date and marry men.

Hopkins does not squarely control the result in *Hively*. Judge Sykes reads it narrowly—and that narrow reading might be supported by a narrower understanding of the statutory purpose, namely, to integrate sex-segregated workplaces and to open up jobs to women who had been excluded from them (as well as men excluded from other jobs). How does a judge determine how broadly to read the statutory purpose?

5. *Congressional Override of* Gilbert. Until the Clinton impeachment in 1998, Congress frequently overrode Supreme Court statutory interpretation decisions. See Mathew Christiansen & William Eskridge Jr., *Congressional Overrides of Supreme Court Statutory Interpretation Decisions, 1967–2011*, 92 Tex. L. Rev. 1317 (2014). One such override was the Pregnancy Discrimination Act of 1978 (PDA), which repudiated *General Electric Co. v. Gilbert*, 429 U.S. 125 (1976). *Gilbert* held that discrimination against pregnant employees was

not sex discrimination, because such policies only affected a subgroup of female employees. The policy did not divide the workforce between men and women and did not treat them all differently. By overwhelming margins, Congress rejected both the result and the reasoning of that precedent—and reaffirmed the liberal workforce, anti-stereotyping purpose of Title VII. See § 701(k).

Enactment of the PDA was the occasion for the Supreme Court to apply Title VII to a matter of relational discrimination. In a guidance to employers soon after the PDA took effect, the EEOC opined that health and medical insurance policies could no longer deny pregnancy benefits to *spouses* of employees, as well as to employees themselves. The guidance targeting relational discrimination could have been justified by the same kinds of associational discrimination or comparator arguments Chief Judge Wood invoked in *Hively*. *Female* employees married to men received pregnancy benefits as part of their family health insurance, but *male* employees married to women did not. As a formal matter, the sex of the employee (the comparator argument) or of the spouse (the associational discrimination argument) is what triggered different treatment. Employers objected that relational discrimination such as this was beyond the coverage of Title VII, even after the PDA.

In *Newport News Shipbuilding & Dry Dock Co. v. EEOC*, 462 U.S. 669 (1983), the Supreme Court agreed with the EEOC. The Court announced that the PDA had not only overridden the *Gilbert* result, but had also renounced its reasoning. Ruling that the company's relational discrimination was "because of sex," *Newport News* relied upon the same kind of comparator argument later deployed by in *Hively*. The majority opinion held that the original Title VII (before the PDA), properly interpreted, barred employment practices "treat[ing] a male employee with dependents 'in a manner which but for that person's sex would be different.' " In other words, Title VII from the beginning had been a legislative endorsement of the liberal workplace. To the extent *Gilbert* was decided under different premises, it had been repudiated by the PDA. *Newport News* also conclusively abrogated the *Gilbert* reasoning that discrimination affecting only a sex-based subgroup is not sex discrimination. As a matter of Title VII doctrine, *Newport News* reflects the Court's application of Title VII to relational discrimination and confirms the comparator argument as a valid form of reasoning about whether there is discrimination because of sex.

6. *Congressional Underwrite as Well as Override of* Hopkins. In addition to overriding the Court, Congress sometimes "underwrites" the Court's decisions, confirming them and codifying their rules and norms. See James Brudney & Ethan Leib, *Legislative Underwrites,* Va. L. Rev. (forthcoming 2017). *Hopkins* is an example of both an override and an underwrite. The Supreme Court handed down several restrictive Title VII decisions in 1989 (the same Term as *Hopkins*)—to withering criticism from legal scholars, workplace experts, civil libertarians, and the Department of Justice. Congressional hearings critically examined all of the Court's recent Title VII decisions, including *Hopkins*. The sponsors of proposed amendments to Title VII and the

witnesses testifying before congressional committees in 1990 and 1991 accepted or endorsed the substantive holding in *Hopkins*, but the sponsors and committees wanted to clarify the burden of proof in mixed-motive cases. Section 107 of the Civil Rights Act of 1991 accepted the basic rule of the *Hopkins* plurality: Once the plaintiff has shown that sex or race discrimination played a significant role in denying job benefits, the burden shifts to the employer to show that it would have made the same decision on legitimate grounds, without the discriminatory considerations. Liberalizing that approach, however, Congress provided that the employer could still be liable if the discriminatory factor was "a motivating factor," even if not the predominant one, but elsewhere in Title VII limited the relief that could be granted in such mixed-motive cases.

In 1990–91, Congress heard testimony that *Hopkins*, despite its problems, was a victory for women "in its acknowledgment that evidence of sex stereotyping is legitimate evidence of gender discrimination."[29] Even those opposing the 1991 amendments recognized that Ann Hopkins had been wronged because the prescriptive sex stereotyping she suffered was "very impermissible" under Title VII.[30] In committee reports, the sponsors were clear that the section aimed at *Hopkins* only "overrules one aspect of the . . . decision."[31] Another report emphasized that these amendments would in no way affect *Hopkins's* holding that "evidence of sex stereotyping is sufficient to prove gender discrimination."[32] The fact that Congress sought out testimony about the effects of sex stereotyping in crafting the 1991 Civil Rights Act is strong evidence that Congress endorsed *Hopkins's* substantive holding.

The foregoing legislative deliberations enrich our understanding of the text and structure of the 1991 Amendments. Section 3(4) of the 1991 Amendments announced Congress's purpose "to respond to recent decisions of the Supreme Court by expanding the scope of relevant civil rights statutes in order to provide adequate protection to victims of discrimination," which assuredly included Ann Hopkins. Consistent with that purpose, Congress examined all the recent Supreme Court Title VII decisions (including *Hopkins*), overrode most of them (including *Hopkins* on the burden of proof issue), and left the substantive discrimination holding of *Hopkins* intact, obviously because even employers accepted the illegitimacy of sex-based stereotypes, including prescriptive stereotypes illustrated by *Hopkins*. This text and history are evidence that the 1991 Act accepted as a building block for future policy the *Hopkins* holding that prescriptive stereotyping (women ought to adhere to

---

29 *Hearings on H.R. 4000, The Civil Rights Act of 1990—Volume 1: Joint Hearings Before the Comm. on Education and Labor and the Subcomm. on Civil and Constitutional Rights of the H. Comm. on the Judiciary,* 101st Cong. 231 (1990) (statement of Judith Lichtman, President, Women's Legal Defense Fund).

30 *Hearings on H.R. 4000, The Civil Rights Act of 1990—Volume 2: Joint Hearings Before the Comm. on Education and Labor and the Subcomm. on Civil and Constitutional Rights of the H. Comm. on the Judiciary,* 101st Cong. 201 (1990) (statement of David A. Maddux, Spokesman, National Retail Federation).

31 H.R. Rep. No. 102–40, pt.1, at 48 (1991).

32 H.R. Rep. No. 101–644, pt.1, at 29 n.17 (1990).

the employer's understanding of the behavior appropriate to being a woman) is actionable under Title VII.

Query: This and earlier notes have presented materials generated by extensive congressional deliberations surrounding the original Title VII (1964) and its amendments (1972, 1978, 1991). None of the judges in *Hively* seemed interested in these materials: Are they relevant to a proper deliberation about the meaning of Title VII? Why or why not?

7. *EEOC's Sexual Harassment Guidelines.* For more than a generation, "sex discrimination" has been synonymous with "sexual harassment." Although lacking the lawmaking authority that Congress has granted the agency under other antidiscrimination statutes, the EEOC in 1980 promulgated sexual harassment guidelines for Title VII. See Guidelines on Sexual Harassment, 45 FR 74677, Nov. 10, 1980, as amended at 64 FR 58334, Oct. 29, 1999. The guidelines interpreted the statute to bar employer tolerance of quid pro quo harassment, where a supervisor demands sexual favors in return for workplace advancement or maintenance, and hostile work environments, where there is pervasive and unwelcome sexual harassment by coworkers. Although typically reluctant to defer to the EEOC in statutory cases, a unanimous Supreme Court wrote the agency's sexual harassment guidelines into law in *Meritor Savings Bank v. Vinson*, 477 U.S. 57 (1986), a decision that revolutionized workplace antidiscrimination law.

The EEOC's sexual harassment guidelines are a classic example of successful administrative policy entrepreneurship. Not only did a conservative Supreme Court unanimously adopt them, but Congress implicitly ratified them in the 1991 Amendments. See *Faragher v. City of Boca Raton,* 524 U.S. 775, 804 n.4 (1998). Title VII's sexual harassment jurisprudence not only represents a major development in the statute's evolution, but also in the nation's small "c" constitutional culture and even its vocabulary. Professor MacKinnon's pathbreaking book, which inspired the EEOC's guidelines, is entitled *Sexual Harassment of Working Women: A Case of Sex Discrimination* (1979).

The most dramatic applications of Title VII in the last generation have been ones that reveal the interconnections among biological sex, gender role, and sexuality. Gay men sexually assaulting male employees have been held to create employer liability under Title VII,[33] and gay men sexually assaulted by straight male coworkers have been afforded relief under Title VII as well.[34] Shortly after the 1991 Amendments had implicitly ratified *Meritor,* the Supreme Court took a case where a straight man claimed he was sexually harassed by his (allegedly) straight coworkers.

---

[33] E.g., *Smith v. Pefanis*, 652 F. Supp. 2d 1308 (N.D. Ga. 2009); *Joyner v. AAA Cooper Transp.*, 597 F. Supp. 537 (M.D. Ala. 1983); *Wright v. Methodist Youth Servs., Inc.*, 511 F. Supp. 307 (N.D. Ill. 1981).

[34] See, e.g., *EEOC v. Boh Bros. Constr. Co.*, 731 F.3d 444 (5th Cir. 2013) (en banc); *Rene v. MGM Grand Hotel, Inc.*, 305 F.3d 1061 (9th Cir. 2002); Reed Abelson, *Men, Increasingly, Are the Ones Claiming Sex Harassment by Men*, N.Y. Times, June 10, 2001.

8. *The* Oncale *Precedent.* Although a case of male-on-male harassment was far beyond the imaginations of the 1964 Congress, a unanimous Supreme Court ruled that this conduct was within the broad statutory language in *Oncale v. Sundowner Offshore Servs., Inc.*, 523 U.S. 75 (1998). Plaintiff Oncale had been physically hazed, sexually taunted and abused, and mock-raped by his male colleagues on an oil rig. He certainly had been "harassed" and the harassment had been "sexual," but had he been sexually harassed "because of sex"? In dicta (but dicta joined by all nine Justices), Justice Scalia's opinion for the Court provided some evidentiary routes, available to Oncale on remand, that also illuminate what discriminate "because of sex" might mean in *Hively*.

First, the Court said that Oncale might offer "direct comparative evidence about how the alleged harasser treated members of both sexes in a mixed-sex workplace." Thus, he could argue that, if he had been a female employee he would not have been subjected to sexual abuse and mock rapes. More on point (because a Title VII lawsuit is filed against the employer, not against fellow employees), Oncale could argue that a female employee complaining to the company that she was being sexually hazed and mock raped would have been taken seriously, and the employer would have remedied the matter. Oncale did claim that his complaints of male-on-male sexual abuse and mock rape had not been taken seriously by the employer ("boys will be boys").

If Oncale had been able to make this kind of showing, he would have been establishing that the company was more intolerant of, and willing to remedy, "heterosexual" assaults (men on a woman) than of "homosexual" assaults (men on a man). Even if neither Oncale nor his harassers self-identified as "gay," the mock rape and other sexual activities were certainly "homosexual" in their operation. Are antihomosexual employer policies or tolerances already suspect under Title VII as interpreted in *Oncale*?

Second, Oncale would have been able to show discrimination because of sex if he could have shown that his attackers were themselves "homosexuals" wanting to molest him (and the employer tolerated that conduct). Lower courts have ruled that same-sex harassment is actionable if motivated by homosexual lust,[35] and the Supreme Court said in *Oncale* that same-sex harassment by a "homosexual" supervisor would meet the because-of-sex criterion. The logic is that "but for" the employee's sex, the sexual harassment would not occur; the gay supervisor would not make sexual advances to a woman. Might this reasoning be extended to cases where the harassers are motivated by homophobia, which is a kind of sexual panic aimed at men or women because of the sex of their preferred partners?

Third, Oncale would probably have succeeded if he could have shown that he was attacked and abused because he was gender deviant. Most of the circuit courts that have ruled on such a case have applied *Hopkins* to support a Title

[35] See, e.g., *Shepherd v. Slater Steels Corp.*, 168 F.3d 998 (7th Cir. 1999); *Yeary v. Goodwill Indus.-Knoxville*, 107 F.3d 443 (6th Cir. 1997); *Wrightson v. Pizza Hut*, 99 F.3d 138 (4th Cir. 1996); *Fry v. Holmes Freight Lines, Inc.*, 72 F.Supp.2d 1074 (W.D. Mo. 1999).

VII claim for workers harassed because of prescriptive gender stereotyping. *E.g., Rene v. MGM Grand Hotel*, 305 F.3d 1061 (9th Cir. 2002).

9. *The Avoidance Canon.* Assume that you are inclined to agree with Judge Sykes, that Title VII gives no relief to claimants alleging discrimination because of their sexual orientation. But if an anti-lesbian policy is nothing more than employer disapproval of women who are not sexually attracted to men, doesn't Professor Hively have the same claim, but stated as prescriptive gender stereotyping (*Hopkins*) rather than sexual orientation? If Judge Sykes says no to that claim, then gay and lesbian employees have been read out of the protections of *Hopkins*, and by extension out of the protections of *Oncale* as well. Is it plausible to interpret Title VII to say that straight women have claims of gender stereotyping (*Hopkins*) but lesbian women do not (the dissent in *Hively*)? And that straight men have claims of sexual harassment by other men (*Oncale*), but not if the victim is gay (*Rene*)?

Such a discriminatory application of Title VII might be unconstitutional under *Romer v. Evans*, 517 U.S. 620 (1996), where the Supreme Court ruled that laws excluding lesbian and gay persons without plausible justification (hence, because of antigay animus) violate the Equal Protection Clause. Under the canon to avoid substantial constitutional questions, a court might avoid a reading of Title VII that seems, gratuitously, to exclude lesbian and gay employees from the protections *Hopkins* and *Oncale* afforded straight employees.

Final Question: If you were a judge on the Seventh Circuit, how would you have decided Professor Hively's challenge? The same issue was heard by the Second Circuit several months later. Read the excerpts below, which we limit to arguments not well-developed in *Hively*. Does any of the analysis change your mind?

Melissa Zarda, Executrix of the Estate of Donald Zarda v. Altitude Express, Inc.

883 F.3d 100 (2d Cir. en banc, Feb. 26, 2018).

The Second Circuit addressed the *Hively* issue, which its earlier precedents had resolved against the lesbian and gay plaintiffs. Thirteen judges participated in the en banc deliberations. The judgment of the Court was delivered by **Chief Judge Katzmann**. Speaking for a majority of the en banc Court, the Chief Judge found that Zarda had made out a case for illegal sex discrimination under Title VII for the following reasons:

- Sexual orientation depends upon "sex" as a referent. One's sexual orientation depends on the "sex" of the person one is attracted to. Therefore sexual orientation discrimination is, definitionally, a subset of sex discrimination. Seven of thirteen judges joined Part IIB1a of the Chief Judge's opinion, and Judge Cabranes (below) seems to have followed that reasoning as well.

- Zarda was a victim of "associational discrimination": he was discriminated against because of the sex of his romantic partner of choice. The Second Circuit had held that discrimination because of the race of a partner is race discrimination, and the Chief Judge extended this reasoning to sex. Eight of thirteen judges joined Part IIB3 of the Chief Judge's opinion.
- The post-1964 statutory history of Title VII supported the plaintiff's claim. Seven of thirteen judges joined Part IIC of the Chief Judge's opinion, which also rejected the Department of Justice's claim that Congress had implicitly ratified lower court decisions rejecting the sex discrimination argument when it amended Title VII in 1991.

Chief Judge Katzmann did not have an en banc majority for his embrace of the comparator argument (Part IIB1b, joined by only five of thirteen) and the gender stereotyping argument (Part IIB2, joined by six of thirteen).

Judge Cabranes concurred only in the judgment, based upon the "sexual orientation depends on sex" argument. "Title VII of the Civil Rights Act of 1964 prohibits discrimination 'because of . . . sex.' Zarda's sexual orientation is a function of his sex. Discrimination against Zarda because of his sexual orientation therefore *is* discrimination because of his sex, and is prohibited by Title VII."

Writing also for Judge Livingston, **Judge Lynch** dissented. He relied on the public meaning of "discrimination because of sex" when Title VII was adopted in 1964. As the coursebook's Story of the Civil Rights Act of 1964 sets forth, Title VII originally targeted employment discrimination because of race, national origin, and color. Representative Smith's amendment to add "sex" to Title VII was controversial, but it reflected the demands of the women's rights movement, which adamantly objected to the exclusion of women from many jobs.

"Discrimination against gay women and men, by contrast, was not on the table for public debate. In those dark, pre-Stonewall days, same-sex sexual relations were criminalized in nearly all states. Only three years before the passage of Title VII, Illinois, under the influence of the American Law Institute's proposed Model Penal Code, had become the first state to repeal laws prohibiting private consensual adult relations between members of the same sex.

"In addition to criminalization, gay men and women were stigmatized as suffering from mental illness. In 1964, both the American Psychiatric Association and the American Psychological Association regrettably classified homosexuality as a mental illness or disorder. As the Supreme Court recently explained, '[f]or much of the 20th century . . . homosexuality was treated as an illness. When the American Psychiatric Association published the first Diagnostic and Statistical Manual of Mental Disorders in 1952, homosexuality was classified as a mental disorder, a position adhered to until 1973.' *Obergefell v. Hodges*, 135 S.Ct. 2584, 2596 (2015). It was not until two years later, in 1975, that the American Psychological Association followed suit and 'adopted the same position [as the American Psychiatric Association], urging all mental health professionals to work to dispel the stigma of mental illness long associated with homosexual orientation.' Because gay identity was viewed as a mental illness and was, in effect, defined by participation in a criminal act, the employment situation for openly gay Americans was bleak." In 1964, persons guilty of "sexual perversion" were still excluded from government service, based upon Exec. Order No. 10450, 18 Fed. Reg. 2,489 (April 27, 1953).

The civil rights and civil liberties organizations in the 1950s and 1960s (including all the women's rights groups) did not consider the rights of "homosexuals" to be part of their agendas. "To the extent that civil rights organizations did begin to engage with gay rights during the early 1960s, they did so through the lens of sexual liberty, rather than equality, grouping the prohibition of laws against same-sex relations with prohibitions of birth control, abortion, and adultery." Even homophile and early gay rights organizations focused on liberty and decriminalization, not equality and job discrimination. It was not until the mid-1970s that job discrimination claims came into focus. See generally James Button et al., *The Politics of Gay Rights at the Local and State Level*, in *The Politics of Gay Rights* 269, 272 (Craig A. Rimmerman et al. eds., 2000).

"In light of that history, it is perhaps needless to say that there was no discussion of sexual orientation discrimination in the debates on Title VII of the Civil Rights Act. If some sexist legislators considered the inclusion of sex discrimination in the bill something of a joke, or perhaps a poison pill to make civil rights legislation even more controversial, evidently no one thought that adding sexual orientation to the list of forbidden categories was worth using even in that way. Nor did those who opposed the sex provision in Title VII include the possibility that prohibiting sex discrimination would also prevent sexual orientation discrimination in their parade of supposed horribles. When Representative Emanuel Celler of New York, floor manager for the Civil Rights Bill in the House, rose to oppose Representative Smith's proposed amendment, he expressed concern that it would lead to such supposed travesties as the elimination of 'protective' employment laws regulating working conditions for women, drafting women for military service, and revisions of rape and alimony laws. *See* 110 Cong. Rec. 2,577 (1964). He did not reference the prohibition of sexual orientation discrimination. The idea was nowhere on the horizon.

"I do not cite this sorry history of opposition to equality for African-Americans, women, and gay women and men, and of the biases prevailing a half-century ago, to argue that the private intentions and motivations of the members of Congress can trump the plain language or clear implications of a legislative enactment. (Still less, of course, do I endorse the views of those who opposed racial equality, ridiculed women's rights, and persecuted people for their sexual orientation.) Although Chief Judge Katzmann has observed elsewhere that judicial warnings about relying on legislative history as an interpretive aid have been overstated, *see* Robert A. Katzmann, *Judging Statutes* 35–39 (2014), I agree with him, and with my other colleagues in the majority, that the implications of legislation flatly prohibiting sex discrimination in employment, duly enacted by Congress and signed by the President, cannot be cabined by citing the private prejudices or blind spots of those members of Congress who voted for it. The above history makes it obvious to me, however, that the majority misconceives the fundamental *public* meaning of the language of the Civil Rights Act. The problem sought to be remedied by adding 'sex' to the prohibited bases of employment discrimination was the pervasive discrimination against women in the employment market, and the chosen remedy was to prohibit discrimination that adversely affected members of one sex or the other. By prohibiting discrimination against people based on their sex, it did not, and does not, prohibit discrimination against people because of their sexual orientation."

Judge Lynch explained the theory underlying his analysis: "The words used in legislation are used for a reason. Legislation is adopted in response to perceived social problems, and legislators adopt the language that they do to address a social evil or accomplish a desirable goal. The words of the statute take meaning from that purpose, and the principles it adopts must be read in light of the problem it was enacted to address. The words may indeed cut deeper than the legislators who voted for the statute fully understood or intended: as relevant here, a law aimed at producing gender equality in the workplace may require or prohibit employment practices that the legislators who voted for it did not yet understand as obstacles to gender equality. Nevertheless, it remains a law aimed at *gender* inequality, and not at other forms of discrimination that were understood at the time, and continue to be understood, as a different kind of prejudice, shared not only by some of those who opposed the rights of women and African-Americans, but also by some who believed in equal rights for women and people of color."

Judge Lynch concluded: "In the end, perhaps all of these arguments, on both sides, boil down to a disagreement about how discrimination on the basis of sexual orientation should be conceptualized. Whether based on linguistic arguments or associational theories or notions of stereotyping, the majority's arguments attempt to draw theoretical links between one kind of discrimination and another: to find ways to reconceptualize discrimination on the basis of sexual orientation as discrimination on the basis of sex. It is hard to believe that there would be much appetite for this kind of recharacterization if the law expressly prohibited sexual orientation discrimination, or that any opponent of sexual orientation discrimination would oppose the addition of sexual orientation to the list of protected characteristics in Title VII on the ground that to do so would be redundant or would express a misunderstanding of the nature of discrimination against men and women who are gay. I believe that the vast majority of people in our society—both those who are hostile to homosexuals and those who deplore such hostility—understand bias against or disapproval of those who are sexually attracted to persons of their own sex as a distinct type of prejudice, and not as merely a form of discrimination against either men or women on the basis of sex."

Judge Livingston and **Judge Raggi** also issued dissenting opinions, substantially agreeing with Judge Lynch.

Judge Lohier concurred in the judgment of the en banc majority and in Part IIb1a of the Chief Judge's opinion. "I agree with the majority opinion that there is no reasonable way to disentangle sex from sexual orientation in interpreting the plain meaning of the words 'because of . . . sex.' The first term clearly subsumes the second, just as race subsumes ethnicity. Oral Arg. Tr. at 53:5–6 (Government conceding that 'ethnicity can be viewed as a subset of race'). From this central holding, the majority opinion explores the comparative approach, the stereotyping rationale, and the associational discrimination rationale to help determine 'when a trait other than sex is . . . a proxy for (or function of) sex.' But in my view, these rationales merely reflect nonexclusive 'evidentiary technique[s],' frameworks, or ways to determine whether sex is a motivating factor in a given case, rather than interpretive tools that apply necessarily across all Title VII cases. Zarda himself has described these three rationales as 'evidentiary theories' or 'routes.' Oral Arg. Tr. at 4:17–18. On this understanding, I join the majority opinion as to Parts II.A and II.B.1.a, which reflect the textualist's approach, and join the remaining parts of the opinion only insofar as they can be said to apply to Zarda's particular case.

"A word about the dissents. My dissenting colleagues focus on what they variously describe as the 'ordinary, contemporary, common meaning' of the words 'because of . . . sex,' or the 'public meaning of [those] words adopted by Congress in light of the social problem it was addressing when it chose those words.' There are at least two problems with this position. First, as the majority opinion points out, cabining the words in this way makes little or no sense of *Oncale* or, for that matter, *Price Waterhouse*. Second, their hunt for the 'contemporary' 'public' meaning of the statute in this case seems to me little more than a roundabout search for legislative history. Judge Lynch's laudable call (either as a way to divine congressional intent or as an interpretive check on the plain text approach) to consider what the legislature would have decided if the issue had occurred to the legislators at the time of enactment is, unfortunately, no longer an interpretive option of first resort. Time and time again, the Supreme Court has told us that the cart of legislative history is pulled by the plain text, not the other way around. The text here pulls in one direction, namely, that sex includes sexual orientation."

Query: How should Judges Lynch, Livingston, and Raggi respond to the arguments raised in the preceding Notes—especially the following questions: How does the interpreter determine "original public meaning" when Congress repeatedly amends the statute and adds relevant text, such as § 703(m)? What is their reason for reading "sex" to mean only one thing in 1964—and why is that binding today? How does their theory account for *Hopkins* and *Oncale*?

CHAPTER 5

CANONS OF STATUTORY INTERPRETATION

■ ■ ■

1. TEXTUAL CANONS

Page 490: Insert the following materials after Problem 5–1:

LOCKHART V. UNITED STATES

United States Supreme Court, 2016.
___ U.S. ___, 136 S.Ct. 958, 194 L.Ed.2d 48.

JUSTICE SOTOMAYOR delivered the opinion of the Court.

Defendants convicted of possessing child pornography in violation of 18 U.S.C. § 2252(a)(4) are subject to a 10-year mandatory minimum sentence and an increased maximum sentence if they have "a prior conviction . . . under the laws of any State relating to aggravated sexual abuse, sexual abuse, or abusive sexual conduct involving a minor or ward." § 2252(b)(2).

The question before us is whether the phrase "involving a minor or ward" modifies all items in the list of predicate crimes ("aggravated sexual abuse," "sexual abuse," and "abusive sexual conduct") or only the one item that immediately precedes it ("abusive sexual conduct"). * * *

II

* * * The issue before us is whether the limiting phrase that appears at the end of that list—"involving a minor or ward"—applies to all three predicate crimes preceding it in the list or only the final predicate crime. We hold that "involving a minor or ward" modifies only "abusive sexual conduct," the antecedent immediately preceding it. Although § 2252(b)(2)'s list of state predicates is awkwardly phrased (to put it charitably), the provision's text and context together reveal a straightforward reading. A timeworn textual canon is confirmed by the structure and internal logic of the statutory scheme.

A

Consider the text. When this Court has interpreted statutes that include a list of terms or phrases followed by a limiting clause, we have typically applied an interpretive strategy called the "rule of the last antecedent." See *Barnhart v. Thomas*, 540 U.S. 20, 26 (2003). The rule provides that "a limiting clause or phrase . . . should ordinarily be read as modifying only the noun or phrase that it immediately follows." *Ibid.*; see also Black's Law Dictionary 1532–1533 (10th ed. 2014) * * * A. Scalia & B. Garner, Reading Law: The Interpretation of Legal Texts 144 (2012).

This Court has applied the rule from our earliest decisions to our more recent * * * . The rule reflects the basic intuition that when a modifier appears at the end of a list, it is easier to apply that modifier only to the item directly before it. That is particularly true where it takes more than a little mental energy to process the individual entries in the list, making it a heavy lift to carry the modifier across them all. For example, imagine you are the general manager of the Yankees and you are rounding out your 2016 roster. You tell your scouts to find a defensive catcher, a quick-footed shortstop, or a pitcher from last year's World Champion Kansas City Royals. It would be natural for your scouts to confine their search for a pitcher to last year's championship team, but to look more broadly for catchers and shortstops.

* * *

Of course, as with any canon of statutory interpretation, the rule of the last antecedent "is not an absolute and can assuredly be overcome by other indicia of meaning. [But h]ere the interpretation urged by the rule of the last antecedent is not overcome by other indicia of meaning. To the contrary, § 2252(b)(2)'s context fortifies the meaning that principle commands.

B

* * * Among the chapters of the Federal Criminal Code that can trigger § 2252(b)(2)'s recidivist enhancement are crimes "under . . . chapter 109A." Chapter 109A criminalizes a range of sexual-abuse offenses involving adults *or* minors and wards. And it places those federal sexual-abuse crimes under headings that use language nearly identical to the language § 2252(b)(2) uses to enumerate the three categories of state sexual-abuse predicates. The first section in Chapter 109A is titled "Aggravated sexual abuse." 18 U.S.C. § 2241. The second is titled "Sexual abuse." § 2242. And the third is titled "Sexual abuse of a minor or ward." § 2243. Applying the rule of the last antecedent, those sections mirror precisely the order, precisely the divisions, and nearly precisely the words used to describe the three state sexual-abuse predicate crimes in § 2252(b)(2): "aggravated sexual abuse," "sexual abuse," and "abusive sexual conduct involving a minor or ward."

This similarity appears to be more than a coincidence. We cannot state with certainty that Congress used Chapter 109A as a template for the list of state predicates set out in § 2252(b)(2), but we cannot ignore the parallel, particularly because the headings in Chapter 109A were in place when Congress amended the statute to add § 2252(b)(2)'s state sexual-abuse predicates. If Congress had intended to limit each of the state predicates to conduct "involving a minor or ward," we doubt it would have followed, or thought it needed to follow, so closely the structure and language of Chapter 109A.

III

A

Lockhart argues, to the contrary, that the phrase "involving a minor or ward" should be interpreted to modify all three state sexual-abuse predicates. He first contends, as does our dissenting colleague, that the so-called series-qualifier principle supports his reading. This principle, Lockhart says, requires a modifier to apply to all items in a series when such an application would represent a natural construction. Brief for Petitioner 12; *post*, at 4.

This Court has long acknowledged that structural or contextual evidence may "rebut the last antecedent inference." [Citing cases] * * * But in none of those cases did the Court describe, much less apply, a countervailing grammatical mandate that could bear the weight that either Lockhart or the dissent places on the series qualifier principle. Instead, the Court simply observed that sometimes context weighs against the application of the rule of the last antecedent. *Barnhart*, 540 U.S., at 26. Whether a modifier is "applicable as much to the first . . . as to the last" words in a list, whether a set of items form a "single, integrated list," and whether the application of the rule would require acceptance of an "unlikely premise" are fundamentally contextual questions.

* * * We take no position today on the meaning of the terms "aggravated sexual abuse," "sexual abuse," and "abusive sexual conduct," including their similarities and differences. But it is clear that applying the limiting phrase to all three items would risk running headlong into the rule against superfluity by transforming a list of separate predicates into a set of synonyms describing the same predicate. See *Bailey v. United States*, 516 U.S. 137, 146 (1995) ("We assume that Congress used two terms because it intended each term to have a particular, nonsuperfluous meaning").

* * * The dissent offers a suggestion rooted in its impressions about how people ordinarily speak and write. *Post*, at 1–4. The problem is that, as even the dissent acknowledges, § 2252(b)(2)'s list of state predicates is hardly intuitive. No one would mistake its odd repetition and inelegant phrasing for a reflection of the accumulated wisdom of everyday speech patterns. It would be as if a friend asked you to get her tart lemons, sour lemons, or sour fruit from Mexico. If you brought back lemons from California, but your friend insisted that she was using customary speech and obviously asked for Mexican fruit only, you would be forgiven for disagreeing on both counts.

Faced with § 2252(b)(2)'s inartful drafting, then, do we interpret the provision by viewing it as a clear, commonsense list best construed as if conversational English? Or do we look around to see if there might be some provenance to its peculiarity? With Chapter 109A so readily at hand, we are unpersuaded by our dissenting colleague's invocation of basic examples from day-to-day life. Whatever the validity of the dissent's broader point, this simply is not a case in which colloquial practice is of much use. Section 2252(b)(2)'s list is hardly the way an average person, or even an average lawyer, would set about to describe the relevant conduct if they had started from scratch.

C

* * * Lockhart and the dissent also rely on a letter sent from the Department of Justice (DOJ) to the House of Representative's Committee on the Judiciary commenting on the proposed "Child Protection and Sexual Predator Punishment Act of 1998." H. R. Rep. No. 105–557, pp. 26–34 (1998). In the letter, DOJ provides commentary on the then-present state of §§ 2252(b)(1) and 2252(b)(2), noting that although there is a "5-year mandatory minimum sentence for individuals charged with receipt or distribution of child pornography and who have prior state convictions for child molestation" pursuant to § 2252(b)(1), there is "no enhanced provision for those individuals charged with possession of child pornography who have prior convictions for child abuse" pursuant to § 2252(b)(2). *Id.*, at 31. That letter, they say, demonstrates that DOJ understood the language at issue here to impose a sentencing enhancement only for prior state convictions involving children.

We doubt that DOJ was trying to describe the full reach of the language in § 2252(b)(1), as the dissent suggests. To the contrary, there are several clues that the letter was relaying on just one of the provision's many salient features. For instance, the letter's references to "child molestation" and "child abuse" do not encompass a large number of state crimes that are unambiguously covered by "abusive sexual conduct involving a minor or ward"—namely, crimes involving "wards." Wards can be minors, but they can also be adults. See, *e.g.*, § 2243(b) (defining "wards" as persons who are "in official detention" and "under . . . custodial, supervisory, or disciplinary authority"). Moreover, we doubt that DOJ intended to express a belief that the potentially broad scope of serious crimes encompassed by "aggravated sexual abuse, sexual abuse, and abusive sexual conduct" reaches no further than state crimes that would traditionally be characterized as "child molestation" or "child abuse."

* * * We therefore think it unnecessary to restrict our interpretation of the provision to the parts of it that DOJ chose to highlight in its letter. Just as importantly, the terse descriptions of the provision in the Senate Report and DOJ letter do nothing to explain *why* Congress would have

wanted to apply the mandatory minimum to individuals convicted in federal court of sexual abuse or aggravated sexual abuse involving an adult, but not to individuals convicted in state court of the same. The legislative history, in short, "hardly speaks with [a] clarity of purpose" through which we can discern Congress' statutory objective. *Universal Camera Corp. v. NLRB*, 340 U.S. 474, 483 (1951). * * *

D

Finally, Lockhart asks us to apply the rule of lenity. We have used the lenity principle to resolve ambiguity in favor of the defendant only "at the end of the process of construing what Congress has expressed" when the ordinary canons of statutory construction have revealed no satisfactory construction. *Callanan v. United States*, 364 U.S. 587, 596 (1961). That is not the case here. To be sure, Lockhart contends that if we applied a different principle of statutory construction—namely, his "series qualifier principle"—we would arrive at an alternative construction of § 2252(b)(2). But the arguable availability of multiple, divergent principles of statutory construction cannot automatically trigger the rule of lenity. Cf. Llewellyn, Remarks on the Theory of Appellate Decision and the Rules or Canons About How Statutes Are To Be Construed, 3 Vand. L. Rev. 395, 401 (1950) ("[T]here are two opposing canons on almost every point"). Here, the rule of the last antecedent is well supported by context and Lockhart's alternative is not. We will not apply the rule of lenity to override a sensible grammatical principle buttressed by the statute's text and structure. * * *

JUSTICE KAGAN, with whom JUSTICE BREYER joins, dissenting.

Imagine a friend told you that she hoped to meet "an actor, director, or producer involved with the new Star Wars movie." You would know immediately that she wanted to meet an actor from the Star Wars cast—not an actor in, for example, the latest Zoolander. Suppose a real estate agent promised to find a client "a house, condo, or apartment in New York." Wouldn't the potential buyer be annoyed if the agent sent him information about condos in Maryland or California? And consider a law imposing a penalty for the "violation of any statute, rule, or regulation relating to insider trading." Surely a person would have cause to protest if punished under that provision for violating a traffic statute. The reason in all three cases is the same: Everyone understands that the modifying phrase—"involved with the new Star Wars movie," "in New York," "relating to insider trading"—applies to each term in the preceding list, not just the last.

That ordinary understanding of how English works, in speech and writing alike, should decide this case. * * * That normal construction finds support in uncommonly clear-cut legislative history, which states in so many words that the three predicate crimes all involve abuse of children. And if any doubt remained, the rule of lenity would command the same result: Lockhart's prior conviction for sexual abuse *of an adult* does not trigger § 2252(b)(2)'s mandatory minimum penalty. I respectfully dissent.

[T]his Court has made clear that the last-antecedent rule does not generally apply to the grammatical construction present here: when "[t]he modifying clause appear[s] . . . at the end of a single, integrated list." *Jama,* 543 U.S., at 344, n. 4. Then, the exact opposite is usually true: As in the examples beginning this opinion, the modifying phrase refers alike to each of the list's terms. A leading treatise puts the point as follows: "When there is a straightforward, parallel construction that involves all nouns or verbs in a series," a modifier at the end of the list "normally applies to the entire series." A. Scalia & B. Garner, Reading Law: The Interpretation of Legal Texts 147 (2012); compare *id.,* at 152 ("When the syntax involves something other than [such] a parallel series of nouns or verbs," the modifier "normally applies only to the nearest reasonable referent"). That interpretive practice of applying the modifier to the whole list boasts a fancy name—the "series-qualifier canon," see Black's Law Dictionary 1574 (10th ed. 2014)—but, as my opening examples show, it reflects the completely ordinary way that people speak and listen, write and read.

Even the exception to the series-qualifier principle is intuitive, emphasizing both its common-sensical basis and its customary usage. When the nouns in a list are so disparate that the modifying clause does not make sense when applied to them all, then the last-antecedent rule takes over. Suppose your friend told you not that she wants to meet "an actor, director, or producer involved with Star Wars," but instead that she hopes someday to meet "a President, Supreme Court Justice, or actor involved with Star Wars." Presumably, you would know that she wants to meet a President or Justice even if that person has no connection to the famed film franchise. But so long as the modifying clause "is applicable as much to the first and other words as to the last," this Court has stated, "the natural construction of the language demands that the clause be read as applicable to all." *Paroline v. United States,* 572 U.S. ___, ___ (2014) (slip op., at 9) (quoting *Porto Rico Railway, Light & Power Co. v. Mor,* 253 U.S. 345, 348 (1920)). In other words, the modifier then qualifies not just the last antecedent but the whole series.

* * *

The majority responds to all this by claiming that the "inelegant phrasing" of § 2252(b)(2) renders it somehow exempt from a grammatical rule reflecting "how people ordinarily" use the English language. *Ante,* at 10. But to begin with, the majority is wrong to suggest that the series-qualifier canon is only about "colloquial" or "conversational" English. *Ibid.* In fact, it applies to both speech and writing, in both their informal and their formal varieties. Here is a way to test my point: Pick up a journal, or a book, or for that matter a Supreme Court opinion—most of which keep "everyday" colloquialisms at a far distance. *Ibid.* You'll come across many sentences having the structure of the statutory provision at issue here: a few nouns followed by a modifying clause. And you'll discover, again and yet again, that the clause modifies every noun in the series, not just the last—in other words, that even (especially?) in formal writing, the series-qualifier principle works.

The majority as well seeks refuge in the idea that applying the series-qualifier canon to § 2252(b)(2) would violate the rule against superfluity. * * * But * * * the majority's approach (as it admits, see *ante,* at 9) produces superfluity too—and in equal measure.

* * * Legislative history confirms what the natural construction of language shows: Each of the three predicate offenses at issue here must involve a minor.* * * The relevant language—again, providing for a mandatory minimum sentence if a person has a prior state-law conviction for "aggravated sexual abuse, sexual abuse, or abusive sexual conduct involving a minor or ward"—first made its appearance in 1996, when Congress inserted it into § 2252(b)(1). See Child Pornography Prevention Act of 1996, § 121(5), 110 Stat. 3009–30, 18 U.S.C. § 2251 note. At that time, the Senate Report on the legislation explained what the new language meant: The mandatory minimum would apply to an "offender with a prior conviction under . . . any *State child abuse law.*" S. Rep. No. 104–358, p. 9 (1996) (emphasis added). It is hard to imagine saying any more directly that the just-added state sexual-abuse predicates all involve minors, and minors only.

Two years later, in urging Congress to include the same predicate offenses in § 2252(b)(2), the Department of Justice (DOJ) itself read the list that way. In a formal bill comment, DOJ noted that proposed legislation on child pornography failed to fix a statutory oddity: Only § 2252(b)(1), and not § 2252(b)(2), then contained the state predicates at issue here. DOJ described that discrepancy as follows: Whereas § 2252(b)(1) provided a penalty enhancement for "individuals charged with receipt or distribution of child pornography *and who have prior state convictions for child molestation,*" the adjacent § 2252(b)(2) contained no such enhancement for those "charged with possession of child pornography *who have prior convictions for child abuse.*" H. R. Rep. No. 105–557, p. 31 (1998) (emphasis added). That should change, DOJ wrote: A possessor of child pornography should also be subject to a 2-year mandatory minimum if he had "a *prior conviction for sexual abuse of a minor.*" *Ibid.* (emphasis added). DOJ thus made clear that the predicate offenses it recommended adding to § 2252(b)(2)—like those already in § 2252(b)(1)—related not to all sexual abuse but only to sexual abuse of children. And Congress gave DOJ just what it wanted: Soon after receiving the letter, Congress added the language at issue to § 2252(b)(2), resulting in the requested 2-year minimum sentence. See Protection of Children From Sexual Predators Act of 1998, § 202(a)(2), 112 Stat. 2977, 18 U.S.C. § 1 note. So every indication, in 1998 no less than in 1996, was that all the predicate crimes relate to children alone.

* * * [T]he majority ventures, the DOJ letter was merely noting "one of the provision's many salient features." *Ibid.* But suppose that you (like the Senate Report's or DOJ letter's authors) had to paraphrase or condense the statutory language at issue here, and that you (like the majority) thought it captured *all* sexual-abuse crimes. Would you then use the phrase "any state child abuse law" as a descriptor (as the Senate Report did)? And would you refer to the whole list of state predicates as involving "sexual abuse of a minor" (as the DOJ letter did)? Of course not. But you might well use such shorthand if, alternatively, you understood the statutory language (as I do) to cover only sexual offenses against children. And so the authors of the Report and letter did here. Such documents of necessity abridge statutory language; but they do not do so by conveying an utterly false impression of what that language is most centrally about—as by describing a provision that (supposedly) covers all sexual abuse as one that reaches only child molestation.

III

[In this Part, the dissent contests the majority's argument about the similarity of Ch. 109A.]

IV

Suppose, for a moment, that this case is not as clear as I've suggested. Assume there is no way to know whether to apply the last-antecedent or the series-qualifier rule. Imagine, too, that the legislative history is not quite so compelling and the majority's "template" argument not quite so strained. Who, then, should prevail? This Court has a rule for how to resolve genuine ambiguity in criminal statutes: in favor of the criminal defendant. As the majority puts the point, the rule of lenity insists that courts side with the defendant "when the ordinary canons of statutory construction have revealed no satisfactory construction." * * * Consider the following sentence, summarizing various points made above: "The series-qualifier principle, the legislative history, and the rule of lenity discussed in this opinion all point in the same direction." Now answer the following question: Has only the rule of lenity been discussed in this opinion, or have the series-qualifier principle and the legislative history been discussed as well? Even had you not read the preceding 16-plus pages, you would know the right answer—because of the ordinary way all of us use language. That, in the end, is why Lockhart should win.

NOTES ON LOCKHART *AND THE DEATH OF JUSTICE SCALIA*

1. *The Last Antecedent Rule vs. the Series-Qualifier Canon. Lockhart* looks like a very different opinion from *King*, doesn't it? Would a battle of micro-focused textual canons have been viewed as a legitimate way to resolve the challenge to the Affordable Care Act? If not, why is this approach permissible for the statute at issue in *Lockhart*, which after all carries with it a serious deprivation of personal liberty? Neither of the two writing justices in *Lockhart*—Sotomayor and Kagan—are textualist-extremists. Why do you think they focused their opinions cases on these narrow arguments? Moreover, is there any principled way to pick among these two canons *without* looking to the broader landscape of statutory structure, legislative history or norms (e.g., lenity)? Note that *both* sides cite the Scalia/Garner treatise as "proof" of the decisive nature of their textual weapon. Textualists argue their formalist approach makes statutory interpretation more predictable and objective, but some of us view cases like *Lockhart* as evidence that the formalist project has failed. See, e.g., Frank Easterbrook, U. Chi. L. Rev. (forthcoming 2016); Abbe R. Gluck, *The CBO Canon, Legislative Reality, and Faint-Hearted Formalism in Statutory Interpretation*, U. Chi. L. Rev. (forthcoming 2016).

2. *The Drafters' Perspective.* There is virtually no chance that anyone drafting the statute at issue in *Lockhart* was focused on (or even knew of) either canon. Should that make a difference in terms of whether the canons should decide the case? The last antecedent rule in particular is often triggered by the placement of a comma at the end of a series. Does it matter to you to learn that grammar is often added to statutes *after* they are passed by the codifying staff? Shouldn't textualists care about that fact, in deciding whether to apply the canon, even if they generally do not wish to delve into how Congress works? See Gluck, The CBO Canon, *supra*.

3. *Lenity as Tiebreaker.* At oral argument, Justice Scalia lamented that some way was needed to choose between these apparently equally applicable "dueling canons," and so suggested the rule of lenity, his favorite policy canon as a tiebreaker. Justice Breyer wondered why the Court would not look to legislative history instead of a canon, given that there was a tie. Justice Scalia's response to this? "You wouldn't delegate such a decision to *staff* would you?" See http://www.supremecourt.gov/oral_arguments/argument_transcripts/14-8358_d1pf.pdf. The opinion also tees up once again the enduring question of when exactly the door is opened to the application of lenity. Lockhart tried to argue that as long as there were two competing canons, that created ambiguity sufficient to trigger the defendant-favoring canon. Do you agree?

4. *Justice Scalia and the Canons.* Although not all textualists embrace canons, Justice Scalia's book *Reading Law* has already had a significant impact in citations alone in lower court cases, a factor suggesting that canons have become a "new interpretive regime" in statutory interpretation. For that insight and the latest contribution to the canon field, see the canon-focused response of Professor Eskridge. See William N. Eskridge's Interpreting Law: A Primer on How to Read Statutes and the Constitution (West 2016).

5. *Statutory Interpretation Without Justice Scalia.* Justice Scalia's profound and enduring influence over the theories and doctrines of statutory interpretation is unquestionable and evident on virtually every page of this coursebook. *Lockhart* was decided just weeks after Justice Scalia's unexpected death on February 13, 2016, but may have been written before it. One mark of Justice Scalia's influence is how fundamentally his approach has altered the *format* of virtually all statutory interpretation briefs and opinions: Everyone now begins with the textualist approach before widening the lens (we tell our students that to do otherwise would be statutory interpretation malpractice in today's legal context!). That alone, together with the desire to rack up as many of the more textualist Justices' votes, may explain the canon-centricity of the *Lockhart* majority and dissent. Going forward, however, the unknowable question is whether we will see some loosening of that approach with the loss of its championing Justice. As lower-courts judges, neither Chief Justice Roberts nor Justice Alito were strict textualists. And *King*, as noted, illustrates the Chief's own willingness to nudge the line. The next few terms will shed light on the durability of Justice Scalia's approach, and with it, the future of textualism.

THE COMMA CASE

The First Circuit's opinion in **O'Connor v. Oakhurst Dairy**, 851 F.3d 69, 70 (1st Cir. 2017) begins: "For want of a comma, we have this case." The case concerned Maine's overtime law, 26 M.R.S.A. § 664(3), which provided that: "[a]n employer may not require an employee to work more than 40 hours in any one week unless 1 1/2 times the regular hourly rate is paid for all hours actually worked in excess of 40 hours in that week." The overtime law exempted certain categories of employees, including employees whose work involves:

The canning, processing, preserving, freezing, drying, marketing, storing, packing for shipment or distribution of:

(1) Agricultural produce;

(2) Meat and fish products; and

(3) Perishable foods.

Oakhurst Dairy contended that, since its delivery drivers distribute dairy products, which are "perishable," they were exempt from the law. The drivers contended that the statute viewed "packing" and "distribution" as a single activity, and since they did not pack the items, they remained protected by the overtime law.

The First Circuit, in an opinion by **Judge David Barron**, concluded the statute was ambiguous and ruled for the drivers. But before the court got there, the case offered a textual canon bonanza. Among other things, Oakhurst relied on the rule against superfluities (can you see why?) and, as the court put it, "on another established linguistic convention in pressing its case—the convention of using a conjunction to mark off the last item on a list." *Oakhurst*, 851 F.3d at 73.

But the starring rule in the case was another grammar rule—the absence of a comma after the word "shipping." The court noted that the Maine Legislative Drafting Manual expressly states that the so-called "Oxford" comma"—the comma between the penultimate and the last item of a series—should not be used. As the court also noted, "Maine statutes invariably omit the serial comma from lists. And this practice reflects a drafting convention that is at least as old as the Maine wage and hour law, even if the drafting manual itself is of more recent vintage." *Id.*

But the court did not find that sufficiently persuasive. (Indeed, later in the opinion the court said it "would be remiss not to note the clarifying virtues of serial commas that other jurisdictions recognize." *Id.* at 75 n.5.). Instead, the court ruled for the drivers after finding the statute ambiguous. The court based its findings on its review of other Maine statutes, which treated "shipment" and "distribution" as separate activities; and on application of what it called the "parallel-usage canon" of grammar which would counsel that "distribution" and "shipment," as the only two non-gerunds in the list, each be read as "playing the same grammatical role—and one distinct from the role that the gerunds play." *Id.* at 74. The court also reviewed some of the other textual arguments by the drivers, including rejecting their *noscitur a sociis* argument as unpersuasive, and declaring it unsatisfying to assume the Maine legislature used the atypical grammatical technique called "asyndeton"—purposeful omission of a conjunction in a list (the court cited the Scalia and Garner treatise here, of course). Finally, the court next turned to the legislative history but found that inconclusive as well.

Thus, finding the statute ambiguous (even as it noted Oakhurst certainly would have won had a comma been present), the court hinged its ruling on a policy canon as a tiebreaker: Namely, the court held that "[t]he default rule of construction under Maine law for ambiguous provisions in the state's wage and hour laws is that they "should be liberally construed to further the beneficent purposes for which they are enacted." *Id.* at 79. That canon tipped the scales for the drivers.

The *New York Times* headline on the write up of this case read: "Lack of Oxford Comma Could Cost Maine Company Millions in Overtime Dispute."

Queries:

- The Supreme Court has cited Congress's own drafting manuals a couple of times in statutory interpretation cases. What justifies the *Oakhurst* court's seeming lack of respect for Maine's own drafting conventions? After all, it is a Maine statute. Cf. Chapter 6, in which we consider the question whether courts should tailor statutory interpretation rules to reflect how Congress actually drafts. Would the answer be any different for a state legislature?

- Isn't it odd that Judge Barron chose not to apply established Maine drafting conventions when interpreting Maine law but *did* choose to rely on Maine's own policy canon favoring remedial construction of overtime laws? What would justify the difference? See also Chapter 4, § 2; cf. Abbe R. Gluck, *Intersystemic Statutory Interpretation: Methodology as "Law" and the Erie Doctrine*, 120 Yale L.J. 1898 (2011) (arguing the *Erie* doctrine requires federal courts to apply state interpretive methods to state law questions.).
- What do you think about the Court's heavy reliance on the absence of a comma and other grammar conventions? Does this case remind you of *Lockhart*, *supra* Chapter 5, § 2? As in that case, the court here references a highly obscure canon (there, the "series-qualifier" canon and here, the "parallel usage" canon as well as "asyndeton"). Why would a court do this? Would a different approach carry more legitimacy?

2. SUBSTANTIVE CANONS

A. THE RULE OF LENITY

Page 512: Add the following Problem 5–2A right after Problem 5–2:

PROBLEM 5–2A: IS A RED GROUPER A "TANGIBLE THING" FOR PURPOSES OF AN OBSTRUCTION OF JUSTICE CRIME?

On August 23, 2007, the *Miss Katie,* a commercial fishing boat, was six days into an expedition in the Gulf of Mexico. Her crew numbered three, including its Captain, John Yates. Engaged in a routine offshore patrol to inspect both recreational and commercial vessels, Officer John Jones of the Florida Fish and Wildlife Conservation Commission decided to board the *Miss Katie* to check on the vessel's compliance with fishing rules. Although the *Miss Katie* was far enough from the Florida coast to be in exclusively federal waters, she was nevertheless within Officer Jones's jurisdiction. Because he had been deputized as a federal agent by the National Marine Fisheries Service, Officer Jones had authority to enforce federal, as well as state, fishing laws.

Upon boarding the *Miss Katie,* Officer Jones noticed three red grouper that appeared to be undersized, hanging from a hook on the deck. At the time, federal conservation regulations required immediate release of red grouper less than 20 inches long. 50 C.F.R. § 622.37(d)(2)(ii) (effective April 2, 2007). Violation of those regulations is a civil offense punishable by a fine or fishing license suspension. See 16 U.S.C. §§ 1857(1)(A), (G), 1858(a), (g).

Suspecting that other undersized fish might be on board, Officer Jones proceeded to inspect the ship's catch, setting aside and measuring only fish that appeared to him to be shorter than 20 inches. Officer Jones ultimately determined that 72 fish fell short of the 20-inch mark. A fellow officer recorded the length of each of the undersized fish on a catch measurement verification form. With few exceptions, the measured fish were between 19 and 20 inches; three were less than 19 inches; none were less than 18.75 inches. After separating the fish measuring below 20 inches from the rest of the catch by placing them in wooden crates, Officer Jones directed Captain **Yates** to leave the fish, thus segregated, in the crates until the *Miss Katie* returned to port. Before departing, Officer Jones issued Captain Yates a citation for possession of undersized fish.

Four days later, after the *Miss Katie* had docked in Cortez, Florida, Officer Jones measured the fish contained in the wooden crates. This time, however, the measured fish, although still less than 20 inches, slightly exceeded the lengths recorded on board. Jones surmised that the fish brought to port were not the same as those he had detected during his initial inspection. Under questioning, one of the crew members admitted that, at Captain Yates's direction, he had thrown overboard the fish Officer Jones had measured at sea, and that he and Captain Yates had replaced the tossed grouper with fish from the rest of the catch.

For this activity, Captain Yates was charged with, and convicted of, violating 18 U.S.C. § 1519, which provides:

> Whoever knowingly alters, destroys, mutilates, conceals, covers up, falsifies, or makes a false entry in any record, document, or tangible object with the intent to impede, obstruct, or influence the investigation or proper administration of any matter within the jurisdiction of any department or agency of the United States or any case filed under title 11, or in relation to or contemplation of any such matter or case, shall be fined under this title, imprisoned not more than 20 years, or both.

Captain Yates was also indicted and convicted under § 2232(a), which provides:

> Destruction or Removal of Property to Prevent Seizure.—Whoever, before, during, or after any search for or seizure of property by any person authorized to make such search or seizure, knowingly destroys, damages, wastes, disposes of, transfers, or otherwise takes any action, or knowingly attempts to destroy, damage, waste, dispose of, transfer, or otherwise take any action, for the purpose of preventing or impairing the Government's lawful authority to take such property into its custody or control or to continue holding such property under its lawful custody and control, shall be fined under this title or imprisoned not more than 5 years, or both.

Captain Yates does not contest his conviction for violating § 2232(a), which has been repeatedly interpreted to include a broad array of tangible objects, but he maintains that fish are not trapped within the term "tangible object," as that term is used in § 1519. Section 1519 was enacted as part of the Sarbanes-

Oxley Act of 2002, 116 Stat. 745, legislation designed to protect investors and restore trust in financial markets following the collapse of Enron Corporation.

Before reading any further, write in the margin your gut reaction to this criminal prosecution: Did Captain Yates conceal or destroy a "tangible object" when he ordered the red groupers tossed back into the sea? How committed are you to this interpretation? Is there further context you'd like to know before announcing your official interpretation of this law (assuming you are a judge or other official)? Jot down some other evidence you would like your law clerk to investigate. Finally, read the following exchange among the Justices and decide how you would vote in the Case of the Red Grouper.

Captain John L. Yates v. United States

___ U.S. ___, 135 S.Ct. 1074, 191 L.Ed.2d 64 (2015).

The Sarbanes-Oxley Act responded to the exposure of Enron's massive fraud on shareholders and others, as well as revelations that the company's outside auditor had systematically destroyed potentially incriminating documents. Congress created § 1519 to prohibit corporate document-shredding to hide evidence of financial wrongdoing. Prior law made it an offense to "intimidat[e], threate[n], or corruptly persuad[e] *another person*" to shred documents. § 1512(b) (emphasis added). Section 1519 cured a conspicuous omission by imposing liability on a person who destroys records himself.

The Government argued that § 1519, as written, plainly extended further than the document-shredding that troubled Congress. Because red groupers are, in ordinary parlance and according to dictionaries, both "tangible" and "objects," Captain Yates violated the plain meaning of the 2002 statute. Additionally, the term "tangible object" has been understood broadly in other statutes, such as Rule 16 of the Federal Rules of Criminal Procedure (discovery of "tangible objects").

Hewing closely to § 1519 and its surrounding statutory context suggested a different analysis to a majority of the Court, however. Writing for three other Justices (Roberts, Breyer, and Sotomayor), **Justice Ginsburg** delivered the judgment of the Court, reversing Captain Yates's conviction for violating § 1519.

"We note first § 1519's caption: 'Destruction, alteration, or falsification of records in Federal investigations and bankruptcy.' That heading conveys no suggestion that the section prohibits spoliation of any and all physical evidence, however remote from records. Neither does the title of the section of the Sarbanes-Oxley Act in which § 1519 was placed, § 802: 'Criminal penalties for altering documents.' 116 Stat. 800. Furthermore, § 1520, the only other provision passed as part of § 802, is titled 'Destruction of corporate audit records' and addresses only that specific subset of records and documents. While these headings are not commanding, they supply cues that Congress did not intend 'tangible object' in § 1519 to sweep within its reach physical objects of every kind, including things no one would describe as records, documents, or devices closely associated with them."

"Section 1519's position within Chapter 73 of Title 18 further signals that § 1519 was not intended to serve as a cross-the-board ban on the destruction of physical evidence of every kind. Congress placed § 1519 (and its companion provision § 1520) at the end of the chapter, following immediately after the pre-existing § 1516, § 1517, and § 1518, each of them prohibiting obstructive acts in specific contexts. See § 1516 (audits of recipients of federal funds); § 1517 (federal examinations of financial institutions); § 1518 (criminal investigations of federal health care offenses). See also S.Rep. No. 107–146, at 7 (observing that § 1517 and § 1518 'apply to obstruction in certain limited types of cases, such as bankruptcy fraud, examinations of financial institutions, and healthcare fraud'). * * *

"The words immediately surrounding 'tangible object' in § 1519—'falsifies, or makes a false entry in any record [or] document'—also cabin the contextual meaning of that term. As explained in *Gustafson v. Alloyd Co.,* 513 U.S. 561, 575, 115 S.Ct. 1061, 131 L.Ed.2d 1 (1995), we rely on the principle of *noscitur a sociis*—a word is known by the company it keeps—to 'avoid ascribing to one word a meaning so broad that it is inconsistent with its accompanying words, thus giving unintended breadth to the Acts of Congress.' In *Gustafson,* we interpreted the word 'communication' in § 2(10) of the Securities Act of 1933 to refer to a public communication, rather than any communication, because the word appeared in a list with other words, notably 'notice, circular, [and] advertisement,' making it 'apparent that the list refer[red] to documents of wide dissemination.' And we did so even though the list began with the word 'any.'

"The *noscitur a sociis* canon operates in a similar manner here. 'Tangible object' is the last in a list of terms that begins 'any record [or] document.' The term is therefore appropriately read to refer, not to any tangible object, but specifically to the subset of tangible objects involving records and documents, *i.e.,* objects used to record or preserve information. See United States Sentencing Commission, Guidelines Manual § 2J1.2, comment., n. 1 (Nov. 2014) (' "Records, documents, or tangible objects" includes (A) records, documents, or tangible objects that are stored on, or that are, magnetic, optical, digital, other electronic, or other storage mediums or devices; and (B) wire or electronic communications.')."This moderate interpretation of 'tangible object' accords with the list of actions § 1519 proscribes. The section applies to anyone who 'alters, destroys, mutilates, conceals, covers up, *falsifies,* or *makes a false entry in* any record, document, or tangible object' with the requisite obstructive intent. (Emphasis added.) The last two verbs, 'falsif[y]' and 'mak[e] a false entry in,' typically take as grammatical objects records, documents, or things used to record or preserve information, such as logbooks or hard drives. See, *e.g.*, Black's Law Dictionary 720 (10th ed. 2014) (defining 'falsify' as '[t]o make deceptive; to counterfeit, forge, or misrepresent; esp., to tamper with (a document, record, etc.)'). It would be unnatural, for example, to describe a killer's act of wiping his fingerprints from a gun as 'falsifying' the murder weapon. But it would not be strange to refer to 'falsifying' data stored on a hard drive as simply 'falsifying' a hard drive. * * *

"Finally, if our recourse to traditional tools of statutory construction leaves any doubt about the meaning of 'tangible object,' as that term is used in § 1519, we would invoke the rule that 'ambiguity concerning the ambit of criminal statutes should be resolved in favor of lenity.' *Cleveland v. United States,* 531 U.S. 12, 25, 121 S.Ct. 365, 148 L.Ed.2d 221 (2000) (quoting *Rewis v. United States,* 401 U.S. 808, 812, 91 S.Ct. 1056, 28 L.Ed.2d 493 (1971)). That interpretative principle is relevant here, where the Government urges a reading of § 1519 that exposes individuals to 20-year prison sentences for tampering with *any* physical object that *might* have evidentiary value in *any* federal investigation into *any* offense, no matter whether the investigation is pending or merely contemplated, or whether the offense subject to investigation is criminal or civil. See *Liparota v. United States,* 471 U.S. 419, 427, 105 S.Ct. 2084, 85 L.Ed.2d 434 (1985) ('Application of the rule of lenity ensures that criminal statutes will provide fair warning concerning conduct rendered illegal and strikes the appropriate balance between the legislature, the prosecutor, and the court in defining criminal liability.'). In determining the meaning of 'tangible object' in § 1519, 'it is appropriate, before we choose the harsher alternative, to require that Congress should have spoken in language that is clear and definite.' *Cleveland,* 531 U.S., at 25, 121 S.Ct. 365 (quoting *United States v. Universal C.I.T. Credit Corp.,* 344 U.S. 218, 222, 73 S.Ct. 227, 97 L.Ed.260 (1952))."

Justice Alito concurred in the Court's judgment (providing five votes to overturn Captain Yates's conviction). He found this a close case and was persuaded to follow the more lenient construction because of the *nouns* (the *noscitur a sociis* argument), the *verbs* (the fit with the verbs describing the criminal action), and the *caption.*

Justice Kagan (joined by Justices Scalia, Kennedy, and Thomas) dissented. "While the plurality starts its analysis with § 1519's heading, I would begin with § 1519's text. When Congress has not supplied a definition, we generally give a statutory term its ordinary meaning. As the plurality must acknowledge, the ordinary meaning of 'tangible object' is 'a discrete thing that possesses physical form.' A fish is, of course, a discrete thing that possesses physical form. See generally Dr. Seuss, One Fish Two Fish Red Fish Blue Fish (1960). So the ordinary meaning of the term 'tangible object' in § 1519, as no one here disputes, covers fish (including too-small red grouper).

"That interpretation accords with endless uses of the term in statute and rule books as construed by courts. Dozens of federal laws and rules of procedure (and hundreds of state enactments) include the term 'tangible object' or its first cousin 'tangible thing'—some in association with documents, others not. [E.g., 18 U.S.C. § 668(a)(1)(D) (defining 'museum' as an entity that owns 'tangible objects that are exhibited to the public').] To my knowledge, no court has ever read any such provision to exclude things that don't record or preserve data; rather, all courts have adhered to the statutory language's ordinary (*i.e.,* expansive) meaning. For example, courts have understood the phrases 'tangible objects' and 'tangible things' in the Federal Rules of Criminal and Civil Procedure to cover everything from guns to drugs to machinery to . . . animals. No surprise, then, that—until today—courts have uniformly applied the term 'tangible object' in § 1519 in the same way."

Justice Kagan agreed (who does not?) that provisions ought to be read within their statutory context—which confirmed the breadth of § 1519. "Section 1519 refers to 'any' tangible object, thus indicating (in line with *that* word's plain meaning) a tangible object 'of whatever kind.' Webster's Third New International Dictionary 97 (2002). This Court has time and again recognized that 'any' has 'an expansive meaning,' bringing within a statute's reach *all* types of the item (here, 'tangible object') to which the law refers. *Department of Housing and Urban Development v. Rucker,* 535 U.S. 125, 131, 122 S.Ct. 1230, 152 L.Ed.2d 258 (2002). And the adjacent laundry list of verbs in § 1519 ('alters, destroys, mutilates, conceals, covers up, falsifies, or makes a false entry') further shows that Congress wrote a statute with a wide scope. Those words are supposed to ensure—just as 'tangible object' is meant to—that § 1519 covers the whole world of evidence-tampering, in all its prodigious variety.

"Still more, 'tangible object' appears as part of a three-noun phrase (including also 'records' and 'documents') common to evidence-tampering laws and always understood to embrace things of all kinds. The Model Penal Code's evidence-tampering section, drafted more than 50 years ago, similarly prohibits a person from 'alter[ing], destroy[ing], conceal[ing] or remov[ing] any *record, document or thing*' in an effort to thwart an official investigation or proceeding. ALI, Model Penal Code § 241.7(1), p. 175 (1962) (emphasis added). The Code's commentary emphasizes that the offense described in that provision is 'not limited to conduct that [alters] a written instrument.' *Id.,* § 241.7, Comment 3, at 179. Rather, the language extends to 'any physical object.' *Ibid.* Consistent with that statement—and, of course, with ordinary meaning—courts in the more than 15 States that have laws based on the Model Code's tampering provision apply them to all tangible objects, including drugs, guns, vehicles and . . . yes, animals. Not a one has limited the phrase's scope to objects that record or preserve information.

"The words 'record, document, or tangible object' in § 1519 also track language in 18 U.S.C. § 1512, the federal witness-tampering law covering (as even the plurality accepts) physical evidence in all its forms. Section 1512, both in its original version (preceding § 1519) and today, repeatedly uses the phrase 'record, document, or other object'—most notably, in a provision prohibiting the use of force or threat to induce another person to withhold any of those materials from an official proceeding. § 4(a) of the Victim and Witness Protection Act of 1982, 96 Stat. 1249, as amended, 18 U.S.C. § 1512(b)(2). That language, which itself likely derived from the Model Penal Code, encompasses no less the bloody knife than the incriminating letter, as all courts have for decades agreed. And typically 'only the most compelling evidence' will persuade this Court that Congress intended 'nearly identical language' in provisions dealing with related subjects to bear different meanings. *Communications Workers v. Beck,* 487 U.S. 735, 754, 108 S.Ct. 2641, 101 L.Ed.2d 634 (1988). Context thus again confirms what text indicates.

"And legislative history, for those who care about it, puts extra icing on a cake already frosted. Section 1519, as the plurality notes, was enacted after the Enron Corporation's collapse, as part of the Sarbanes-Oxley Act of 2002, 116 Stat. 745. But the provision began its life in a separate bill, and the drafters emphasized that Enron was 'only a case study exposing the shortcomings in our current laws' relating to both 'corporate and criminal' fraud. S. Rep. No. 107–146, pp. 2, 11 (2002). The primary 'loophole[ ]' Congress identified, see *id.,* at 14, arose from limits in the part of § 1512 just described: That provision, as uniformly construed, prohibited a person from inducing another to destroy 'record[s], document[s], or other object[s]'—of every type—but not from doing so himself. § 1512(b)(2). Congress (as even the plurality agrees) enacted § 1519 to close that yawning gap. But § 1519 could fully achieve that goal only if it covered all the records, documents, and objects § 1512 did, as well as all the means of tampering with them. And so § 1519 was written to do exactly that—'to apply broadly to any acts to destroy or fabricate physical evidence,' as long as performed with the requisite intent. S. Rep. No. 107–146, at 14. 'When a person destroys evidence,' the drafters explained, 'overly technical legal distinctions should neither hinder nor prevent prosecution.' *Id.,* at 7. Ah well: Congress, meet today's Court, which here invents just such a distinction with just such an effect."

Justice Kagan was unimpressed with the arguments from the caption, nouns, and verbs, all relied upon by the plurality and concurring opinions. Because titles are almost always abridgments, shortcuts to give only a general impression of statutory ambits, Justice Kagan opined that there is "no other case in which we have *begun* our interpretation of a statute with the title, or relied on a title to override the law's clear terms. Instead, we have followed 'the wise rule that the title of a statute and the heading of a section cannot limit the plain meaning of the text.' *Trainmen v. Baltimore & Ohio R. Co.,* 331 U.S. 519, 528–529, 67 S.Ct. 1387, 91 L.Ed. 1646 (1947)."

Noscitur a sociis is only relevant if there were a statutory ambiguity, Justice Kagan suggested. "Anyway, assigning 'tangible object' its ordinary meaning comports with *noscitur a sociis* and *ejusdem generis* when applied, as they should be, with attention to § 1519's subject and purpose. Those canons require identifying a common trait that links all the words in a statutory phrase. In responding to that demand, the plurality characterizes records and documents as things that preserve information—and so they are. But just as much, they are things that provide information, and thus potentially serve as evidence relevant to matters under review. And in a statute pertaining to obstruction of federal investigations, that evidentiary function comes to the fore. The destruction of records and documents prevents law enforcement agents from gathering facts relevant to official inquiries. And so too does the destruction of tangible objects—of whatever kind. Whether the item is a fisherman's ledger or an undersized fish, throwing it overboard has the identical effect on the administration of justice. For purposes of § 1519, records, documents, and (all) tangible objects are therefore alike."

The argument from verbs was, likewise, mystifying to the dissenters. "The plurality observes that § 1519 prohibits 'falsif[ying]' or 'mak[ing] a false entry in' a tangible object, and no one can do those things to, say, a murder weapon (or a fish). But of course someone can alter, destroy, mutilate, conceal, or cover up such a tangible object, and § 1519 prohibits those actions too. The Court has never before suggested that all the verbs in a statute need to match up with all the nouns. See *Robers v. United States,* 572 U.S. ___, ___, 134 S.Ct. 1854, 1858, 188 L.Ed.2d 885 (2014) ('[T]he law does not require legislators to write extra language specifically exempting, phrase by phrase, applications in respect to which a portion of a phrase is not needed'). And for good reason. It is exactly when Congress sets out to draft a statute broadly—to include every imaginable variation on a theme—that such mismatches will arise. To respond by narrowing the law, as the plurality does, is thus to flout both what Congress wrote and what Congress wanted."

Can the rule of lenity justify a narrowing of § 1519, in light of so much evidence that the statute, as a matter of law, covers Captain Yates's destruction of the undersized red grouper? No, argued Justice Kagan, but the rule of lenity does suggest what is afoot in the plurality and concurring opinions—a judicial concern with "overcriminalization and excessive punishment in the U.S. Code.

"Now as to this statute, I think the plurality somewhat—though only somewhat—exaggerates the matter. The plurality omits from its description of § 1519 the requirement that a person act 'knowingly' and with 'the intent to impede, obstruct, or influence' federal law enforcement. And in highlighting § 1519's maximum penalty, the plurality glosses over the absence of any prescribed minimum. (Let's not forget that Yates's sentence was not 20 years, but 30 days.) Congress presumably enacts laws with high maximums and no minimums when it thinks the prohibited conduct may run the gamut from major to minor. That is assuredly true of acts obstructing justice. Most district judges, as Congress knows, will recognize differences between such cases and prosecutions like this one, and will try to make the punishment fit the crime. Still and all, I tend to think, for the reasons the plurality gives, that § 1519 is a bad law—too broad and undifferentiated, with too-high maximum penalties, which give prosecutors too much leverage and sentencers too much discretion. And I'd go further: In those ways, § 1519 is unfortunately not an outlier, but an emblem of a deeper pathology in the federal criminal code.

"But whatever the wisdom or folly of § 1519, this Court does not get to rewrite the law. 'Resolution of the pros and cons of whether a statute should sweep broadly or narrowly is for Congress.' *Rodgers,* 466 U.S., at 484, 104 S.Ct. 1942. If judges disagree with Congress's choice, we are perfectly entitled to say so—in lectures, in law review articles, and even in dicta. But we are not entitled to replace the statute Congress enacted with an alternative of our own design."

NOTES AND QUESTIONS ON YATES V. UNITED STATES

None of the opinions in *Yates* emphasizes the legislative evidence, but Representative Oxley filed an *amicus* brief with strong arguments supporting the plurality opinion's conclusion that Congress had no purpose to create a general obstruction of justice statute in section 1519. Should courts reject legislative evidence in favor of canons? Should canons come before consideration of legislative evidence or after? If they come after, then canons may become infused with purposivist assumptions. Notice that Justice Ginsburg first notes the purpose of section 1519 before she applies the canons. Is this consistent with the idea of canons of construction?

Relatedly, some of us believe that the Oxley *amicus* informed Justice Ginsburg's text-based canonical arguments by deploying legislative history as a mechanism to argue for a narrow interpretation based upon the statutory caption and title, the placement of § 1519 in the Criminal Code, and the relationship of § 1519 to other obstruction of justice provisions. Should the Court have cited the Oxley brief? Why do you suppose no one did cite it?

Canons Versus Legislative Evidence: Textualists decry legislative evidence because they argue Congress has a conflict of interest in both legislating and interpreting law: Do courts have a similar conflict of interest in relying upon canons since courts create canons?

Latin Canons and Counter-Canons: Canons have been criticized because they lead to counter-canons, but Karl Lewellyn's famous article on this point (excerpted Chapter 5, pp. 553–558) did not focus on the Latin canons with as much intensity as the Justices did in *Yates*. Does Lewellyn's argument apply to the seemingly more technical semantic canons? Both *ejusdem generis* and *noscitur a sociis* require the interpreter to find a common generality, as Justice Kagan notes. Query whether that move to generality predictably triggers canons focused on specificity? Can we predict that every time *ejusdem generis* or *noscitur a sociis* is used, that the other side can make an argument based on canons against surplusage (that each and every word of a statute should have meaning), or the canon on meaningful variation (that different words in a statute mean different things). So, for example, in *Yates,* by reading tangible object as something like a document, as did the plurality opinion, the interpreter seems to either read out the term "tangible object" or gives it less of a meaningful variation? Of course, as did the dissent, the same argument can be flipped. By reading the statute to say any "tangible object," as did the dissent, does that read out the words "record" and "document"?

B. INTERPRETATION TO AVOID CONSTITUTIONAL PROBLEMS

Page 517: Insert the following case right after *National Federation of Independent Business v. Sebelius*:

McDonnell v. United States
___ U.S. ___, 136 S.Ct. 2355, 195 L.Ed.2d 639 (2016).

Former Virginia Governor Robert McDonnell was convicted of fraud and extortion; the federal statutory theory was that he had committed (or agreed to commit) an "official act" in exchange for the loans and gifts. Federal criminal law defines "official act" as "any decision or action on any question, matter, cause, suit, proceeding or controversy, which may at any time be pending, or which may by law be brought before any public official, in such official's official capacity, or in such official's place of trust or profit." 18 U.S.C. § 201(a)(3). According to the prosecutors, Governor McDonnell accepted $175,000 from a Virginia businessman seeking public university testing of a nutritional supplement his firm wanted to market. In return for the gifts, prosecutors argued that McDonnell committed at least five "official acts," including "arranging meetings" for the businessman with other Virginia officials to discuss the product, "hosting" events for the company at the Governor's Mansion, and "contacting other government officials" concerning the research studies.

The trial judge instructed the jury that "official act" encompasses "acts that a public official customarily performs," including acts "in furtherance of longer-term goals" or "in a series of steps to exercise influence or achieve an end." The judge rejected Governor McDonnell's request to instruct the jury that "merely arranging a meeting, attending an event, hosting a reception, or making a speech are not, standing alone, 'official acts'."

Reversing the Governor's convictions and remanding for a new trial, **Chief Justice Roberts** wrote for a unanimous Court. Invoking the *noscitur a sociis* canon (Coursebook, pp. 454–456), the statutory definition of "official act" suggests that the public official's action must involve a formal exercise of governmental power, and must also be something specific and focused that is "pending" or "may by law be brought" before a public official. To qualify as an "official act," the public official must make a decision or take an action on that question or matter, or agree to do so. Setting up a meeting, talking to another official, or organizing an event—without more—does not fit that definition of "official act."

In support of the Court's reading, the Chief Justice invoked the avoidance canon. Section 201 defines a bribe in *quid pro quo* terms, and the Government's theory would include a lot of official activities as "quos." "But conscientious public officials arrange meetings for constituents, contact other officials on their behalf, and include them in events all the time. The basic compact underlying representative government *assumes* that public officials will hear from their constituents and act appropriately on their concerns—whether it is the union official worried about a plant closing or the homeowners who wonder why it took five days to restore power to their neighborhood after a storm. The Government's position could cast a pall of potential prosecution over these relationships if the union had given a campaign contribution in the past or the homeowners invited the official to join them on their annual outing to the ballgame. Officials might wonder whether they could respond to even the most commonplace requests for assistance, and citizens with legitimate concerns might shrink from participating in democratic discourse.

"This concern is substantial. White House counsel who worked in every administration from that of President Reagan to President Obama warn that the Government's "breathtaking expansion of public-corruption law would likely chill federal officials' interactions with the people they serve and thus damage their ability effectively to perform their duties." Brief for Former Federal Officials as *Amici Curiae* 6. Six former Virginia attorneys general—four Democrats and two Republicans—also filed an *amicus* brief in this Court echoing those concerns, as did 77 former state attorneys general from States other than Virginia—41 Democrats, 35 Republicans, and 1 independent. Brief for Former Virginia Attorneys General as *Amici Curiae* 1–2, 16; Brief for 77 Former State Attorneys General (Non-Virginia) as *Amici Curiae* 1–2."

In addition to these First Amendment governance concerns, the Chief Justice found the Government's interpretation was so broad that it raised due process notice concerns as well. See *Skilling* (Coursebook, pp. 513–516). "The Government's position also raises significant federalism concerns. A State defines itself as a sovereign through "the structure of its government, and the character of those who exercise government authority." *Gregory v. Ashcroft* (Coursebook, pp. 533–546). That includes the prerogative to regulate the permissible scope of interactions between state officials and their constituents. Here, where a more limited interpretation of 'official act' is supported by both text and precedent, we decline to 'construe the statute in a manner that leaves its outer boundaries ambiguous and involves the Federal Government in setting standards "of 'good government for local and state officials.' *McNally v. United States,* 483 U.S. 350, 360, 107 S.Ct. 2875, 97 L.Ed.2d 292 (1987)."

Note how the Chief Justice's deployment of the avoidance canon here is different from his deployment in *Sebelius*, the previous case. In *McDonnell*, the Chief Justice does not actually say that the Government's reading of § 201 would be actually unconstitutional. This "modern" version of the avoidance canon is explored in the Notes.

Page 532: Insert the following new case and problem before Subsection C:

NEW SKIRMISHES OVER THE SEVERABILITY DOCTRINE

Murphy, Governor of New Jersey, et al. v. National Collegiate Athletic Association, et. al.

584 U.S. ____, 138 S.Ct. 1461, 200 L.Ed.2d 854 (2018).

In **Murphy v. NCAA,** the Court considered whether a provision of the Professional and Amateur Sports Protection Act (PASPA) prohibiting state authorization of sports gambling violated the anti-commandeering rule of the Constitution. Finding that the statute was not an ordinary congressional act of preemption, the Court, through an opinion by **Justice Alito**, found the provision unconstitutional.

Having done so, the Court then turned to the severability question, or, as Justice Alito put it, "whether, as petitioners maintain, our decision regarding PASPA's prohibition of the authorization and licensing of sports gambling operations dooms the remainder of the Act. In order for other PASPA provisions to fall, it must be 'evident that [Congress] would not have enacted those provisions which are within its power, independently of [those] which [are] not.' *Alaska Airlines, Inc. v. Brock,* 480 U.S. 678, 684 (1987) (internal quotation marks omitted). In conducting that inquiry, we ask whether the law remains 'fully operative' without the invalid provisions, *Free Enterprise Fund v. Public Company Accounting Oversight*

Bd., 561 U.S. 477, 509 (2010) (internal quotation marks omitted), but 'we cannot rewrite a statute and give it an effect altogether different from that sought by the measure viewed as a whole' " (citation omitted).

The Court took an aggressive stance toward severability in concluding that the entire statute functioned as a coherent whole, and struck the entire law down, over the dissent's objection, courtesy of **Justice Ginsburg,** that so doing was "deploy[ing] a wrecking ball destroying the [PAPSA]." The dissent continued:

"When a statute reveals a constitutional flaw, the Court ordinarily engages in a salvage rather than a demolition operation: It 'limit[s] the solution [to] severing any problematic portions while leaving the remainder intact.' *Free Enterprise Fund v. Public Company Accounting Oversight Bd.*, 561 U.S. 477, 508 (2010) (internal quotation marks omitted). The relevant question is whether the Legislature would have wanted unproblematic aspects of the legislation to survive or would want them to fall along with the infirmity. . . . On no rational ground can it be concluded that Congress would have preferred no statute at all if it could not prohibit States from authorizing or licensing such schemes. Deleting the alleged 'commandeering' direction would free the statute to accomplish just what Congress legitimately sought to achieve: stopping sports gambling regimes while making it clear that the stoppage is attributable to federal, not state, action."

Justice Thomas concurred to express his "growing discomfort with our modern severability precedents" and urged the Court to reconsider its precedents on the topic.

"Those precedents appear to be in tension with traditional limits on judicial authority. Early American courts did not have a severability doctrine. See [Kevin] Walsh, Partial Unconstitutionality, 85 N.Y.U. L. Rev. 738, 769 (2010) (Walsh). They recognized that the judicial power is, fundamentally, the power to render judgments in individual cases. . . . Thus, when early American courts determined that a statute was unconstitutional, they would simply decline to enforce it in the case before them. See Walsh 755–766. '[T]here was no "next step" in which courts inquired into whether the legislature would have preferred no law at all to the constitutional remainder.' *Id.*, at 777."

Arguing that "courts cannot take a blue pencil to statutes," Justice Thomas concluded that "the severability doctrine must be an exercise in statutory interpretation. . . . But even under this view, the severability doctrine is still dubious for at least two reasons. First, the severability doctrine does not follow basic principles of statutory interpretation. Instead of requiring courts to determine what a statute means, the severability doctrine requires courts to make 'a nebulous inquiry into hypothetical congressional intent.' . . . It requires judges to determine what Congress would have intended had it known that part of its statute was unconstitutional. . . . It seems unlikely that the enacting Congress had any intent on this question; Congress typically does not pass statutes with the expectation that some part will later be deemed unconstitutional. . . . More fundamentally, even if courts could discern Congress' hypothetical intentions, intentions do not count unless they are enshrined in a text that makes it through the constitutional processes of bicameralism and presentment. See *Wyeth v. Levine*, 555 U.S. 555, 586–588 (2009) (Thomas, J., concurring in judgment). Because we have 'a Government of laws, not of men,' we are governed by 'legislated text,' not 'legislators' intentions'—and especially not legislators' *hypothetical* intentions. *Zuni Public School Dist. No. 89 v. Department of Education*, 550 U.S. 81, 119 (2007) (Scalia, J., dissenting). Yet hypothetical intent is exactly what the severability doctrine turns on, at least when Congress has not expressed its fallback position in the text."

Justice Thomas went on to discuss questions related to the intersection of standing doctrine and severability and then concluded: "In sum, our modern severability precedents are in tension with longstanding limits on the judicial power. And, though no party in this case has asked us to reconsider these precedents, at some point, it behooves us to do so."

The severability doctrine has been around, and applied without controversy by jurists of all methodological stripes for decades. See William N. Eskridge, Jr., *Interpreting* Law*: A Primer on How to Read Statutes and the Constitution* 337 (2017). On the other hand, some scholars have argued that a strong presumption in favor of severability lowers the cost of legislating too much and puts too much of the onus on courts to effectively engage in legislative surgery when part of a statute is found unconstitutional. Is Justice Thomas justified to so casually suggest overturning years of precedent here?

Do you see the connection between textualism and Justice Thomas's objection to modern severability doctrine? How do you suggest courts determine whether to sever a statute if they will not consider congressional intent?

PROBLEM 5–4: SEVERABILITY AND THE AFFORDABLE CARE ACT (AGAIN)

In 2018, Texas, leading almost two dozen states, brought suit in federal district court arguing that the entire Affordable Care Act (ACA) was unconstitutional in a filing that hinged on a severability argument. See Texas v. United States, No. 4:18-cv-00167-O (N.D. Tex. 2018). Specifically, Texas's argument looked to the 2017 tax reform legislation passed by the Republican-controlled Congress (and supported by President Trump) after numerous failed attempts to "repeal and replace" the ACA earlier in the year. As relevant to the

ACA, the tax reform legislation made just one change: it reduced the penalty for failure to buy health insurance under the ACA from $695 to $0.

Recall that the requirement to purchase health insurance—the so-called insurance-purchase mandate—was the focal point of the original challenge to the ACA's constitutionality in 2012. In *NFIB v. Sebelius*, discussed earlier in this Chapter, four Justices would have voted to strike down the mandate as an unconstitutional exercise of the Commerce Power. The Chief Justice, however, applying the canon of constitutional avoidance, read the mandate as a tax and so a valid exercise of the Taxing Power. In *Texas v. United States*, the states argue that the mandate no longer functions as a tax without the penalty, *ergo*, it is no longer constitutional and, *double ergo*, under the severability doctrine the entire 2,000-page law falls with it.

The Department of Justice has declined to defend the law, a position controversial in and of itself. But it also has argued that Texas has it only partially right when it comes to severability. DOJ would not argue that *all* of the ACA falls with the mandate—the ACA contains many provision unrelated to insurance, such as calorie-count posting requirements, amendments to Medicare's coverage of pharmaceutical drugs, public health funding, and so on—but it agrees with Texas that the key insurance reforms in the statute, namely those requirements that insurers accept all consumers at relatively equal rates regardless of health status, go down with the mandate.

The basis for DOJ's argument, and part of Texas's argument, is that the 2010 Congress, in enacting the ACA, included a findings section (in the section of the law justifying the mandate as a valid exercise of the Commerce Power) in which it describes the mandate as essential to supporting the insurance reforms. See Patient Protection and Affordable Care Act, sec. 1501, Pub. L. 111–148, 124 Stat. 119, 242–243 (2010). (The mandate sustains the insurance markets in the face of these expensive requirements by introducing new health customers in those markets.) What is more, in 2012, the Obama-led DOJ argued in *NFIB* before the Supreme Court that the mandate was not severable from the insurance reforms for those same reasons. Brief for the Respondents (Severability), *NFIB v. Sebelius*, Nos. 11-393 AND 11-400 (Jan. 2012).

In response, the opposing states, acting as intervenors friendly to the ACA in the lawsuit, as well as *amici*, argue that opponents have it wrong. Whatever the intent of the 2010 Congress and the circumstances of the 2012 insurance markets, they argue, Congress in *2017* made a decision to repeal the mandate and the mandate alone, thereby signaling its clear intent that the rest of the statute could and should stand without it.

How would you decide the severability issue? As you think it over, consider these questions:

Which Congress Matters? Is this really a fight between the 2010 and 2017 Congresses? Which Congress's intent should control?

How to Understand Congressional Intent More Generally? Indeed, are we even talking about Congressional "intent" anymore? Normally, when severability arises it is because a *court* has made the decision that part of a statute must go, and the question is what it should do with the rest. Is that the same situation here? Do we really need get into the kind of hypsometrical guessing game about intent that Justice Thomas was worried about in *Murphy* here?

The Relevance of Political Realities and Constraints? At one point, Texas argues, in support for its argument to strike the entire statute down, that the 2017 Congress really *wanted* to repeal the entire law but didn't have the votes. The only reason Congress was able to pass even the mandate-penalty-amendment was that it used the special budget-related procedure of reconciliation, which we discuss in Chapter 6 of the casebook, to do so. Under Congress's rules, that budget procedure bypasses the filibuster, so only 50 votes—not the usual 60 in the Senate—are required, but only laws relating to the budget can be passed under that rule, which is why nothing else in the ACA was affected. Which way does Texas's argument cut? Also, should the courts be taking these kinds of political realities into account when deciding such questions?

C. THE NEW FEDERALISM CANONS

Page 552: Insert the following Note and case before Section 3:

NOTE ON THE FUTURE OF INTERPRETATION IN THE ROBERTS COURT

King v. Burwell, the 2015 challenge to the Affordable Care Act, raises a host of provocative, cutting edge questions related to the themes of this Chapter. *King* was briefed as a barrage of textualist, policy-based, and administrative canon-fire, but the Court, per the Chief Justice, gave us an opinion that has stronger echoes to the old Legal Process school's vision of a reasonable, purposive Congress—a Congress with a "plan" that the Court can understand—than we have seen in a long time. At the same time, the Chief Justice refers to no legislative history, and confines his views on purpose to the four corners of the document. Is *King* a textualist opinion? A pragmatic, functional opinion? A new textualism-influenced purposivism?

King also has major significance for the themes in Chapters 6 (the modern lawmaking context) and 8 (administrative deference). *King* is the most explicit statement by the Court yet that realities of the modern lawmaking process might have implications for the applicability of many canons of interpretation. Do the canons impose a simplicity and perfection on Congress that statutes like the ACA, with its highly unorthodox history, simply cannot bear? What, if anything, does *King* tell us about how the Court should approach messy, long, modern statutes? The Court seems rueful that the statute did not go through the usual textbook legislative process; yet how did it respond? The Court also does not acknowledge that the kind of unorthodox legislative process it laments in *King* is increasingly the norm, not the exception. What does that mean for the canons and other approaches to statutory interpretation? *See* Gluck,

O'Connell & Po, *Unorthodox Lawmaking, Unorthodox Rulemaking*, 115 Colum. L. Rev. 1789 (2015).

Keep the deference themes in mind as well. The Court rejects *Chevron* deference—ask yourself why? Is it because the IRS is not the proper expert? What if HHS had issued the rule instead? Was the Court justified to conclude that it was unreasonable to assume that Congress would have delegated such a significant question? We return to these points in Chapter 8.

DAVID KING ET AL. v. SYLVIA BURWELL, SECRETARY OF HEALTH AND HUMAN SERVICES, ET AL.

United States Supreme Court, 2015.
__ U.S. __, 135 S.Ct. 2480, 192 L.Ed.2d 483.

[Excerpted in Chapter 1 of this Supplement. Please refer to Chapter 1 for notes on *King*'s place in the textualism v. purposivism debate and its approach to the realities of the legislative process.]

CHAPTER 6

LEGISLATIVE HISTORY AND LAWMAKING CONTEXT

■ ■ ■

1. SHOULD JUDGES OR AGENCIES CONSULT LEGISLATIVE CONTEXT?

Page 616: Insert the following Notes and new case on legislative history before Problem 6–1:

5. *Textualist Theory Versus Practice in the Gorsuch Era.* While on the Tenth Circuit, then-Judge Gorsuch wrote, like other textualists, that he worried about whether looking at legislative materials amounted to improper "psychoanalysis of Congress," see *In re Dawes*, 652 F.3d 1236, 1244 (2011). However, in other opinions, then-Judge Gorsuch seemed perfectly willing to look at legislative history. See, e.g., *Almond v. Unified School District,* 665 F.3d 1174, 1183 (10th Cir. 2011) (Gorsuch opinion relying on a House committee report and the statement of a Senate sponsor); *United States v. Dolan,* 571 U.S. 1022, 1025 (10th Cir. 2009) (Gorsuch opinion: "The plain language of the Act, longstanding canons of construction, the [statute's] legislative history, and our own case law all plot against [the defendant's] interpretation.").

At his confirmation hearings, then-judge Gorsuch seemed of two minds—that legislative history may or may not have value. *Hearing on the Nomination of Neil Gorsuch to be an Associate Justice of the U.S. Supreme Court, March 22, 2017 Morning Session, Before the S. Comm. on the Judiciary*, 115th Cong. 37 (2017) (statement of J. Neil Gorsuch). He resisted trying to divine the contents of "535" minds, *Hearing on the Nomination of Neil Gorsuch to be an Associate Justice of the U.S. Supreme Court, March 22, 2017 Afternoon Session, Before the S. Comm. on the Judiciary*, 115th Cong. 33 (2017) (statement of J. Neil Gorsuch), a standard textualist criticism of legislative evidence but, at the same time, admitted that he had "used legislative history from time to time." *Hearing on the Nomination of Neil Gorsuch to be an Associate Justice of the U.S. Supreme Court, March 21, 2017 Afternoon Session, Before the S. Comm. on the Judiciary*, 115th Cong. 124 (2017) (statement of J. Neil Gorsuch). He expressed his concern about legislative history based on two principles: notice and the separation of powers. Individuals have "notice" of the statute's terms and focusing on legislative history turns judges into legislators.

> Before I put a person in prison, before I deny someone of their liberty or property, I want to be very sure that I can look them square

> in the eye and say you should have known, you were on notice, that the law prohibited that which you're doing. . . . I don't want to have him . . . say how am I supposed to tell? I need an army of lawyers to figure that out. Some people can afford armies of lawyers, most Americans can't. It's a matter of fair notice and due process. The other part again is separation of powers considerations. . . . If I start importing my feelings, if I treat statues or laws as workshop [sic] ink block tests, I've usurped your role. I've taken the right of self government by the people, for the people.

Hearing on the Nomination of Neil Gorsuch to be an Associate Justice of the U.S. Supreme Court, March 21, 2017 Afternoon Session, Before the S. Comm. on the Judiciary, 115th Cong. 17 (2017) (statement of J. Neil Gorsuch). Are there responses to this account?

Criminal cases. Is this example misleading? First, many modern criminal laws have no legislative history because crime bills are typically very controversial. Committee chairmen and leaders will agree to move the bill directly to the Senate floor and, in the House, through the Rules Committee. See Chapter 1, § 1(B) (The Rules of the House and Senate). Second, do the same concerns apply when Apple is fighting Microsoft? When a case reaches the Supreme Court on statutory interpretation involving economic titans, does the criminal case rationale dissolve? Particularly in the new high-tech age of Congress.gov, does it take a battery of lawyers to read the Congressional Record—simply "Control F" and you can locate any particular statutory phrase. Finally, in criminal cases, the rule of lenity, see Chapter 5, § 2(A), protects just these values (discussing notice and separation of powers bases for the rule of lenity canon). Then why should we need a rule against legislative history to accomplish the same ends?

Notice. How often do you think criminal defendants "read" statutes? Isn't "notice" just a legal fiction? If the average person does not read statutes or the congressional record, then why is there a reason to elevate one over the other? Moreover, the "notice" argument assumes that legislative history is unavailable, but in fact the Constitution requires that the Congress keep a journal. U.S. Const. art. I, § 5. Surely, the Congressional Record is a public document. If accessibility to the public is the issue, would not the better rule be to look at the documents created by Congress, such as "section-by-section" analyses in committee reports, which explain the bill in non-legalese?

Separation of powers. "Legislating from the bench" is a slogan deserving some scrutiny. As we noted in Chapter 1, § 2 (Note on the Separation of Powers), functional adjectives like "judicial" or "legislative" are notoriously difficult to apply. In cases where statutory meaning is truly plain, there is no conflict between these ideas. But plain meaning cases are few and far between. Most cases arriving in appellate courts or the Supreme Court involve ambiguous or disputed meanings. In such cases, *there is no definitive text to apply*. The question then becomes how to resolve two contestable meanings of the text. In the absence of an agreed upon meaning, the judge who refuses to look to more evidence (the legislative history) is faced with 2 unpalatable possibilities: (1) declaring the meaning plain when it is not; or (2) adding her preferred meaning without acknowledging it. In either case, could the judge be said to be "legislating from the bench" if we know, from the evidence, that Congress's meaning was different? For just such a case, consider Problem 6–1 below.

6. *Rhetorical Ambivalence Toward Legislative History in the Post-Scalia Era.* Justice Scalia's arguments against legislative evidence have had a notable effect on the rhetoric involving its use. While he was on the Supreme Court, Justices would refer to legislative history with caveats, such as "for those who find it useful," to forestall a dissent or concurrence from Justice Scalia objecting to the use of legislative history. As Professor Brudney dubbed it, this seemed to generate "confirmatory legislative history," the history being used to confirm a conclusion achieved by textual analysis. James J. Brudney, *Confirmatory Legislative History*, 76 Brook. L. Rev. 901, 901–02 (2011).

Ambivalence about legislative evidence still casts a shadow on the Supreme Court even after Justice Scalia's death. It was on display in the 2016–17 Term in a much-awaited case involving pensions for religiously-affiliated entities. *Advocate Health Care Network v. Stapleton*, 137 S.Ct. 1652 (2017). For decades, multi-million dollar religiously-affiliated hospitals and similar entities had enjoyed a regulatory exemption—called the "church plan" exemption from ERISA—the statute that regulates pensions to ensure that pensioners do in fact receive benefits upon retirement. *Id.* at 1655–56. Employees brought suit using a textual argument: the religiously affiliated entities were not covered because the plans were not created by churches as required under the statute's definitions. 29 U.S.C. § 1002(33).

Ruling in favor of the hospitals, Justice Kagan wrote a brilliantly simplified explanation of a very difficult statute. She felled the employees' microcosmic textual analysis with various textual maneuvers, easily puncturing the employees' hypothetical arguments with her own hypothetical linguistic constructions, deliberately wielding canons like the canon against surplusage to support the result. *Stapleton*, 137 S.Ct. at 1658–61. So much for the text. Her approach toward legislative evidence was decidedly less enthusiastic and seemingly contradictory. Although she called the materials proffered "lowly,"—"the sort of stuff we have called 'among the least illuminating forms of legislative history,' " *id.* at 1661 (citing *NLRB v. SW General, Inc.*, 137 S.Ct. 929, 943 (2017)),—Justice Kagan proceeded to consider the legislative evidence to support her textual conclusions. *Id.* at 1661–62. As far as the hierarchy of legislative history is concerned, she was on solid ground: hearings are typically very low in the pecking order and isolated floor statements are not always the best of evidence. The question, though, is why one would bother to entertain the evidence if in fact it was so "lowly."

What possible purpose lies in saying one thing and doing another? One answer is that given by Justice Gorsuch (who did not participate in this case) in his confirmation hearings on his own "no . . . but . . . I've done it" ambivalent attitude on legislative evidence: judges really do want to know what Congress was trying to do. See *Hearing on the Nomination of Neil Gorsuch to be an Associate Justice of the U.S. Supreme Court, March 21, 2017 Afternoon Session, Before the S. Comm. on the Judiciary*, 115th Cong. 124 (2017). They do not want to find themselves overruled by materials showing they were totally off-base (see *Pepper v. Hart*, Coursebook pp. 617–627), but they feel themselves not terribly well-suited to evaluate the evidence proffered. One answer could be that, although illogical, the ambivalence conveys messages to two different audiences: to the Supreme Court bar, "watch out if you rely on legislative evidence"; but to the litigants in the individual case, "we have heard your arguments."

Meanwhile, Justice Sotomayor showed no hesitation in looking to legislative evidence. *Stapleton*, 137 S.Ct. at 1663 (Sotomayor, J., concurring). She concurred for the sole purpose of explaining that ERISA's church exemption had grown far beyond the bounds of what the legislative history described, yielding a result she invited Congress to reconsider. She wrote:

> As the majority acknowledges . . . the available legislative history does not clearly endorse this result. That silence gives me pause: The decision to exempt plans neither established nor maintained by a church could have the kind of broad effect that is usually thoroughly debated during the legislative process and thus recorded in the legislative record. And to the extent that Congress acted to exempt plans established by orders of Catholic Sisters . . . it is not at all clear that Congress would take the same action today with respect to some of the largest health-care providers in the country. Despite their relationship to churches, organizations such as petitioners operate for-profit subsidiaries; employ thousands of employees; earn billions of dollars in revenue; and compete in the secular market with companies that must bear the cost of complying with ERISA. These organizations thus bear little resemblance to those Congress considered when enacting the 1980 amendment to the church plan definition. This current reality might prompt Congress to take a different path. *Stapleton*, 137 S.Ct. at 1663 (Sotomayor, J., concurring) (citations omitted).

Query: Would Congress be more likely to review the statute if the Court had ruled in favor of the employees rather than the employers?

Digital Realty Trust, Inc. v. Paul Somers

583 U.S. ____, 138 S.Ct. 767, 200 L.Ed.2d 15 (2018).

The legislative history debate has continued after Justice Gorsuch joined the Court. In **Digital Realty Trust, Inc. v. Somers**, Paul Somers, vice president of Digital Realty Trust, alleged that he was terminated shortly after he reported the securities-law violations by his employer to senior management. Somers argued that such termination violated the whistleblower provisions in the 2010 Dodd-Frank Wall Street Reform and Consumer Protection Act.

The Dodd-Frank Act defines "whistleblower" to mean a person who provides "information relating to a violation of the securities laws to the [Securities and Exchange] Commission." 15 U.S.C. § 78u–6(a)(6). Under the Act, whistleblowers are protected from retaliation for, *inter alia*, "making disclosures that are required or protected under" Sarbanes-Oxley, the Securities Exchange Act of 1934, the criminal anti-retaliation proscription at 18 U.S.C. § 1513(e), or any other law subject to the SEC's jurisdiction. 15 U.S.C. § 78u–6(h)(1)(A)(iii). The question before the Court was: "Does the anti-retaliation provision of Dodd-Frank extend to an individual who has not reported a violation of the securities laws to the SEC and therefore falls outside the Act's definition of 'whistleblower' "?

Justice Ginsburg's majority opinion held emphatically "no," based on the plain text of the definition and the canon *exclusio unius*. For flavor, and extra support, however, she also relied on legislative history: "At issue in this case is the Dodd-Frank anti-retaliation provision enacted in 2010, eight years after the enactment of Sarbanes-Oxley. Passed in the wake of the 2008 financial crisis, Dodd-Frank aimed to 'promote the financial stability of the United States by improving accountability and transparency in the financial system.' 124 Stat. 1376. Dodd-Frank responded to numerous perceived shortcomings in financial regulation. Among them was the SEC's need for additional 'power, assistance and money at its disposal' to regulate securities markets. Rep. No. 111–176, pp. 36, 37 (2010). To assist the Commission 'in identifying securities law violations,' the Act established 'a new, robust whistleblower program designed to motivate people who know of securities law violations to tell the SEC.' *Id.,* at 38. And recognizing that 'whistleblower often face the difficult choice between telling the truth and . . . committing "career suicide," ' Congress sought to protect whistleblowers from employment discrimination. *Id.,* at 111, 112."

Looking first to text, the Court held: "The definition section of the statute supplies an unequivocal answer: A 'whistleblower' is 'any individual who provides . . . information relating to a violation of the securities laws *to the Commission*.' § 78u–6(a)(6) (emphasis added). Leaving no doubt as to the definition's reach, the statute instructs that the 'definitio[n] shall apply' '[i]n this section,' that is, throughout § 78u–6. § 78u–6(a)(6). . . . Reinforcing our reading, another whistleblower protection provision in Dodd-Frank imposes no requirement that information be conveyed to a government agency. Title 10 of the statute, which created the Consumer Financial Protection Bureau (CFPB), prohibits discrimination against a 'covered employee' who, among other things, 'provide[s] . . . information to [his or her] employer, the Bureau, or any other State, local, or Federal, government authority or law enforcement agency relating to' a violation of a law subject to the CFPB's jurisdiction. 12 U.S.C. § 5567(a)(1). To qualify as a 'covered employee,' an individual need not provide information to the CFPB, or any other entity. See § 5567(b).... '[W]hen Congress includes particular language in one section of a statute but omits it in another[,] . . . this Court presumes that Congress intended a difference in meaning.' *Loughrin v. United States*, 573 U.S. ___, ___ (2014) (slip op., at 6) (internal quotation marks and alteration omitted). Congress placed a government-reporting requirement in § 78u–6(h), but not elsewhere in the same statute. Courts are not at liberty to dispense with the condition—tell the SEC—Congress imposed."

But the Court then returned to statutory purpose, a section of the opinion that prompted an outcry by the concurrence. As the Court wrote: "Dodd-Frank's purpose and design corroborate our comprehension of § 78u–6(h)'s reporting requirement. The 'core objective' of Dodd-Frank's robust whistleblower program, as Somers acknowledges, Tr. of Oral Arg. 45, is 'to motivate people who know of securities law violations to *tell the SEC*,' S. Rep. No. 111–176, at 38 (emphasis added).... Financial inducements alone, Congress recognized, may be insufficient to encourage certain employees, fearful of employer retaliation, to come forward with evidence of wrongdoing. Congress therefore complemented the Dodd-Frank monetary incentives for SEC reporting by heightening protection against retaliation.... Dodd-Frank's award program and anti-retaliation provision thus work synchronously to motivate individuals with knowledge of illegal activity to 'tell the SEC.' S. Rep. No. 111–176, at 38."

Justice Thomas concurred in part and concurred in the judgment, joined by Justices Alito and Gorsuch, to take on the majority's use of legislative history and purpose: "I join the Court's opinion only to the extent it relies on the text of the Dodd-Frank Wall Street Reform and Consumer Protection Act (Dodd-Frank), 124 Stat. 1376. As the Court observes, th[e] statutory definition 'resolves the question before us.' The Court goes on, however, to discuss the supposed 'purpose' of the statute, which it primarily derives from a single Senate Report. Even assuming a majority of Congress read the Senate Report, agreed with it, and voted for Dodd-Frank with the same intent, 'we are a government of laws, not of men, and are governed by what Congress enacted rather than by what it intended.' *Lawson v. FMR LLC*, 571 U.S. 429, ___ (2014) (Scalia, J., concurring in part and concurring in judgment) (slip op., at 1). And 'it would be a strange canon of statutory construction that would require Congress to state in committee reports . . . that which is obvious on the face of a statute.' *Harrison v. PPG Industries, Inc.*, 446 U.S. 578, 592 (1980). For these reasons, I am unable to join the portions of the Court's opinion that venture beyond the statutory text."

In a lengthy footnote, Justice Thomas also reproduced an infamous (and very, very old!) dialogue between Senators Armstrong and Dole over reliance on committee reports:

"Mr. ARMSTRONG. Mr. President, will the Senator tell me whether or not he wrote the committee report?

"Mr. DOLE. Did I write the committee report?

"Mr. ARMSTRONG. Yes.

"Mr. DOLE. No; the Senator from Kansas did not write the committee report.

"Mr. ARMSTRONG. Did any Senator write the committee report?

"Mr. DOLE. I have to check.

"Mr. ARMSTRONG. Does the Senator know of any Senator who wrote the committee report?

"Mr. DOLE. I might be able to identify one, but I would have to search. I was here all during the time it was written, I might say, and worked carefully with the staff as they worked. . . .

"Mr. ARMSTRONG. Mr. President, has the Senator from Kansas, the chairman of the Finance Committee, read the committee report in its entirety?

"Mr. DOLE. I am working on it. It is not a bestseller, but I am working on it.

"Mr. ARMSTRONG. Mr. President, did members of the Finance Committee vote on the committee report?

"Mr. DOLE. No.

"Mr. ARMSTRONG. . . . The report itself is not considered by the Committee on Finance. It was not subject to amendment by the Committee on Finance. It is not subject to amendment now by the Senate. . . . If there were matter within this report which was disagreed to by the Senator from Colorado or even by a majority of all Senators, there would be no way for us to change the report. I could not offer an amendment tonight to amend the committee report. . . . [L]et me just make the point that this is not the law, it was not voted on, it is not subject to amendment, and we should discipline ourselves to the task of expressing congressional intent in the statute."

(This dialogue is from 1982 (!), even before the heyday of textualism and its impact on more responsible use of legislative history. It seems time for textualists to retire it as is tells us little about the way either Congress or the courts use legislative history today.

Justice Sotomayor, joined by Justice Breyer, concurred to take on Justice Thomas's argument and to put in a plug for the value of courts considering how Congress actually operates when interpreting statutes.

She wrote: "Legislative history is of course not the law, but that does not mean it cannot aid us in our understanding of a law. Just as courts are capable of assessing the reliability and utility of evidence generally, they are capable of assessing the reliability and utility of legislative-history materials. Committee reports, like the Senate Report the Court discusses here are a particularly reliable source to which we can look to ensure our fidelity to Congress' intended meaning. Bills presented to Congress for consideration are generally accompanied by a committee report. Such reports are typically circulated at least two days before a bill is to be considered on the floor and provide Members of Congress and their staffs with information about 'a bill's context, purposes, policy implications, and details,' along with information on its supporters and opponents. R. Katzmann, Judging Statutes 20, and n. 62 (2014) (citing A. LaRue, Senate Manual Containing the Standing Rules, Orders, Laws, and Resolutions Affecting the Business of the United States Senate, S. Doc. No. 107–1, p. 17 (2001)). These materials 'have long been important means of informing the whole chamber about proposed legislation,' Katzmann, Judging Statutes, at 19, a point Members themselves have emphasized over the years. It is thus no surprise that legislative staffers view committee and conference reports as the most reliable type of legislative history. See Gluck & Bressman, Statutory Interpretation From the Inside—An Empirical Study of Congressional Drafting, Delegation and the Canons: Part I, 65 Stan. L. Rev. 901, 977 (2013)."

"Legislative history can be particularly helpful when a statute is ambiguous or deals with especially complex matters. But even when, as here, a statute's meaning can clearly be discerned from its text, consulting reliable legislative history can still be useful, as it enables us to corroborate and fortify our understanding of the text. Moreover, confirming our construction of a statute by considering reliable legislative history shows respect for and promotes comity with a coequal branch of Government. For these reasons, I do not think it wise for judges to close their eyes to reliable legislative history—and the realities of how Members of Congress create and enact laws—when it is available."

Justice Sotomayor countered Justice Thomas's footnote with a lengthy one of her own, citing Senator Charles Grassley's comment at Justice Scalia's Supreme Court confirmation hearing: "[A]s one who has served in Congress for 12 years, legislative history is very important to those of us here who want further detailed expression of that legislative intent," 99th Cong., 2d Sess., 65–66 (1986); as well as Abner Mikva, *Reading and Writing Statutes*, 28 S. Tex. L. Rev. 181, 184 (1986) ("The committee report is the bone structure of the legislation. It is the roadmap that explains why things are in and things are out of the statute") and academic work reporting members' and staff reliance on committee reports in their understandings of statutes. See Brudney, *Congressional Commentary on*

Judicial Interpretations of Statutes: Idle Chatter or Telling Response? 93 Mich. L. Rev. 1, 28; Gluck & Bressman, *Statutory Interpretation from the Inside—An Empirical Study of Congressional Drafting, Delegation, and the Canon: Part I,* 65 Stan. L. Rev. 901, 968 (2013).

3. LAWMAKING CONTEXT: MICRO TO MACRO

A. CONGRESSIONAL CONTEXT: HOW CONGRESS'S STRUCTURE AND PROCESSES AFFECT LEGISLATION

Page 684: Delete both paragraphs of Note 4 and insert the following:

Query: Revisit **King v. Burwell**, excerpted in Chapter 1 of this Supplement, and our note on the Legislative Process and the ACA. Consider how the case and the note reflects on the themes of this chapter.

PART 3

AGENCIES AND ADMINISTRATIVE IMPLEMENTATION

■ ■ ■

CHAPTER 7

INTRODUCTION TO ADMINISTRATIVE LAW

■ ■ ■

1. AGENCY RULEMAKING

A. PROCEDURAL REQUIREMENTS FOR LEGISLATIVE RULEMAKING

Page 723: Insert the following after Section 1(A) on regulatory restraints by statute:

4. ***Requirements Imposed by Post-Regulation Congressional Review.*** When first enacted, some believed the Congressional Review Act (CRA) was a dead letter. Without the Act, Congress already had the authority to reject a rule or regulation: all it had to do was pass a law rejecting that regulation. So, too, all the President had to do was to instruct an agency to pass a repealing rule. Others insisted the Act was a "transition" measure, which is to say that it allowed an incoming President to reject a set of "midnight" rules created by an outgoing President. Outgoing Presidents have an incentive to support regulations that are controversial—since the President is leaving office, he will no longer suffer electoral consequences if the regulation fails. Moreover, the CRA provides subtle, but potentially crucial, procedural advantages: it bars use of the Senate filibuster and allows for limited debate and thus speedier congressional action.

In 2017, the CRA made a dramatic appearance in Washington. It had only been used once since its passage—when a unified Republican Congress gave it new life. In 2017, under the authority of the CRA, the House and Senate voted to eliminate 13 regulations, and these laws were signed by President Trump in the first 100 days of his Administration. The laws rejected regulations submitted by the Securities and Exchange Commission, the Department of Interior, the Department of Education, and several other federal agencies. See, e.g., H.R.J. Res. 69, 115th Cong. (2017); H.R.J. Res. 58, 115th Cong. (2017); H.R.J. Res. 41, 115th Cong. (2017). Among the regulations overturned were a gun safety rule requiring the Social Security Administration to share information to reduce mentally ill individuals' access to firearms, H.R.J. Res. 40, 115th Cong. (2017), and a Department of Interior "Stream Protection Rule" that restricted what mining companies dumped into waterways, H.R.J. Res. 38, 115th Cong.

(2017). Advocates of the CRA insist that it still has unnoticed deregulatory power: the clock for CRA review, they contend, depends upon notice to Congress. Apparently, many agencies failed to comply with the law when regulations were first promulgated and so, in theory, once those agencies notify Congress, the 60 days might begin to run on hundreds of regulations that have been in effect for some time, perhaps years.

Although some members of Congress have drafted new legislation to repeal the CRA, regulatory opponents are also seeking to increase Congress's general authority to review regulations, pushing the Regulations from the Executive in Need of Scrutiny Act of 2017 (H.R. 26, 115th Cong. (2017)) (REINS Act). The REINS Act would require that major regulations would not go into effect unless Congress passed a joint resolution in their support. Proponents urge, in legislative language, that Congress has "excessively delegated" constitutional power to the executive over time, *id.* at § 2, and that the Act is a necessary claw-back of legislative power which will lead to better regulation and a more accountable system. On the delegation question, see Chapter 1, § 2. Query whether this Act would pass muster under the Supreme Court's decision in *INS v. Chadha*, 462 U.S. 919 (1983) that a one House veto is unconstitutional.

3. INFORMAL ADJUDICATIONS, GUIDANCES, AND INACTION

C. ADMINISTRATIVE GUIDANCES, INCLUDING POLICY STATEMENTS AND INTERPRETIVE RULES

Page 848: Insert the following case at the end of the Notes and Questions on Guidance Documents:

THOMAS E. PEREZ, SECRETARY OF LABOR V. MORTGAGE BANKERS ASS'N ET AL.

United States Supreme Court, 2015.
572 U.S. ___, 135 S.Ct. 1199, 191 L.Ed.2d 186.

JUSTICE SOTOMAYOR delivered the opinion of the Court. * * *

The APA establishes the procedures federal administrative agencies use for "rule making," defined as the process of "formulating, amending, or repealing a rule." § 551(5). "Rule," in turn, is defined broadly to include "statement [s] of general or particular applicability and future effect" that are designed to "implement, interpret, or prescribe law or policy." § 551(4).

Section 4 of the APA, 5 U.S.C. § 553, prescribes a three-step procedure for so-called "notice-and-comment rulemaking." First, the agency must issue a "[g]eneral notice of proposed rule making," ordinarily by publication in the Federal Register. § 553(b). Second, if "notice [is] required," the agency must "give interested persons an opportunity to participate in the rule making through submission of written data, views, or arguments." § 553(c). An agency must consider and respond to significant comments received during the period for public comment. Third, when the agency promulgates the final rule, it must include in the rule's text "a concise general statement of [its] basis and purpose." § 553(c). Rules issued through the notice-and-comment process are often referred to as "legislative rules" because they have the "force and effect of law."

Not all "rules" must be issued through the notice-and-comment process. Section 4(b)(A) of the APA provides that, unless another statute states otherwise, the notice-and-comment requirement "does not apply" to "interpretative rules, general statements of policy, or rules of agency organization, procedure, or practice." 5 U.S.C. § 553(b)(A). The term "interpretative rule," or "interpretive rule," is not further defined by the APA, and its precise meaning is the source of much scholarly and judicial debate. See generally Pierce, Distinguishing Legislative Rules From Interpretive Rules, 52 Admin. L. Rev. 547 (2000); Manning, Nonlegislative Rules, 72 Geo. Wash. L. Rev. 893 (2004). We need not, and do not, wade into that debate here. For our purposes, it suffices to say that the critical feature of interpretive rules is that they are "issued by an agency to advise the public of the agency's construction of the statutes and rules which it administers." *Shalala v. Guernsey Memorial Hospital,* 514 U.S. 87, 99, 115 S.Ct. 1232, 131 L.Ed.2d 106 (1995) (internal quotation marks omitted). The absence of a notice-and-comment obligation makes the process of issuing interpretive rules comparatively easier for agencies than issuing legislative rules. But that convenience comes at a price: Interpretive rules "do not have the force and effect of law and are not accorded that weight in the adjudicatory process." *Ibid.*

[The Department of Labor administers the Fair Labor Standards Act of 1938, which guarantees extra wages for "overtime" work. The statute exempts employees who are administrative and authorizes the Department to fill in the details of who might be included in this exemption. The Department for years interpreted the statute and its own regulations not to exempt mortgage-loan officers, but in 2006 the Department changed its interpretation and promulgated its new view in an opinion letter publicized to the industry, but not subject to notice-and-comment. Applying *Paralyzed Veterans* [Coursebook, pp. 845–846], the Court of Appeals for the D.C. Circuit ruled that this change of position had to go through the full APA rulemaking process.]

The *Paralyzed Veterans* doctrine is contrary to the clear text of the APA's rulemaking provisions, and it improperly imposes on agencies an obligation beyond the "maximum procedural requirements" specified in the APA, *Vermont Yankee Nuclear Power Corp. v. Natural Resources Defense Council, Inc.,* 435 U.S. 519, 524, 98 S.Ct. 1197, 55 L.Ed.2d 460 (1978).

The text of the APA answers the question presented. Section 4 of the APA provides that "notice of proposed rule making shall be published in the Federal Register." 5 U.S.C. § 553(b). When such notice is required by the APA, "the agency shall give interested persons an opportunity to participate in the rule making." § 553(c). But § 4 further states that unless "notice or hearing is required by statute," the Act's notice-and-comment requirement "does not apply . . . to interpretative rules." § 553(b)(A). This exemption of interpretive rules from the notice-and-comment process is categorical, and it is fatal to the rule announced in *Paralyzed Veterans*.

Rather than examining the exemption for interpretive rules contained in § 4(b)(A) of the APA, the D.C. Circuit in *Paralyzed Veterans* focused its attention on § 1 of the Act. That section defines "rule making" to include not only the initial issuance of new rules, but also "repeal[s]" or "amend[ments]" of existing rules. See § 551(5). Because notice-and-comment requirements may apply even to these later agency actions, the court reasoned, "allow[ing] an agency to make a fundamental change in its interpretation of a substantive regulation without notice and comment" would undermine the APA's procedural framework.

This reading of the APA conflates the differing purposes of §§ 1 and 4 of the Act. Section 1 defines what a rulemaking is. It does not, however, say what procedures an agency must use when it engages in rulemaking. That is the purpose of § 4. And § 4 specifically exempts interpretive rules from the notice-and-comment requirements that apply to legislative rules. So, the D.C. Circuit correctly read § 1 of the APA to mandate that agencies use the same procedures when they amend or repeal a rule as they used to issue the rule in the first instance. See *FCC v. Fox Broadcasting I* (2009) [Coursebook, pp. 790–796] (the APA "make[s] no distinction . . . between initial agency action and subsequent agency action undoing or revising that action"). Where the court went wrong was in failing to apply that accurate understanding of § 1 to the exemption for interpretive rules contained in § 4: Because an agency is not required to use notice-and-comment procedures to issue an initial interpretive rule, it is also not required to use those procedures when it amends or repeals that interpretive rule.

The straightforward reading of the APA we now adopt harmonizes with longstanding principles of our administrative law jurisprudence. Time and again, we have reiterated that the APA "sets forth the full extent of judicial authority to review executive agency action for procedural correctness." *Fox Broadcasting I.* Beyond the APA's minimum requirements, courts lack authority "to impose upon [an] agency its own notion of which procedures are 'best' or most likely to further some vague, undefined public good." *Vermont Yankee.* To do otherwise would violate "the very basic tenet of administrative law that agencies should be free to fashion their own rules of procedure." *Id.*

These foundational principles apply with equal force to the APA's procedures for rulemaking. We explained in *Vermont Yankee* that § 4 of the Act "established the maximum procedural requirements which Congress was willing to have the courts impose upon agencies in conducting rulemaking procedures." *Id.,* at 524, 98 S.Ct. 1197. "Agencies are free to grant additional procedural rights in the exercise of their discretion, but reviewing courts are generally not free to impose them if the agencies have not chosen to grant them." *Ibid.*

JUSTICE ALITO, concurring in part and in the judgment.

[Justice Alito agreed that the *Paralyzed Veterans* doctrine was inconsistent with the APA but was sympathetic to the impulse that inspired that line of cases.] The creation of that doctrine may have been prompted by an understandable concern about the aggrandizement of the power of administrative agencies as a result of the combined effect of (1) the effective delegation to agencies by Congress of huge swaths of lawmaking authority, (2) the exploitation by agencies of the uncertain boundary between legislative and interpretive rules, and (3) this Court's cases holding that courts must ordinarily defer to an agency's interpretation of its own ambiguous regulations. See *Bowles v. Seminole Rock & Sand Co.,* 325 U.S. 410, 65 S.Ct. 1215, 89 L.Ed. 1700 (1945). I do not dismiss these concerns, but the *Paralyzed Veterans* doctrine is not a viable cure for these problems. At least one of the three factors noted above, however, concerns a matter that can be addressed by this Court. The opinions of Justice Scalia and Justice Thomas offer substantial reasons why the *Seminole Rock* doctrine may be incorrect. See also *Christopher v. SmithKline Beecham Corp.,* 567 U.S. ___, ___–___, 132 S.Ct. 2156, 2168–2169, 183 L.Ed.2d 153 (2012) (citing, *inter alia,* Manning, Constitutional Structure and Judicial Deference to Agency Interpretations of Agency Rules, 96 Colum. L. Rev. 612 (1996)). I await a case in which the validity of *Seminole Rock* may be explored through full briefing and argument.

[We omit the separate concurring opinions from JUSTICE SCALIA and JUSTICE THOMAS.]

Query: If you were a lawyer for the Alaska Professional Hunters Association, challenging the FAA's 1998 notice regarding Alaska fish and wildlife guides who pilot light aircraft as part of their guiding duties (see pp. 843–844 of the Coursebook), *Perez* would take away *Paralyzed Veterans* as a legal reason for a court to invalidate the FAA's approach. Is there another good legal argument that you could make against the extension of the agency's commercial pilot rules to these guides?

Page 853: Insert the following note at the end of Chapter 7:

NOTE: REVIEW OF BASIC GROUNDS FOR ADMINISTRATIVE CHALLENGE—THE CASE OF IMMIGRATION GUIDANCE

Immigration questions are high profile topics. Recent issues regarding immigration help to illustrate how important administrative law may be to individual lives—and how intertwined administrative law questions are with the constitutional exercise of executive power.

In 2012, President Obama proposed "deferred action" for a class of individuals who had come to the United States as children. This program is known as Deferred Action for Children or DACA (hereinafter DACA or the Children's program). The program was issued by Memorandum, otherwise known as administrative "guidance" to the agency about how to implement the immigration laws. Thus begins a process in which there are Four Phases to consider.

First phase: the original 2012 Obama DACA guidance.

Second phase: the 2014 Obama guidance extending DACA and creating DAPA, the program for the parents of children of U.S. citizens or lawful permanent residents (hereinafter DAPA or the Parent's program).

Third phase: the states' successful challenge to the second DAPA guidance in *Texas v. United States*, 809 F.3d 134 (5th Cir. 2015), *aff'd by an equally divided court*, United States v. Texas, 136 S.Ct. 2271 (2016).

Fourth phase: the Rescission of DAPA by the Trump Administration.

As we write, we are in Phase Five—an administrative law challenge to the Trump guidance rescinding DACA.

Phase One: Creating the Children's Program (DACA)

Here is the guidance that created DACA on June 15, 2012:

MEMORANDUM FOR:	David Aguilar Acting Commissioner, U.S. Border Protection
FROM:	Janet Napolitano Secretary of Homeland Security

Exercising Prosecutorial Discretion with Respect to Individuals Who Came to the United States as Children

By this memorandum, I am setting forth how, in the exercise of our prosecutorial discretion, the Department of Homeland Security (DHS) should enforce the Nation's immigration laws against certain young people who were brought to this country as children and know only this country as home. As a general matter, these individuals lacked the intent to violate the law and our ongoing review of pending removal cases is already offering administrative closure to many of them. However, additional measures are necessary to ensure that our enforcement resources are not expended on these low priority cases but are instead appropriately focused on people who meet our enforcement priorities.

The following criteria should be satisfied before an individual is considered for an exercise of prosecutorial discretion pursuant to this memorandum:

- came to the United States under the age of sixteen;
- has continuously resided in the United States for at least five years preceding the date of this memorandum and is present in the United States on the date of this memorandum;
- is currently in school, has graduated from high school, has obtained a general education development certificate, or is an honorably discharged veteran * * *;
- has not been convicted of a felony offense, a significant misdemeanor offense, multiple misdemeanor offenses, or otherwise poses a threat to national security or public safety; and
- is not above the age of thirty.

Our Nation's immigration laws must be enforced in a strong and sensible manner. They are not designed to be blindly enforced without consideration given to the individual circumstances of each case. Nor are they designed to remove productive young people to countries where they may not have lived or even speak the language. Indeed, many of these young people have already contributed to our country in significant ways. Prosecutorial discretion, which is used in so many other areas, is especially justified here. * * * *

No individual should receive deferred action under this memorandum unless they first pass a background check and requests for relief pursuant to this memorandum are to be decided on a case by case basis. DHS cannot provide any assurance that relief will be granted in all cases.

[Ed: There follow rules based on the use of "prosecutorial discretion" to apply these criteria in cases where the individual is encountered by immigration authorities, in removal proceedings, or subject to removal.]

This memorandum confers no substantive right, immigration status or pathway to citizenship. Only the Congress, acting through its legislative authority, can confer these rights. It remains for the executive branch, however, to set forth policy for the exercise of discretion within the framework of the existing law. I have done so here.

Janet Napolitano

Phase Two: Extending DACA and Instituting the Parent's Program (DAPA)

Two years later, on November 20, 2014, the Obama administration aimed to expand the program to the parents of the children covered by DACA. This order is known as DAPA, or the Parent's Program.

MEMORANDUM FOR: Léon Rodriguez
Director
U.S. Citizenship and Immigration Services

FROM: Jeh Johnson
Secretary of Homeland Security

SUBJECT:

Exercising Prosecutorial Discretion with Respect to Individuals Who Came to the United States as Children and with Respect to Certain Individuals Who Are the Parents of U.S. Citizens or Permanent Residents

* * * *

Secretary Napolitano noted two years ago, when she issued her prosecutorial discretion guidance regarding children that "[o]ur Nation's immigration laws must be enforced in a strong and sensible manner. They are not designed to be blindly enforced without consideration given to the individual circumstances of each case."

Deferred action is a long-standing administrative mechanism dating back decades by which the Secretary of Homeland Security may defer the removal of an undocumented immigrant for a period of time. A form of administrative relief similar to deferred action, known then as "indefinite voluntary departure," was originally authorized by the Reagan and Bush Administrations to defer the deportations of an estimated 1.5 million undocumented spouse and minor children who did not qualify for legalization under the Immigration Reform and Control Act of 1986. Known as the "Family Fairness" program, the policy was specifically implemented to promote the humane enforcement of the law and ensure family unity.

Deferred action is a form of prosecutorial discretion by which the Secretary deprioritizes an individual's case for humanitarian reasons, administrative convenience, or in the interest of the Department's overall enforcement mission. As an act of prosecutorial discretion, deferred action is legally available so long as it is granted on a case-by-case basis, and it may be terminated at any time at the agency's direction. Deferred action does not confer any form of legal status in this country, much less citizenship; it simply means that, for a specified period of time, an individual is permitted to be lawfully present in the United States. Nor can deferred action itself lead to a green card. Although deferred action is not expressly conferred by statute, the practice is referenced and therefore endorsed by implication in several federal statutes.[36] * * * *

By this memorandum, I am now expanding certain parameters of DACA and issuing guidance for case-by-case use of deferred action for those adults who have been in this country since January 1, 2010, are the parents of U.S. citizens or lawful permanent residents, and who are otherwise not enforcement priorities, as set forth in the November 20, 2014 [DACA memo].

Case-by-case exercises of deferred action for children and long-standing members of American society who are not enforcement priorities are in this Nation's security and economic interest and make common sense, because they encourage these people to come out of the shadows, submit to background checks, pay fees, apply for work authorization (which by separate authority I may grant), and be counted.

[The memorandum thereafter expands the persons eligible for DACA, removing the age cap, extending renewal and work authorization to 3 years.]

I hereby direct USCIS to establish a process, similar to DACA, for exercising prosecutorial discretion through the use of deferred action, on a case-by-case basis, to those individuals who:

- have, on the date of this memorandum, a son or daughter who is a U.S. citizen or lawful permanent resident;
- have continuously resided in the United States since before January 1, 2010;

[36] The footnote in the Memorandum cites references in the immigration laws to "deferred" status, such as a provision in the immigration law providing that petitioners under the Violence Against Women Act may be "eligible for deferred action and employment authorization." Other citations include references to T or U Visa applicants (victims of human trafficking and domestic violence) not precluding an application for "deferred action status"; the REAL ID Act, requiring states to examine documentary evidence of lawful status, including "approved deferred action status," and the National Defense Authorization Act of 2004, providing that a spouse or child of a U.S. citizen who has died as a result of honorable service "shall be eligible for deferred action." Note that these cross-references presume the viability of an existing deferred action program.

- are physically present in the United States on the date of this memorandum, and at the time of making a request for consideration of deferred action with USCIS;
- have no lawful status on the date of this memorandum;
- are not an enforcement priority as reflected in the November 20, 2014 [guidance];
- present no other factors that, in the exercise of discretion, makes a grant of deferred action inappropriate. * * * *

Applicants must submit biometrics for USCIS to conduct background checks similar to the background check that is required for DACA applications. Each person who applies for deferred action pursuant to the criteria above shall also be eligible to apply for work authorization for the period of deferred action, pursuant to my authority to grant such authorization [under the Immigration and Nationality Act]. * * * *

This memorandum confers no substantive right, immigration status or pathway to citizenship. Only an Act of Congress can confer these rights. It remains within the authority to the Executive Branch, however, to set forth policy for the exercise of prosecutorial discretion and deferred action within the framework of existing law. This memorandum is an exercise of that authority. * * * *

Phase Three: The States Challenge the DAPA Order and the Fifth Circuit Agrees

Twenty-six states, including Texas, challenged the DACA extension and DAPA program (the 2014 order above). They argued that the program, as applied, did not involve prosecutorial discretion—that as actually implemented the program was binding upon immigration agents. They asserted that the program would cost states significant monies, for example, by providing drivers' licenses. They also claimed the immigration laws did not give discretion to the President to create such orders, that the matter had to be resolved by Congress. They estimated that the DACA extension and the Parents program would cover 4 million people.

The states' legal claims provide a good review of the principal kinds of arguments we have seen in this Chapter and earlier in the book. The essential arguments were:

(1) that the order was inconsistent with the immigration statutes (see *FDA v. Brown & Williamson Tobacco*, Chapter 2, § 3);

(2) that the order was arbitrary and capricious under the APA (see *Motor Vehicle Manufacturers Ass'n v. State Farm Mutual Automobile Ins.*, Chapter 7, § 1);

(3) that the government failed to follow the proper procedures for notice-and comment under the APA (*see, e.g., American Mining*

Congress v. Mine Safety & Health Administration, Chapter 7 § 3, note pp. 838–39); and

(4) that the order exceeded the President's executive power under the Constitution (see Chapter 2, § 2).

The Obama Administration responded by contending, among other things:

(1) that the states had no standing (see Chapter 3, § 1, pp. 230–33);

(2) that the program was purely discretionary so that there was no law to apply and the action should be dismissed under APA section 701 (see *Heckler v. Chaney*, *Norton v. Southern Utah Wilderness Alliance*, Chapter 7 § 3B).

In the Fifth Circuit decision, the court enjoined the DAPA order because it was likely that the states would succeed in arguing that the program was unauthorized by existing immigration laws. The court found that the Immigration and Nationality Act "flatly does not permit the reclassification of millions of illegal aliens as lawfully present and thereby make them newly eligible for a host of federal and state benefits, including work authorization." *Texas v. United States*, 809 F.2d 134, 183 (5th Cir. 2015). According to the court, "DAPA is foreclosed by Congress's careful plan; the program is 'manifestly contrary to the statute' and therefore was properly enjoined." *Id.* at 186.

The Fifth Circuit also ruled that the guidance failed under the Administrative Procedure Act, because the agency had not used the proper procedures. Homeland Security had issued the order as guidance, rather than after notice-and-comment, asserting that the rule was nonbinding on individuals subject to removal and to the agency. In fact, held the Fifth Circuit, the actual practice within the agency, based on testimony from agency personnel in the district court, was that deferred action was determined by rote without the agency actually exercising discretion, so that the guidance was "binding" in fact. *Texas v. United States*, 809 F. 3d at 171–74. Any language in the order to the contrary was deemed "pretextual." *Id.* at 173. Such an order was what is called a "legislative rule," which requires notice-and-comment and cannot be issued by guidance. (For a discussion of legislative rules, see Chapter 7 § 3, note pp. 838–39). The court rejected arguments that the states lacked standing because the states would incur significant costs by providing services like drivers' licenses. The Court did not reach the constitutional question.

The Supreme Court, by equally divided vote, United States v. Texas, 136 S.Ct. 2271 (2016) (per curiam), affirmed the decision of the Fifth Circuit.

Phase Four: Trump Issues Guidance to Rescind the DACA Order

The DACA/DAPA saga has not ended. The DAPA order was suspended, but DACA remained in force. When President Trump took office, he attempted to rescind the Children's 2012 order with administrative guidance as follows:

Elaine C. Duke
Acting Secretary

SUBJECT:

Rescission of the June 15, 2012 Memorandum Entitled "Exercising Prosecutorial Discretion with Respect to Individuals Who Came to the United States as Children"

This memorandum rescinds the June 15, 2012 memorandum entitled "Exercising Prosecutorial Discretion with Respect to Individuals Who Came to the United States as Children," which established the program known as Deferred Action for Childhood Arrivals ("DACA"). For the reasons and in the manner outlined below, Department of Homeland Security personnel shall take all appropriate actions to execute a wind-down of the program, consistent with the parameters established in this memorandum.

Background

The Department of Homeland Security established DACA through the issuance of a memorandum on June 15, 2012. The program purported to use deferred action—an act of prosecutorial discretion meant to be applied only on an individualized case-by-case basis—to confer certain benefits to illegal aliens that Congress had not otherwise acted to provide by law. Specifically, DACA provided certain illegal aliens who entered the United States before the age of sixteen a period of deferred action and eligibility to request employment authorization.

On November 20, 2014, the Department issued a new memorandum, expanding the parameters of DACA and creating a new policy called Deferred Action for Parents of Americans and Lawful Permanent Residents ("DAPA"). Among other things—such as the expansion of the coverage criteria under the 2012 DACA policy to encompass aliens with a wider range of ages and arrival dates, and lengthening the period of deferred action and work authorization from two years to three—the November 20, 2014 memorandum directed USCIS "to establish a process, similar to DACA, for exercising prosecutorial discretion through the use of deferred action, on a case-by-case basis," to certain aliens who have "a son or daughter who is a U.S. citizen or lawful permanent resident."

Prior to the implementation of DAPA, twenty-six states—led by Texas—challenged the policies announced in the November 20, 2014 memorandum in the U.S. District Court for the Southern District of Texas. In an order issued on February 16, 2015, the district court preliminarily enjoined the policies nationwide. The district court held that the plaintiff states were likely to succeed on their claim that the DAPA program did not comply with relevant authorities.

The United States Court of Appeals for the Fifth Circuit affirmed, holding that Texas and the other states had demonstrated a substantial likelihood of success on the merits and satisfied the other requirements for a preliminary injunction. The Fifth Circuit concluded that the Department's DAPA policy conflicted with the discretion authorized by Congress. In considering the DAPA program, the court noted that the Immigration and Nationality Act "flatly does not permit the reclassification of millions of illegal aliens as lawfully present and thereby make them newly eligible for a host of federal and state benefits, including work authorization." According to the court, "DAPA is foreclosed by Congress's careful plan; the program is 'manifestly contrary to the statute' and therefore was properly enjoined."

Although the original DACA policy was not challenged in the lawsuit, both the district and appellate court decisions relied on factual findings about the implementation of the 2012 DACA memorandum. The Fifth Circuit agreed with the lower court that DACA decisions were not truly discretionary, and that DAPA and expanded DACA would be substantially similar in execution. Both the district court and the Fifth Circuit concluded that implementation of the program did not comply with the Administrative Procedure Act because the Department did not implement it through notice-and-comment rulemaking.

The Supreme Court affirmed the Fifth Circuit's ruling by equally divided vote (4–4). The evenly divided ruling resulted in the Fifth Circuit order being affirmed. The preliminary injunction therefore remains in place today. In October 2016, the Supreme Court denied a request from DHS to rehear the case upon the appointment of a new Justice. After the 2016 election, both parties agreed to a stay in litigation to allow the new administration to review these issues.

On January 25, 2017, President Trump issued Executive Order No. 13,768, "Enhancing Public Safety in the Interior of the United States." In that Order, the President directed federal agencies to "[e]nsure the faithful execution of the immigration laws . . . against all removable aliens," and established new immigration enforcement priorities." * * *

The Attorney General sent a letter to the Department on September 4, 2017, articulating his legal determination that DACA "was effectuated by the previous administration through executive action, without proper statutory authority and with no established end-date, after Congress' repeated rejection of proposed legislation that would have accomplished a similar result. Such an open-ended circumvention of immigration laws was an unconstitutional exercise of authority by the Executive Branch." The letter further stated that because DACA "has the same legal and constitutional defects that the courts recognized as to DAPA, it is likely that potentially imminent litigation would yield similar results with respect to DACA." Nevertheless, in light of the administrative complexities associated with ending the program, he recommended that the Department wind it down in an efficient and orderly fashion, and his office has reviewed the terms on which our Department will do so.

Taking into consideration the Supreme Court's and the Fifth Circuit's rulings in the ongoing litigation, and the September 4, 2017 letter from the Attorney General, it is clear that the June 15, 2012 DACA program should be terminated. In the exercise of my authority in establishing national immigration policies and priorities, except for the purposes explicitly identified below, I hereby rescind the June 15, 2012 memorandum.

Recognizing the complexities associated with winding down the program, the Department will provide a limited window in which it will adjudicate certain requests for DACA and associated applications meeting certain parameters specified below. Accordingly, effective immediately, the Department:

- Will adjudicate—on an individual, case-by-case basis—properly filed pending DACA initial requests and associated applications for Employment Authorization Documents that have been accepted by the Department as of the date of this memorandum.
- Will reject all DACA initial requests and associated applications for Employment Authorization Documents filed after the date of this memorandum.
- Will adjudicate—on an individual, case by case basis—properly filed pending DACA renewal requests and associated applications for Employment Authorization Documents from current beneficiaries that have been accepted by the Department as of the date of this memorandum, and from current beneficiaries whose benefits will expire between the date of this memorandum and March 5, 2018 that have been accepted by the Department as of October 5, 2017.
- Will reject all DACA renewal requests and associated applications for Employment Authorization Documents filed outside of the parameters specified above.
- Will not terminate the grants of previously issued deferred action or revoke Employment Authorization Documents solely based on the directives in this memorandum for the remaining duration of their validity periods. * * * *
- Will continue to exercise its discretionary authority to terminate or deny deferred action at any time when

immigration officials determine termination or denial of deferred action is appropriate.

This document is not intended to, does not, and may not be relied upon to create any right or benefit, substantive or procedural, enforceable at law by any party in any administrative, civil, or criminal matter. Likewise, no limitations are placed by this guidance on the otherwise lawful enforcement or litigation prerogatives of DHS.

Review of Administrative Law Claims. Critics quickly took to the courts to challenge the Trump Rescission Order. Janet Napolitano, now head of the UC California school system (but once the author of DACA as Secretary of Homeland Security) filed suit, as did individuals in the state of New York. What administrative law arguments do you think that they are using? Reread the Rescission Order. Jot down your thoughts in the margin. Hint: take a look at the arguments Texas and other states used to challenge the Obama 2014 guidance. Can all those same arguments be used to challenge the Trump guidance? What arguments will the Trump administration make to sustain its new policy under the Administrative Procedure Act?

Statutory Considerations to Note. In considering whether existing immigration law permitted the Trump order, there are divergent views. Some claim that the 5th Circuit ruling wrongly relied upon the term "lawful presence," when "deferred action" is not "lawful presence" because it only delays removal. On the other hand, the Fifth Circuit found that Congress had created by statute specific procedures for parents of U.S. citizen children to obtain a visa (similar to temporary presence) and that these were inconsistent with the DAPA order. "In general, an applicant must (i) have a U.S. citizen child who is at least twenty-one years old, (ii) leave the United States, (iii) wait ten years, and then (iv) obtain one of the limited number of family-preference visas from a United States consulate." *Texas v. United States*, 809 F.3d at 179–80. The Court also found that Congress had only granted deferred action in limited circumstances, for victims of human trafficking, domestic violence, terrorism, or family members of persons killed in service to the country. *Id.* at 179.

Administrative Law and Presidential Power. Take particular note of the fact that the Trump guidance repeats a claim by the Attorney General that the DAPA order was unconstitutional. It also states that the Fifth Circuit held DAPA was an unconstitutional exercise of Presidential power. In fact, the Fifth Circuit did not strike down DAPA on constitutional grounds, but under the Administrative Procedure Act. See *Texas v. United States*, 809 F.3d 134 (5th Cir. 2015). Does that make the Trump order arbitrary and capricious? To sustain the order, will the Trump administration have to convince a court that the Obama order was unconstitutional? If you were going to make a constitutional argument that the Obama order was unconstitutional, what precedent would you cite? For some help, refer to Chapter 2, § 2, and the President's power to "take care" that the laws be faithfully executed under

Article II of the Constitution. Should Obama's order get a "pass" on constitutionality because the Congress had refused to act? Should Trump deploy the same "necessity" defense?

CHAPTER 8

DELEGATION, DEFERENCE, AND JUDICIAL TREATMENT OF AGENCY STATUTORY INTERPRETATIONS

■ ■ ■

1. THE EMERGENCE OF MODERN DEFERENCE PRACTICE

B. INTRODUCTION TO *CHEVRON*

Page 894: Insert the following materials before Section 1(C):

David King et al. v. Sylvia Burwell, Secretary of Health and Human Services, et al.

___ U.S. ___, 135 S.Ct. 2480, 192 L.Ed.2d 483 (2015).

[Excerpted in Chapter 1 of this Supplement.]

Recall that the issue in this case was whether the Affordable Care Act's tax credits are available in States that have a Federal Exchange rather than a State Exchange. The Act provides that tax credits "shall be allowed" for any "applicable taxpayer." 26 U.S.C. § 36B(a). The Act then directs that the amount of the tax credit depends in part on whether the taxpayer has enrolled in an insurance plan through "an Exchange established by the State under section 1311" of the Act, [i.e., 42 U.S.C. sec. 18031, 26 U.S.C. secs. 36B(b)–(c)]."

Implementing the ACA, the IRS, after notice-and-comment, promulgated a rule making subsidies available on both State and Federal Exchanges. 77 Fed. Reg. 30378 (2012). The rule provides that a taxpayer is eligible for a tax credit if he enrolled in an insurance plan through "an Exchange," 26 CFR § 1.36B–2 (2013), which is defined as "an Exchange serving the individual market . . . regardless of whether the Exchange is established and operated by a State . . . or by HHS," 45 CFR § 155.20 (2014). At this point, approximately half the states have established their own Exchanges; the others have elected to have HHS do so.

The issue before the Court was whether Section 36B authorizes tax credits for individuals who enroll in an insurance plan through a Federal Exchange. The challengers argued that a Federal Exchange is not "an Exchange established by the State under [42 U.S.C. § 18031]," and that the IRS Rule therefore contradicts Section 36B. The Government responded that the IRS Rule is lawful because the phrase "an Exchange established by the State under [42 U.S.C. § 18031]" should be read to include Federal Exchanges and that, in any event, the ACA is ambiguous on this score and the Court's *Chevron* jurisprudence was inapplicable to sustain the agency rule.

The Fourth Circuit, below, had found the statute ambiguous and had deferred to the IRS pursuant to *Chevron*. The Chief Justice opened the legal analysis with a different approach. "When analyzing an agency's interpretation of a statute, we often apply the two-step framework announced in *Chevron*. Under that framework, we ask whether the statute is ambiguous and, if so, whether the agency's interpretation is reasonable. This approach 'is premised on the theory that a statute's ambiguity constitutes an implicit delegation from Congress to the agency to fill in the statutory gaps.' *FDA v. Brown & Williamson Tobacco Corp.,* 529 U.S. 120, 159 (2000) (Coursebook, pp. 884–894). 'In extraordinary cases, however, there may be reason to hesitate before concluding that Congress has intended such an implicit delegation.' Ibid.

"This is one of those cases. The tax credits are among the Act's key reforms, involving billions of dollars in spending each year and affecting the price of health insurance for millions of people. Whether those credits are available on Federal Exchanges is thus a question of deep 'economic and political significance' that is central to this statutory scheme; had Congress wished to assign that question to an agency, it surely would have done so expressly. *Utility Air Regulatory Group v. EPA,* 134 S.Ct. 2427, 2444 (2014) (quoting Brown & Williamson). It is especially unlikely that Congress would have delegated this decision to the IRS, which has no expertise in crafting health insurance policy of this sort. See *Gonzales v. Oregon,* 546 U.S. 243, 266–267 (2006) (Coursebook, pp. 927–935). This is not a case for the IRS."

As excerpted in Chapter 1 of this Supplement, the Chief Justice's opinion for the Court then interpreted the ACA without deference to the IRS. Finding the specific language ambiguous, the Court resolved the ambiguity not by deferring to the agency, but by considering the statutory plan. Writing for the three dissenting Justices, Justice Scalia strongly disagreed with the Court's finding of ambiguity and its application of the statutory plan and design but followed the Court in not applying the *Chevron* framework.

NOTE ON THE "MAJOR QUESTIONS DOCTRINE"

King v. Burwell confirms the following structure for the Supreme Court's *Chevron* jurisprudence: The Court will defer to agency rules and orders promulgated pursuant to delegated lawmaking authority (*Mead*) and following the required procedures of the APA (*Perez*, excerpted in Chapter 7 of this Supplement). That the agency is interpreting its own jurisdiction or authority does not bar *Chevron* deference (*City of Arlington, Texas v. FCC,* Coursebook, pp. 893–894)—but the Court will not defer if the agency is resolving an issue of "deep economic or political significance" (*Utility Air*, quoted in *King*). *King* may cement in place the important "major questions doctrine," whose entrenchment had been in some question previously. The Court in *King* did not defer to the IRS, but why exactly? Was it because the question was too big to assume delegation? Or was it because the big question in particular was the kind of "elephant in a mousehole" that the Court assumes Congress does not delegate without some express statement?

Or perhaps there really is something different going on. Some view the Court's decision as based more on *expertise* than on anything related to the type of question at issue. The question in *King* may properly have been a question for *another* agency (i.e., HHS), but it was not within the IRS's own expertise. One can see something similar going on in *Gonzales v. Oregon,* the aid-in-dying case, in Chapter 8. So understood, this reading of *King* raises another question about the Court's deference jurisprudence: it reveals a continuing resistance toward resolving the open question whether deference to *multiple* agencies simultaneously is ever appropriate and how exactly those questions should be resolved when one agency is the favored interpreter. See discussion in Chapter 8. In an era in which overlapping delegations is the norm, isn't the Court going to have to address this question sooner rather than later? For more on *King* and *Chevron*, see Gluck, *Imperfect Statutes, Imperfect Courts*, 129 Harv. L. Rev. at 93–96.

Thus, as in *King*, the agency view might still prevail, but only by coincidence—i.e., because the Court's independent interpretation of the statute is the same as the agency's view. (We think it goes without saying that the agency's views will still receive *Skidmore* deference, whether the Court says so or not, because the Justices will read the Solicitor General's brief with great attention to its account of the regulatory history, facts in the world, and the statutory language and plan.)

So that is the doctrine. Is the major questions exception (or loophole) to *Chevron* justified? The major questions canon is a potentially elastic loophole to *Chevron*'s broad commitment of judicial deference to agency interpretations pursuant to congressional delegations of lawmaking authority, because many issues can be understood as either "major questions" or "routine applications." Indeed, the Supreme Court has applied the doctrine erratically, at best. Sometimes, when the agency is making a big move, the Court ignores the doctrine. See Abigail R. Moncrieff, *Reincarnating the "Major Questions" Exception to Chevron Deference as a Doctrine of Non-Interference (Or Why*

Massachusetts v. EPA *Got it Wrong)*, 60 Admin. L. Rev. 593 (2008). Lisa Heinzerling argues that the major question doctrine as applied in *King v. Burwell* and *Utility Air Regulatory Group v. EPA*, 134 S.Ct. 2427 (2014) reflects a "power canons" approach hostile to the regulatory state, requiring "clear congressional language to enable an ambitious regulatory agenda, but not to disable one." Lisa Heinzerling, *The Power Canons* (forthcoming 2017, William and Mary Law Review, volume 58). Gluck argues that *King* was yet another sign that there is a contingent of the Court interested in destabilizing *Chevron* and taking more power back for the Court. Gluck, *Imperfect Statutes, Imperfect Courts*, 129 Harv. L. Rev. at 94. After all, remember that when the Court holds the question too big to give to an agency, it does not remand the matter to Congress but rather decides the major question for *itself*. *Id.*

When the Court does invoke the major questions doctrine, it does so in very different ways. In *King*, the Chief Justice invokes the major questions doctrine at Step Zero: *Chevron*'s framework does not apply at all. In *MCI v. ATT*, the Court seems to invoke major questions as support for its conclusion that the FCC failed Step One (Congress directly addressed the issue). In *Utility Air Regulatory Group v. EPA*, the Court invoked the doctrine at Step Two! The issue was whether the Clean Air Act authorized EPA to regulate the emission of greenhouse gases for all stationary sources, including those not otherwise regulated by the Act. As in *Chevron* itself, the Court applied the two-step *Chevron* deference regime, hence ruling that Step Zero was satisfied. As in *Chevron*, the Court at Step One found the statute ambiguous and therefore ruled that Congress had not directly addressed the issue. But at Step Two, which had been perfunctory in *Chevron*, the *Utility Air Regulatory Group* Court held that the EPA's interpretation was unreasonable. Citing *Brown and Williamson*, the Court held that Congress did not intend EPA to regulate this broadly.

In short, major questions concerns can show up at any stage of the *Chevron* analysis—and in some cases it is not clear even where the major questions doctrine is having force. E.g., *Gonzales v. Oregon* (perhaps Step Zero, but the Court is not clear). Notice, also, the tension between the major questions doctrine in Step Zero and the Court's holding in *City of Arlington*, which says that *Chevron* applies to agency interpretation of its own jurisdiction. The Chief Justice dissented in *City of Arlington*, in which he protested the ceding of so much power to agencies, and then he writes for the Court in *King v. Burwell.*

Finally, it is not clear what constitutes a "major" question. Is it a major question because of the impact on the economy? Is it a major question because of political controversy? Is it a major question because of the impact on the regulatory schemes? Is it a major question because of the impact on the number of citizens? For example, would a change to any federal voting rule, for example, be a major question by definition because it covered all voters? Does it matter that there is a mismatch between the issue at stake and the agency doing the regulating as in *King v. Burwell*?

On the other hand, the major questions canon might be defensible along precisely the same lines as *Chevron* itself. The key reason is the strong presumption of continuity for major policies unless and until Congress has deliberated about and enacted a change in those major policies. David Shapiro, *Continuity and Change in Statutory Interpretation,* 67 N.Y.U. L. Rev. 921 (1992); accord, William N. Eskridge Jr., *Interpreting Law: A Primer on How to Read Statutes and the Constitution* 287–90 (2016); John F. Manning, *Continuity and the Legal Design,* 79 Notre Dame L. Rev. 1863 (2004). Because a major policy change would disrupt reliance interests, continuity is consistent with rule of law values.

Additionally, one might say that a major policy change should be made by the most democratically accountable process—Article I, Section 7 legislation. Thus, the major questions doctrine might be consistent with democratic values. See Theodore W. Ruger, *The Story of* FDA v. Brown & Williamson*: The Norm of Agency Continuity*, in *Statutory Interpretation Stories* 334 (Eskridge, Frickey & Garrett eds., 2011). Although Congress is sometimes criticized for booting controversial issues to agencies to avoid political accountability, congressional drafting staff overwhelmingly support the premise of the major questions canon, because they do not view lawmaking delegations as reaching policy shifts not explicitly made by statute. Abbe Gluck & Lisa Schultz Bressman, *Statutory Interpretation from the Inside: An Empirical Study of Congressional Drafting, Delegation and the Canons: Part I,* 65 Stan. L. Rev. 901, 994, 1003–04 (2014).

Thomas E. Perez, Secretary of Labor v. Mortgage Bankers Ass'n et al.
572 U.S. ___, 135 S.Ct. 1199, 191 L.Ed.2d 186 (2015).

[Excerpted in Chapter 7 of this Supplement.]

The Supreme Court held that an agency is not required to use notice and comment rulemaking when revising an interpretation of its own rule. **Justice Sotomayor**'s majority decision in *Mortgage Bankers* does not reach the issue of deference, but both Justice Scalia and Justice Thomas authored concurring opinions expressing concern for the implications of the decision in light of *Seminole Rock* and *Auer*, two leading Supreme Court cases requiring strong deference to agency interpretations of their own substantive rules (Coursebook, pp. 893–894). Justice Alito also wrote a concurring opinion suggesting a willingness to reconsider *Auer*.

Concurring only in the judgment, **Justice Scalia** expressed alarm: "Considered alongside our law of deference to administrative determinations, however, today's decision produces a balance between power and procedure quite different from the one Congress chose when it enacted the APA.

" 'The [APA] was framed against a background of rapid expansion of the administrative process as a check upon administrators whose zeal might otherwise have carried them to excesses not contemplated in legislation creating their offices.'" *United States v. Morton Salt Co.,* 338 U.S. 632, 644 (1950). The Act guards against excesses in rulemaking by requiring notice and comment. Before an agency makes a rule, it normally must notify the public of the proposal, invite them to comment on its shortcomings, consider and respond to their arguments, and explain its final decision in a statement of the rule's basis and purpose. 5 U.S.C. § 553(b)–(c).

"The APA exempts interpretive rules from these requirements. § 553(b)(A). But this concession to agencies was meant to be more modest in its effects than it is today. For despite exempting interpretive rules from notice and comment, the Act provides that "the *reviewing court* shall . . . interpret constitutional and statutory provisions, and determine the meaning or applicability of the terms of an agency action." § 706 (emphasis added). The Act thus contemplates that courts, not agencies, will authoritatively resolve ambiguities in statutes and regulations. In such a regime, the exemption for interpretive rules does not add much to agency power. An agency may use interpretive rules to *advise* the public by explaining its interpretation of the law. But an agency may not use interpretive rules to *bind* the public by making law, because it remains the responsibility of the court to decide whether the law means what the agency says it means.

"Heedless of the original design of the APA, we have developed an elaborate law of deference to agencies' interpretations of statutes and regulations. Never mentioning § 706's directive that the "reviewing court . . . interpret . . . statutory provisions," we have held that *agencies* may authoritatively resolve ambiguities in statutes. *Chevron.* And never mentioning § 706's directive that the 'reviewing court . . . determine the meaning or applicability of the terms of an agency action,' we have—relying on a case decided before the APA, *Bowles v. Seminole Rock & Sand Co.,* 325 U.S. 410 (1945)—held that *agencies* may authoritatively resolve ambiguities in regulations. *Auer v. Robbins,* 519 U.S. 452, 461 (1997).

"By supplementing the APA with judge-made doctrines of deference, we have revolutionized the import of interpretive rules' exemption from notice-and-comment rulemaking. Agencies may now use these rules not just to advise the public, but also to bind them. After all, if an interpretive rule gets deference, the people are bound to obey it on pain of sanction, no less surely than they are bound to obey substantive rules, which are accorded similar deference. Interpretive rules that command deference *do* have the force of law.

"The Court's reasons for resisting this obvious point would not withstand a gentle breeze. Even when an agency's interpretation gets deference, the Court argues, 'it is the court that ultimately decides whether [the text] means what the agency says.' That is not quite so. So long as the agency does not stray beyond the ambiguity in the text being interpreted, deference *compels* the reviewing court to "decide" that the text means what the agency says. The Court continues that 'deference is not an inexorable command in all cases,' because (for example) it does not apply to plainly erroneous interpretations. *Ibid.* True, but beside the point. Saying *all* interpretive rules lack force of law because plainly erroneous interpretations do not bind courts is like saying *all* substantive rules lack force of law because arbitrary and capricious rules do not bind courts. Of course an interpretive rule must meet certain conditions before it gets deference—the interpretation must, for instance, be reasonable—but once it does so it is every bit as binding as a substantive rule. So the point stands: By deferring to interpretive rules, we have allowed agencies to make binding rules unhampered by notice-and-comment procedures.

"The problem is bad enough, and perhaps insoluble if *Chevron* is not to be uprooted, with respect to interpretive rules setting forth agency interpretation of statutes. But an agency's interpretation of its own regulations is another matter. By giving that category of interpretive rules *Auer* deference, we do more than allow the agency to make binding regulations without notice and comment. Because the agency (not Congress) drafts the substantive rules that are the object of those interpretations, giving them deference allows the agency to control the extent of its notice-and-comment-free domain. To expand this domain, the agency need only write substantive rules more broadly and vaguely, leaving plenty of gaps to be filled in later, using interpretive rules unchecked by notice and comment. The APA does not remotely contemplate this regime."

According to Justice Scalia, adhering to *Auer* deference for interpretive rules "allows the agency to control the extent of its notice-and-comment-free domain" because an agency can simply issue a vague rule and then subsequently fill in the gaps through interpretive rules, knowing that those rules will go "unchecked." This result, he concludes, "produces a balance between power and procedure quite different from the one Congress chose when it enacted the APA."

Also concurring only in the judgment, **Justice Thomas** expressed concern for the constitutional implications of the Court's holding in light of *Seminole Rock*. "I write separately because these cases call into question the legitimacy of our precedents requiring deference to administrative interpretations of regulations. That line of precedents, beginning with *Bowles v. Seminole Rock & Sand Co.,* 325 U.S. 410 (1945), requires judges to defer to agency interpretations of regulations, thus, as happened in these cases, giving legal effect to the interpretations rather than the regulations themselves. Because this doctrine effects a transfer of the judicial power to an executive agency, it raises constitutional concerns. This line of precedents undermines our obligation to provide a judicial check on the other branches, and it subjects regulated parties to precisely the abuses that the Framers sought to prevent."

Although *Seminole Rock* has yet to be directly reconsidered by the Supreme Court, is it possible that the Court avoids the consequences decried by Justices Scalia and Thomas in other ways? (Recall, by the way, that Justice Scalia authored *Auer*, the leading statement of *Seminole Rock* in the post-*Chevron* era.) With Justice Scalia's death in February 2016, *Auer*'s once-fragile future seems somewhat harder to predict.

2. AGENCY DEFERENCE AND *STARE DECISIS*

Page 924: Insert the following after the Note on Administrative Overrides of Supreme Court Statutory Interpretation Decisions:

NOTE ON CHEVRON, BRAND X *AND JUSTICE GORSUCH*

During Senate confirmation hearings for Justice Neil Gorsuch, *Chevron* and *Brand X* were much discussed by the Senate Judiciary Committee and on the floor of the Senate. Although Senator Hatch joked that members of the public might wonder why there was so much legislative angst about a gas station, Senator Franken reminded the committee: "This is a big deal. During the entire 114th Congress, *Chevron* deference was mentioned only twice on the Senate floor. But between the announcement of [the Gorsuch] nomination on January 31 and last week, that decision was mentioned 30 times by 4 different Senators. Each of those four senators discussed the case while speaking in support of your nomination. Three of those senators are members of this committee." *Hearing on the Nomination of Neil Gorsuch to be an Associate Justice of the U.S. Supreme Court, March 21, 2017 Afternoon Session, Before the S. Comm. on the Judiciary*, 115th Cong. 59 (2017) (statement of Sen. Al Franken, Member, S. Comm. on the Judiciary (D-Minn.)).

One of Gorsuch's most controversial opinions written as a Circuit Court judge was a concurrence (to his own majority opinion) in which he suggested that *Chevron* and *Brand X* were misguided. In *Gutierrez-Brizuela v. Lynch*, 834 F.3d 1142 (10th Cir. 2016) (Gorsuch, J., concurring) then-judge Gorsuch wrote:

> There's an elephant in the room with us today. We have studiously attempted to work our way around it and even left it unremarked. But the fact is *Chevron* and *Brand X* permit executive bureaucracies to swallow huge amounts of core judicial and legislative power and concentrate federal power in a way that seems more than a little difficult to square with the Constitution of the framers' design. Maybe the time has come to face the behemoth.

Gorsuch argued that, under *Nat'l Cable & Telecomms. Ass'n v. Brand X Internet Servs.,* 545 U.S. 967 (2005) [*Brand X*], judges were forced to substitute an agency's interpretation of law for their own judicial interpretation, reprising some of the themes in Justice Scalia's *Brand X* dissent. "Under *Brand X*'s terms, after all, courts are required to overrule their own declarations about the meaning of existing law in favor of interpretations dictated by executive agencies." *Gutierrez-Brizuela*, 834 F.3d at 1150 (Gorsuch, J., concurring).

> That's exactly what happened to Mr. Padilla-Caldera. First this court read the relevant immigration statutes to permit an alien who has entered the country illegally to seek a discretionary adjustment of status from the Attorney General. Then we remanded the case to allow the Attorney General to make that discretionary decision in Mr. Padilla-Caldera's case. But instead of undertaking that task, the BIA interpreted the statutory scheme to reach the opposite conclusion we had, applied its new statutory interpretation to Mr. Padilla-Caldera, and held him categorically forbidden from receiving a discretionary adjustment of status. When the case returned to this court, we conceded that the relevant statutes were indeed ambiguous and acknowledged that *Brand X* required us to defer to the BIA's new interpretation, in the end holding that Mr. Padilla-Caldera was, as the agency said, categorically prohibited from applying for a discretionary adjustment of status. Quite literally then, after this court declared the statutes' meaning and issued a final decision, *an executive agency was permitted to (and did) tell us to reverse our decision like some sort of super court of appeals.* If that doesn't qualify as an unconstitutional revision of a judicial declaration of the law by a political branch, I confess I begin to wonder whether we've forgotten what might. *Id.* (emphasis added) (citations omitted).

Questioned closely by members of the Senate Judiciary Committee, Judge Gorsuch defended his opinion, arguing that critics failed to appreciate the technical nature of the argument and the impact of the case on the litigant's individual rights to due process. As far as questions or determinations of fact, he testified, judges should defer to agencies, leaving a substantial space for *Chevron*-type arguments. *Hearing on the Nomination of Neil Gorsuch to be an Associate Justice of the U.S. Supreme Court, March 21, 2017 Afternoon Session, Before the S. Comm. on the Judiciary*, 115th Cong. 97 (2017) (statement of J. Neil Gorsuch). But for questions of law, Gorsuch indicated that the court's holdings were in tension with the Administrative Procedure Act itself which provides that questions of law deserve *judicial* review. *Id.*

The *Gutierrez-Brizuela* concurring opinion goes quite a bit further than indicting *Brand X* or focusing on the law/fact distinction that Gorsuch emphasized at his confirmation hearing. A good deal of the opinion is a full-throated criticism of *Chevron* as based on a legal fiction. Judge Gorsuch writes, *Gutierrez-Brizuela*, 834 F.3d at 1152–53 (Gorsuch, J., concurring):

Chevron step two tells us we must allow an executive agency to resolve the meaning of any ambiguous statutory provision. In this way, *Chevron* seems no less than a judge-made doctrine for the abdication of the judicial duty. Of course, some role remains for judges even under *Chevron*. At *Chevron* step one, judges decide whether the statute is "ambiguous," and at step two they decide whether the agency's view is "reasonable." But where in all this does a court *interpret* the law and say what it *is*? When does a court independently decide what the statute means and whether it has or has not vested a legal right in a person? Where *Chevron* applies that job seems to have gone extinct.

* * * *

For whatever the agency may be doing under *Chevron*, the problem remains that *courts* are not fulfilling their duty to interpret the law and declare invalid agency actions inconsistent with those interpretations in the cases and controversies that come before them. A duty expressly assigned to them by the APA and one often likely compelled by the Constitution itself. That's a problem for the judiciary. And it is a problem for the people whose liberties may now be impaired not by an independent decisionmaker seeking to declare the law's meaning as fairly as possible—the decisionmaker promised to them by law—but by an avowedly politicized administrative agent seeking to pursue whatever policy whim may rule the day. Those problems remain uncured by this line of reply.

Maybe as troubling, this line of reply invites a nest of questions even taken on its own terms. *Chevron* says that we should infer from any statutory ambiguity Congress's "intent" to "delegate" its "legislative authority" to the executive to make "reasonable" policy choices. But where exactly has Congress expressed this intent? Trying to infer the intentions of an institution composed of 535 members is a notoriously doubtful business under the best of circumstances. And these are not exactly the best of circumstances. *Chevron* suggests we should infer an intent to delegate not because Congress has anywhere expressed any such wish, not because anyone anywhere in any legislative history even hinted at that possibility, but because the legislation in question is silent (ambiguous) on the subject. Usually we're told that "an agency literally has no power to act . . . unless and until Congress confers power upon it." *La. Pub. Serv. Comm'n v. FCC*, 476 U.S. 355, 374, 106 S.Ct. 1890, 90 L.Ed.2d 369 (1986). Yet *Chevron* seems to stand this ancient and venerable principle nearly on its head.

Maybe worse still, *Chevron*'s inference about hidden congressional intentions seems belied by the intentions Congress has made textually manifest. After all and again, in the APA Congress expressly vested the courts with the responsibility to "interpret . . .

> statutory provisions" and overturn agency action inconsistent with those interpretations. 5 U.S.C. § 706. Meanwhile not a word can be found here about delegating legislative authority to agencies. On this record, how can anyone fairly say that Congress "intended" for courts to abdicate their statutory duty under [section 706] and instead "intended" to delegate away its legislative power to executive agencies? The fact is, *Chevron*'s claim about legislative intentions is no more than a fiction—and one that requires a pretty hefty suspension of disbelief at that.

From there, the opinion moves even further, suggesting that *Chevron* may be unconstitutional under what is generally considered a long-dead non-delegation doctrine, *Gutierrez-Brizuela*, 834 F.3d at 1154–55 (Gorsuch, J., concurring); see Chapter 1, § 2:

> [E]ven supposing we somehow had something resembling an authentic congressional delegation of legislative authority—you still might wonder: *can* Congress really delegate its legislative authority—its power to write new rules of general applicability—to executive agencies? The Supreme Court has long recognized that under the Constitution "congress cannot delegate legislative power to the president" and that this "principle [is] universally recognized as vital to the integrity and maintenance of the system of government ordained by the constitution." *Marshall Field & Co. v. Clark*, 143 U.S. 649, 692, 12 S.Ct. 495, 36 L.Ed. 294 (1892). Yet on this account of *Chevron* we're examining, its whole point and purpose seems to be exactly that—to delegate legislative power to the executive branch.
>
> * * * *
>
> But even taking the forgiving intelligible principle test as a given, it's no small question whether *Chevron* can clear it. For if an agency can enact a new rule of general applicability affecting huge swaths of the national economy one day and reverse itself the next (and that is exactly what *Chevron* permits, *see* 467 U.S. at 857–59, 104 S.Ct. 2778), you might be forgiven for asking: where's the "substantial guidance" in that? And if an agency can interpret the scope of its statutory jurisdiction one way one day and reverse itself the next (and that is exactly what *City of Arlington's* application of *Chevron* says it can), you might well wonder: where are the promised "clearly delineated boundaries" of agency authority? The Supreme Court once unanimously declared that a statute affording the executive the power to write an industrial code of competition for the poultry industry violated the separation of powers. *A.L.A. Schechter Poultry Corp. v. United States*, 295 U.S. 495, 537–42, 55 S.Ct. 837, 79 L.Ed. 1570 (1935). And if that's the case, you might ask how is it that *Chevron*—a rule that invests agencies with pretty unfettered power to regulate a lot more than chicken—can evade the chopping block.

> Even under the most relaxed or functionalist view of our separated powers some concern has to arise, too, when so much power is concentrated in the hands of a single branch of government. *See* The Federalist No. 47 (James Madison) ("The accumulation of all powers, legislative, executive, and judiciary, in the same hands . . . may justly be pronounced the very definition of tyranny."). After all, *Chevron* invests the power to decide the meaning of the law, and to do so with legislative policy goals in mind, in the very entity charged with enforcing the law. Under its terms, an administrative agency may set and revise policy (legislative), override adverse judicial determinations (judicial), and exercise enforcement discretion (executive). Add to this the fact that today many administrative agencies "wield[ ] vast power" and are overseen by political appointees (but often receive little effective oversight from the chief executive to whom they nominally report), and you have a pretty potent mix. . . . Under any conception of our separation of powers, I would have thought powerful and centralized authorities like today's administrative agencies would have warranted less deference from other branches, not more. None of this is to suggest that *Chevron* is "the very definition of tyranny." But on any account it certainly seems to have added prodigious new powers to an already titanic administrative state—and spawned along the way more than a few due process and equal protection problems of the sort documented in the court's opinion today . . . . It's an arrangement, too, that seems pretty hard to square with the Constitution of the founders' design and, as Justice Frankfurter once observed, "[t]he accretion of dangerous power does not come in a day. It does come, however slowly, from the generative force of unchecked disregard of the restrictions" imposed by the Constitution. *Youngstown Sheet & Tube Co. v. Sawyer*, 343 U.S. 579, 594, 72 S.Ct. 863, 96 L.Ed. 1153 (1952) (Frankfurter, J., concurring).

Asked at his confirmation hearings whether he could possibly be unbiased toward *Chevron*, Gorsuch insisted that he would keep as open a mind as possible, citing the experience of the judge for whom he clerked, Judge Sentelle on the D.C. Circuit, who once wrote an opinion that he himself later reversed in an *en banc* opinion. *Hearing on the Nomination of Neil Gorsuch to be an Associate Justice of the U.S. Supreme Court, March 21, 2017 Afternoon Session, Before the S. Comm. on the Judiciary*, 115th Cong. 39–40 (2017) (statement of J. Neil Gorsuch). When asked whether he would wish *Chevron* overturned, then-judge Gorsuch refused to answer. *Id.* at 39. When asked what could replace *Chevron*, Gorsuch explained that *Skidmore* deference would still exist. *Id.*

Chevron and the Regulatory State. Senator Hatch and other conservatives have introduced legislation to amend the Administrative Procedure Act to require that courts undertake *de novo* review of all relevant questions of law relating to agency rules. See, e.g., Separation of Powers Restoration Act of

2017, H.R. 76, 115th Cong. (2017); Separation of Powers Restoration Act of 2016, H.R. 4768, 114th Cong. (2016); Separation of Powers Restoration Act of 2016, S. 2724, 114th Cong. (2016). Why do you think conservative politicians care about *Chevron* and/or *Brand X*? Remember that the Obama administration was famously stymied in Congress and so moved a good deal of its agenda through the executive branch. Senator Franken attempted to link Judge Gorsuch's position to the Trump administration's claims to unravel the regulatory state. *Hearing on the Nomination of Neil Gorsuch to be an Associate Justice of the U.S. Supreme Court, March 21, 2017 Afternoon Session, Before the S. Comm. on the Judiciary*, 115th Cong. 57–58 (2017) (statement of Sen. Al Franken, Member, S. Comm. on the Judiciary (D-Minn.)). Do you think that reversing *Brand X* or even *Chevron* would have a significant effect on the regulatory state? Or is it less about the doctrine than the concurring opinion's dicta about the "titanic administrative state"?

Political Versus Judicial Decisionmakers. The *Gutierrez-Brizuela* concurrence finds fault with the Bureau of Immigration Appeals, as a "political" decisionmaker, putatively "overturning" the Tenth Circuit's legal interpretation. But doesn't this kind of "reversal" happen all the time? For example, anytime Congress dislikes a judicial interpretation of a statute, it can override that interpretation. See Matthew R. Christiansen & William N. Eskridge Jr., *Congressional Overrides of Supreme Court Statutory Interpretation Decisions, 1967–2011*, 92 Tex. L. Rev. 1317, 1317 (2014). Overrides are most common when a judicial ruling is politically salient: the more "political," the more likely the interpretation will be overruled. If that is true, what is the real problem with a political body reversing a judicial ruling? Are not such reversals more democratically legitimate? Then-Judge Gorsuch emphasizes the costs to individuals, namely due process and notice. Is the real problem in *Gutierrez-Brizuela* that the individual has been subject to the same kind of dangers that come from bills of attainder, U.S. Const. art. I, § 9, which is to say, a political body deciding individual cases? See *INS v. Chadha*, 462 U.S. 919 (1983) (Powell, J., concurring), Chapter 1, § 2(A).

Intention to Delegate. Are you persuaded by Gorsuch's critique that Congress has not delegated authority to an agency simply because the statute is ambiguous? What if, as *Mead* shows (Coursebook, p. 897), a specific section of the agency's organic statute delegated rule-making authority to the agency? Cf. Abbe R. Gluck & Lisa Schultz Bressman, *Statutory Interpretation from the Inside—An Empirical Study of Congressional Drafting, Delegation and the Canons—Part I,* 65 Stan. L. Rev. 901, 990–101 (2013) (finding that congressional drafters know of *Chevron* but leave ambiguities in statutes for many different reasons, but also largely agreeing with *Mead's* assumption about delegation when specific rule-making authority is given). Should a more specific grant of authority to implement the statute be more persuasive evidence of congressional delegation than the more general Administrative Procedure Act? Or does the more general APA control?

Is Chevron *Unintelligible*? Is *Chevron* so unintelligible as to violate the non-delegation doctrine? Since the New Deal, the Supreme Court has upheld entirely vague delegations and many believe any attempt by the Court to police the boundaries of delegation are long gone. Reconsider Chapter 1, § 2 (Note on the Nondelegation Doctrine, Coursebook, pp. 87–89). Could one find the delegation of legislative power "unintelligible" when it yields opposite results, that is when agencies change positions dramatically? Is that the precise opposite of the view that ambiguity amounts to a delegation of power from Congress to agencies?

BRETT M. KAVANAUGH, BOOK REVIEW, FIXING STATUTORY INTERPRETATION

129 Harv. L. Rev. 2118 (2016)

As this supplement went to press, President Trump announced that his nominee to fill retiring Justice Anthony Kennedy's seat on the Supreme Court would be Judge Brett M. Kavanaugh of the D.C. Circuit. Judge Kavanaugh has written many important statutory interpretation opinions, several of which are discussed in this Casebook. But recently, in a review of Judge Robert A. Katzmann's book, *Judging Statutes*, Judge Kavanaugh also offered some interesting new views about substantive canons and the *Chevron* doctrine, and what he views as the problematic way in which those rules turn on a threshold determination of ambiguity:

> In my view, one primary problem stands out. Several substantive principles of interpretation—such as constitutional avoidance, use of legislative history, and *Chevron*—depend on an initial determination of whether a text is clear or ambiguous. But judges often cannot make that initial clarity versus ambiguity decision in a settled, principled, or evenhanded way. The upshot is that judges sometimes decide (or appear to decide) high-profile and important statutory cases not by using settled, agreed upon rules of the road, but instead by selectively picking from among wealth of canons of construction. Those decisions leave the bar and the public understandably skeptical that courts are really acting as neutral, impartial umpires in certain statutory interpretation cases.
>
> *Id.* at 2118–2119 (citations omitted).

Judge Kavanaugh argues that "[u]nfortunately, there is often no good or predictable way for judges to determine whether statutory text contains 'enough' ambiguity to cross the line beyond which courts may resort to the constitutional avoidance canon, legislative history, or *Chevron* deference." *Id.* at 2136. The problem this produces is that "it is harder for judges to ensure that they are separating their policy views from what the law requires of them. * * * After nearly a decade on the bench, I have a firm sense that the clarity versus ambiguity determination—is the statute clear or ambiguous?—is too often a barrier to the ideal that statutory interpretation should be neutral, impartial, and predictable among judges of different partisan backgrounds and ideological predilections." *Id.* at 2128–39 & 2143.

Judge Kavanaugh suggests instead that:

> "[J]udges should strive to find the best reading of the statute. They should not be diverted by an arbitrary initial inquiry into whether the statute can be characterized as clear or ambiguous. . . . Instead, statutory interpretation could proceed in a two-step process. First, courts could determine the best reading of the text of the statute by interpreting the words of the statute, taking account of the context of the whole statute, and applying any other appropriate semantic canons of construction. Second, once judges have arrived at the best reading of the text, they can apply—openly and honestly—any substantive canons (such as plain statement rules or the absurdity doctrine) that may justify departure from the text. Under this two-step approach, few if any statutory interpretation cases would turn on an initial finding of clarity versus ambiguity in the way that they do now." *Id.* at 2144.

Possible implications of this approach, among others, Judge Kavanaugh writes, might be "jettisoning" the canon of constitutional avoidance (because it turns on a finding of ambiguity); legislative history would be useful to buttress a textual reading rather than be utilized as a relevant tool only when text is ambiguous; he would "toss" the *ejusdem generis* canon because it turns too much on judges having to "devise the connective tissue or common denominator"; eliminate the superfluities rule because it leads judges to read statutes atextually (giving different meanings to what really are repetitive words); and turn other substantive canons, such as the federalism canon, into plain statement rules (because plain statement rules are not triggered by a finding of ambiguity).

With respect to *Chevron*, Judge Kavanaugh, unlike Justice Gorsuch, is more of two minds about the benefits and drawbacks of the doctrine as currently applied:

> "*Chevron* makes a lot of sense in certain circumstances. It affords agencies discretion over how to exercise authority delegated to them by Congress * * * . The theory is that Congress delegates the decision to an executive branch agency that makes the policy decision, and that the courts should stay out of it for the most part * * * But *Chevron* has not been limited to those kinds of cases. It can also apply whenever a statute is ambiguous. * * * The key move from step one (if clear) to step two (if ambiguous) of *Chevron* is not determinate because it depends on the threshold clarity versus ambiguity determination." *Id.* at 2152.

Judge Kavanaugh's tentative suggestion is to look for evidence of delegation rather than ambiguity:

"To begin with, courts should still defer to agencies in cases involving statues using broad and open-ended terms like 'reasonable,' 'appropriate,' 'feasible,' or 'practicable.' In those cases, courts should say that the agency may choose among reasonable options allowed by the text of the statute. In those circumstances, courts should be careful not to unduly second-guess the agency's choice of regulation.* * * But in cases where an agency is instead interpreting a specific statutory term or phrase, courts should determine whether the agency's interpretation is the best reading of the statutory text. Judges are trained to do that, and it can be done in a neutral and impartial manner in most cases. *Id.* at 2153–54.

Judge Kavanaugh is far from the first to suggest problems with the ambiguity threshold, see, e.g., Ward Farnsworth et al., *Ambiguity about Ambiguity: An Empirical Inquiry into Legal Interpretation*,2 J. LEG. ANALYSIS 257 (2010) or the first to focus on delegation—indeed *Mead* is arguably a case about precisely that. Only time will tell how his potential presence on the Court will affect statutory and administrative law cases.

3. MORE COMPLEX AGENCY INTERPRETATION QUESTIONS IN THE MODERN ADMINISTRATIVE STATE

A. MULTIPLE AGENCIES AND STATE AND PRIVATE IMPLEMENTERS OF FEDERAL LAW

Page 939: Insert the following new case and notes before Subsection B:

THE MOST RECENT BATTLE BETWEEN STATUTES: LABOR LAW VERSUS THE FEDERAL ARBITRATION ACT

Like *Gonzales*, this labor law case brings together many of the themes of this book and raises questions about the future of *Chevron* deference.

EPIC SYSTEMS CORP. V. LEWIS

United States Supreme Court, 2018.
584 U.S. ____, 138 S.Ct. 1612, 200 L.Ed.2d 899.

JUSTICE GORSUCH delivered the opinion of the Court.

Should employees and employers be allowed to agree that any disputes between them will be resolved through one-on-one arbitration? Or should employees always be permitted to bring their claims in class or collective actions, no matter what they agreed with their employers?

As a matter of policy these questions are surely debatable. But as a matter of law the answer is clear. In the Federal Arbitration Act [FAA], Congress has instructed federal courts to enforce arbitration agreements according to their terms—including terms providing for individualized proceedings. Nor can we agree with the employees' suggestion that the National Labor Relations Act (NLRA) offers a conflicting command. It is this Court's duty to interpret Congress's statutes as a harmonious whole rather than at war with one another. And abiding that duty here leads to an unmistakable conclusion. The NLRA secures to employees rights to organize unions and bargain collectively, but it says nothing about how judges and arbitrators must try legal disputes that leave the workplace and enter the courtroom or arbitral forum. This Court has never read a right to class actions into the NLRA—and for three quarters of a century neither did the National Labor Relations Board. Far from conflicting, the Arbitration Act and the NLRA have long enjoyed separate spheres of influence and neither permits this Court to declare the parties' agreements unlawful.

I

[The Court granted certiorari to resolve a Circuit split on this question coming out of the Fifth, Seventh and Ninth Circuits. In each case, employees entered into agreements providing that they would arbitrate any disputes that might arise between them and their employers, and their agreements specified individualized arbitration, with claims "pertaining to different [e]mployees [to] be heard in separate proceedings." (slip op., at 3). In each case, the employees tried to bring their claims as class actions under Federal Rule of Civil Procedure 23.]

[The Ninth and Seventh Circuits refused to allow employers to compel arbitration. Specifically, they held that requiring individualized arbitration proceedings violates federal labor law—the National Labor Relations Act—by barring employees from engaging in the "concerted activit[y]," 29 U.S.C. § 157, of pursuing claims as a class or collective action. The Fifth Circuit adopted the opposite position. Another aspect of the case involved claims that the agency position had shifted. The National Labor Relations Board (NLRB) had not previously alleged a conflict between the FAA and NLRA. In 2012, the Board changed its position, a position subsequently disavowed by the Trump Administration.]

II

* * * Congress adopted the Arbitration Act in 1925 in response to a perception that courts were unduly hostile to arbitration. * * * Before 1925, English and American common law courts routinely refused to enforce agreements to arbitrate disputes. *Scherk* v. *Alberto-Culver Co.*, 417 U.S. 506, 510, n. 4 (1974). But in Congress's judgment arbitration had more to offer than courts recognized—not least the promise of quicker, more

informal, and often cheaper resolutions for everyone involved. *Id.*, at 511. So Congress directed courts to abandon their hostility and instead treat arbitration agreements as "valid, irrevocable, and enforceable." 9 U.S.C. § 2. The Act, this Court has said, establishes "a liberal federal policy favoring arbitration agreements." *Moses H. Cone Memorial Hospital v. Mercury Constr. Corp.*, 460 U.S. 1, 24 (1983) (citing *Prima Paint Corp. v. Flood & Conklin Mfg. Co.*, 388 U.S. 395 (1967)). * * *

Not only did Congress require courts to respect and enforce agreements to arbitrate; it also specifically directed them to respect and enforce the parties' chosen arbitration procedures. * * * Indeed, we have often observed that the Arbitration Act requires courts "rigorously" to "enforce arbitration agreements according to their terms, including terms that specify *with whom* the parties choose to arbitrate their disputes and *the rules* under which that arbitration will be conducted." *American Express Co. v. Italian Colors Restaurant*, 570 U.S. 228, 233 (2013) (some emphasis added; citations, internal quotation marks, and brackets omitted).

On first blush, these emphatic directions would seem to resolve any argument under the Arbitration Act. The parties before us contracted for arbitration. They proceeded to specify the rules that would govern their arbitrations, indicating their intention to use individualized rather than class or collective action procedures. And this much the Arbitration Act seems to protect pretty absolutely [citations omitted]. You might wonder if the balance Congress struck in 1925 between arbitration and litigation should be revisited in light of more contemporary developments. You might even ask if the Act was good policy when enacted. But all the same you might find it difficult to see how to avoid the statute's application.

Still, the employees suggest the Arbitration Act's saving clause creates an exception for cases like theirs. By its terms, the saving clause allows courts to refuse to enforce arbitration agreements "upon such grounds as exist at law or in equity for the revocation of any contract." § 2. That provision applies here, the employees tell us, because the NLRA renders their particular class and collective action waivers illegal. In their view, illegality under the NLRA is a "ground" that "exists at law . . . for the revocation" of their arbitration agreements, at least to the extent those agreements prohibit class or collective action proceedings.

The problem with this line of argument is fundamental. Put to the side the question whether the saving clause was designed to save not only state law defenses but also defenses allegedly arising from federal statute [citation omitted]. Put to the side the question of what it takes to qualify as a ground for "revocation" of a contract [citation omitted]. Put to the side for the moment, too, even the question whether the NLRA actually renders class and collective action waivers illegal. Assuming (but not granting) the employees could satisfactorily answer all those questions, the saving clause still can't save their cause.

It can't because the saving clause recognizes only defenses that apply to "any" contract. In this way the clause establishes a sort of "equal-treatment" rule for arbitration contracts [citation omitted]. The clause "permits agreements to arbitrate to be invalidated by 'generally applicable contract defenses, such as fraud, duress, or unconscionability.'" *Concepcion*, 563 U. S., at 339. At the same time, the clause offers no refuge for "defenses that apply only to arbitration or that derive their meaning from the fact that an agreement to arbitrate is at issue." *Ibid.* Under our precedent, this means the saving clause does not save defenses that target arbitration either by name or by more subtle methods, such as by "interfer[ing] with fundamental attributes of arbitration." *Id.*, at 344; see *Kindred Nursing, supra,* at ___ (slip op., at 5).

* * *

III

But that's not the end of it. Even if the Arbitration Act normally requires us to enforce arbitration agreements like theirs, the employees reply that the NLRA overrides that guidance in these cases and commands us to hold their agreements unlawful yet.

This argument faces a stout uphill climb. When confronted with two Acts of Congress allegedly touching on the same topic, this Court is not at "liberty to pick and choose among congressional enactments" and must instead strive "to give effect to both." *Morton v. Mancari*, 417 U.S. 535, 551 (1974). A party seeking to suggest that two statutes cannot be harmonized, and that one displaces the other, bears the heavy burden of showing "a clearly expressed congressional intention" that such a result should follow. *Vimar Seguros y Reaseguros, S. A. v. M/V Sky Reefer*, 515 U.S. 528, 533 (1995). The intention must be "clear and manifest." *Morton, supra*, at 551. And in approaching a claimed conflict, we come armed with the "stron[g] presum[ption]" that repeals by implication are "disfavored" and that "Congress will specifically address" preexisting law when it wishes to suspend its operations in a later statute. *United States v. Fausto*, 484 U.S. 439, 452, 453 (1988).

These rules exist for good reasons. Respect for Congress as drafter counsels against too easily finding irreconcilable conflicts in its work. More than that, respect for the separation of powers counsels restraint. Allowing judges to pick and choose between statutes risks transforming them from expounders of what the law *is* into policymakers choosing what the law *should be*. Our rules aiming for harmony over conflict in statutory interpretation grow from an appreciation that it's the job of Congress by legislation, not this Court by supposition, both to write the laws and to repeal them.

Seeking to demonstrate an irreconcilable statutory conflict even in light of these demanding standards, the employees point to Section 7 of the NLRA. That provision guarantees workers "the right to self-organization, to form, join, or assist labor organizations, to bargain collectively through representatives of their own choosing, and to engage in other concerted activities for the purpose of collective bargaining or other mutual aid or protection." 29 U.S.C. § 157. From this language, the employees ask us to infer a clear and manifest congressional command to displace the Arbitration Act and outlaw agreements like theirs.

But that much inference is more than this Court may make. Section 7 focuses on the right to organize unions and bargain collectively. It may permit unions to bargain to prohibit arbitration. But it does not express approval or disapproval of arbitration. It does not mention class or collective action procedures. It does not even hint at a wish to displace the Arbitration Act—let alone accomplish that much clearly and manifestly, as our precedents demand.

Neither should any of this come as a surprise. The notion that Section 7 confers a right to class or collective actions seems pretty unlikely when you recall that procedures like that were hardly known when the NLRA was adopted in 1935. Federal Rule of Civil Procedure 23 didn't create the modern class action until 1966; class arbitration didn't emerge until later still; and even the Fair Labor Standards Act's collective action provision postdated Section 7 by years. See Rule 23—Class Actions, 28 U. S. C. App., p. 1258 (1964 ed., Supp. II) * * *. And while some forms of group litigation existed even in 1935, Section 7's failure to mention them only reinforces that the statute doesn't speak to such procedures [citations omitted].

* * * Still another contextual clue yields the same message. The employees' underlying causes of action involve their wages and arise not under the NLRA but under an entirely different statute, the Fair Labor Standards Act. The FLSA allows employees to sue on behalf of "themselves and other employees similarly situated," 29 U.S.C. § 216(b), and it's precisely this sort of collective action the employees before us wish to pursue. Yet they do not offer the seemingly more natural suggestion that the FLSA overcomes the Arbitration Act to permit their class and collective actions. Why not? Presumably because this Court held decades ago that an identical collective action scheme (in fact, one borrowed from the FLSA) does *not* displace the Arbitration Act or prohibit individualized arbitration proceedings. *Gilmer v. Interstate/Johnson* (discussing Age Discrimination in Employment Act). * * *

Perhaps worse still, the employees' theory runs afoul of the usual rule that Congress "does not alter the fundamental details of a regulatory scheme in vague terms or ancillary provisions—it does not, one might say, hide elephants in mouseholes." *Whitman* v. *American Trucking Assns., Inc.*, 531 U.S. 457, 468 (2001). Union organization and collective bargaining in the workplace are the bread and butter of the NLRA, while the particulars of dispute resolution procedures in Article III courts or arbitration proceedings are usually left to other statutes and rules—not least the Federal Rules of Civil Procedure, the Arbitration Act, and the FLSA. It's more than a little doubtful that Congress would have tucked into the mousehole of Section 7's catchall term an elephant that tramples the work done by these other laws; flattens the parties' contracted-for dispute resolution procedures; and seats the Board as supreme superintendent of claims arising under a statute it doesn't even administer. Nor does it help to fold yet another statute into the mix.

[The Court then discussed its many recent arbitration-favoring precedents at length.] If all the statutes in all those cases did not provide a congressional command sufficient to displace the Arbitration Act, we cannot imagine how we might hold that the NLRA alone and for the first time does so today.

* * * With so much against them in the statute and our precedent, the employees end by seeking shelter in *Chevron*. Even if this Court doesn't see what they see in Section 7, the employees say we must rule for them anyway because of the deference this Court owes to an administrative agency's interpretation of the law. To be sure, the employees do not wish us to defer to the general counsel's judgment in 2010 that the NLRA and the Arbitration Act coexist peaceably; they wish us to defer instead to the Board's 2012 opinion suggesting the NLRA displaces the Arbitration Act. No party to these cases has asked us to reconsider *Chevron* deference. But even under *Chevron*'s terms, no deference is due. To show why, it suffices to outline just a few of the most obvious reasons.

The *Chevron* Court justified deference on the premise that a statutory ambiguity represents an "implicit" delegation to an agency to interpret a "statute which it administers." 467 U.S., at 841, 844. Here, though, the Board hasn't just sought to interpret its statute, the NLRA, in isolation; it has sought to interpret this statute in a way that limits the work of a second statute, the Arbitration Act. And on no account might we agree that Congress implicitly delegated to an agency authority to address the meaning of a second statute it does not administer. One of *Chevron*'s essential premises is simply missing here.

It's easy, too, to see why the "reconciliation" of distinct statutory regimes "is a matter for the courts," not agencies. *Gordon v. New York Stock Exchange, Inc.*, 422 U.S. 659, 685–686 (1975). An agency eager to advance its statutory mission, but without any particular interest in or expertise with a second statute, might (as here) seek to diminish the second statute's scope in favor of a more expansive interpretation of its own—effectively "bootstrap[ping] itself into an area in which it has no jurisdiction." *Adams Fruit Co. v. Barrett*, 494 U.S. 638, 650 (1990). All of which threatens to undo rather than honor legislative intentions. To preserve the balance Congress struck in its statutes, courts must exercise independent interpretive judgment. * * *

Another justification the *Chevron* Court offered for deference is that "policy choices" should be left to Executive Branch officials "directly accountable to the people." 467 U.S., at 865. But here the Executive seems of two minds, for we have received competing briefs from the Board and from the United States (through the Solicitor General) disputing the meaning of the NLRA. And whatever argument might be mustered for deferring to the Executive on grounds of political accountability, surely it becomes a garble when the Executive speaks from both sides of its mouth, articulating no single position on which it might be held accountable. * * *

Finally, the *Chevron* Court explained that deference is not due unless a "court, employing traditional tools of statutory construction," is left with an unresolved ambiguity. 467 U.S., at 843, n. 9. And that too is missing: the canon against reading conflicts into statutes is a traditional tool of statutory construction and it, along with the other traditional canons we have discussed, is more than up to the job of solving today's interpretive puzzle. Where, as here, the canons supply an answer, "*Chevron* leaves the stage." *Alternative Entertainment*, 858 F. 3d, at 417 (opinion of Sutton, J.).

IV

* * * The dissent imposes a vast construction on Section 7's language. *Post,* at 9. But a statute's meaning does not always "turn solely" on the broadest imaginable "definitions of its component words." Linguistic and statutory context also matter. We have offered an extensive explanation why those clues support our reading today. By contrast, the dissent rests its interpretation on legislative history. *Post,* at 3–5; see also *post,* at 19–21. But legislative history is not the law. "It is the business of Congress to sum up its own debates in its legislation," and once it enacts a statute "[w]e do not inquire what the legislature meant; we ask only what the statute means." *Schwegmann Brothers v. Calvert Distillers Corp.*, 341 U.S. 384, 396, 397 (1951) (Jackson, J., concurring) (quoting Justice Holmes). Besides, when it comes to the legislative history here, it seems Congress "did not discuss the right to file class or consolidated claims against employers." *D. R. Horton*, 737 F. 3d, at 361. So the dissent seeks instead to divine messages from congressional commentary directed to different questions altogether—a project that threatens to "substitute [the Court] for the Congress." *Schwegmann, supra*, at 396.

The policy may be debatable but the law is clear: Congress has instructed that arbitration agreements like those before us must be enforced as written. While Congress is of course always free to amend this judgment, we see nothing suggesting it did so in the NLRA—much less that it manifested a clear intention to displace the Arbitration Act. Because we can easily read Congress's statutes to work in harmony, that is where our duty lies. The judgments in *Epic*, No. 16–285, and *Ernst & Young*, No. 16–300, are reversed, and the cases are remanded for further proceedings consistent with this opinion. The judgment in *Murphy Oil*, No. 16–307, is AFFIRMED.

[We omit the concurring opinion of JUSTICE THOMAS]

JUSTICE GINSBURG, with whom JUSTICE BREYER, JUSTICE SOTOMAYOR, and JUSTICE KAGAN join, dissenting.

* * * The Court today subordinates employee protective labor legislation to the Arbitration Act. In so doing, the Court forgets the labor market imbalance that gave rise to the NLGA and the NLRA, and ignores the destructive consequences of diminishing the right of employees to band together in confronting an employer. [quotation marks and citation omitted]. Congressional correction of the Court's elevation of the FAA over workers' rights to act in concert is urgently in order. * * *

I

* * *

A

[Justice Ginsburg first details the history of tumultuous labor relations culminating in the FAA.] * * * Early legislative efforts to protect workers' rights to band together were unavailing. * * * As the Great Depression shifted political winds further in favor of worker-protective laws, Congress passed two statutes aimed at protecting employees' associational rights. First, in 1932, Congress passed the NLGA, which regulates the employer-employee relationship indirectly. Section 2 of the Act declares:

> "Whereas . . . the individual unorganized worker is commonly helpless to exercise actual liberty of contract and to protect his freedom of labor, . . . it is necessary that he have full freedom of association, self organization, and designation of representatives of his own choosing, . . . and that he shall be free from the interference, restraint, or coercion of employers . . . in the designation of such representatives or in self organization or in other concerted activities for the purpose of collective bargaining or other mutual aid or protection." 29 U.S.C. § 102.

Section 3 provides that federal courts shall not enforce "any . . . undertaking or promise in conflict with the public policy declared in [§ 2]." § 103.1 In adopting these provisions, Congress sought to render ineffective employer imposed contracts proscribing employees' concerted activity of any and every kind. See 75 Cong. Rec. 4504–4505 (remarks of Sen. Norris) ("[o]ne of the objects" of the NLGA was to "outlaw" yellow-dog contracts). While banning court enforcement of contracts proscribing concerted action by employees, the NLGA did not directly prohibit coercive employer practices. But Congress did so three years later, in 1935, when it enacted the NLRA. Relevant here, § 7 of the NLRA guarantees employees "the right to self-organization, to form, join, or assist labor organizations, to bargain collectively through representatives of their own choosing, *and to engage in other concerted activities for the purpose of collective bargaining or other mutual aid or protection.*" 29 U.S.C. § 157 (emphasis added). Section 8(a)(1) safeguards those rights by making it an "unfair labor practice" for an employer to "interfere with, restrain, or coerce employees in the exercise of the rights guaranteed in [§ 7].

C

* * * Although the NLRA safeguards, first and foremost, workers' rights to join unions and to engage in collective bargaining, the statute speaks more embracively. In addition to protecting employees' rights "to form, join, or assist labor organizations" and "to bargain collectively through representatives of their own choosing," the Act protects employees' rights "to engage in *other* concerted activities for the purpose of . . . mutual aid or protection." 29 U.S.C. § 157 (emphasis added). * * *

Suits to enforce workplace rights collectively fit comfortably under the umbrella "concerted activities for the purpose of . . . mutual aid or protection." 29 U.S.C. § 157. "Concerted" means "[p]lanned or accomplished together; combined." American Heritage Dictionary 381 (5th ed. 2011). "Mutual" means "reciprocal." *Id.,* at 1163. When employees meet the requirements for litigation of shared legal claims in joint, collective, and class proceedings, the litigation of their claims is undoubtedly "accomplished together." By joining hands in litigation, workers can spread the costs of litigation and reduce the risk of employer retaliation. See *infra,* at 27–28.

* * * Crucially important here, for over 75 years, the Board has held that the NLRA safeguards employees from employer interference when they pursue joint, collective, and class suits related to the terms and conditions of their employment. See, *e.g., Spandsco Oil and Royalty Co.*, 42 N. L. R. B. 942, 948–949 (1942) (three employees' joint filing of FLSA suit ranked as concerted activity protected by the NLRA); *Poultrymen's Service Corp.*, 41 N.L.R.B. 444, 460–463, and n. 28 (1942) (same with respect to employee's filing of FLSA suit on behalf of himself and others similarly situated), enf'd, 138 F. 2d 204 (CA3 1943); *Sarkes Tarzian, Inc.*, 149 N. L. R. B. 147, 149, 153 (1964) (same with respect to employees' filing class libel suit); *United Parcel Service, Inc.*, 252 N. L. R. B. 1015, 1018(1980) (same

with respect to employee's filing class action regarding break times), enf'd, 677 F. 2d 421 (CA6 1982); *Harco Trucking, LLC*, 344 N.L.R.B. 478, 478–479 (2005) (same with respect to employee's maintaining class action regarding wages). For decades, federal courts have endorsed the Board's view, comprehending that "the filing of a labor related civil action by a group of employees is ordinarily a concerted activity protected by § 7." *Leviton Mfg. Co. v. NLRB*, 486 F. 2d 686, 689 (CA1 1973); see, *e.g., Brady v. National Football League*, 644 F. 3d 661, 673 (CA8 2011) (similar). The Court pays scant heed to this longstanding line of decisions.

D

* * *

1

The Court relies principally on the *ejusdem generis* canon. See *ante,* at 12. Observing that § 7's "other concerted activities" clause "appears at the end of a detailed list of activities," the Court says the clause should be read to "embrace" only activities "similar in nature" to those set forth first in the list, *ibid.* (internal quotation marks omitted), *i.e.,* " 'self-organization,' 'form[ing], join[ing], or assist[ing] labor organizations,' and 'bargain[ing] collectively,' " *ibid.* The Court concludes that § 7 should, therefore, be read to protect "things employees 'just do' for themselves." . . . In any event, there is no sound reason to employ the *ejusdem generis* canon to narrow § 7's protections in the manner the Court suggests.

The *ejusdem generis* canon may serve as a useful guide where it is doubtful Congress intended statutory words or phrases to have the broad scope their ordinary meaning conveys. See *Russell Motor Car Co. v. United States*, 261 U.S. 514, 519 (1923). Courts must take care, however, not to deploy the canon to undermine Congress' efforts to draft encompassing legislation [citation omitted]. Nothing suggests that Congress envisioned a cramped construction of the NLRA. Quite the opposite, Congress expressed an embracive purpose in enacting the legislation, *i.e.,* to "protec[t] the exercise by workers of full freedom of association." 29 U.S.C. § 151; see *supra,* at 9.

* * *

3

* * * In a related argument, the Court maintains that the NLRA does not "even whispe[r]" about the "rules [that] should govern the adjudication of class or collective actions in court or arbitration." *Ante,* at 13. The employees here involved, of course, do not look to the NLRA for the procedures enabling them to vindicate their employment rights in arbitral or judicial forums. They assert that the Act establishes their right to act in concert using existing, generally available procedures, see *supra,* at 7, n. 3, and to do so free from employer interference. The FLSA and the Federal

Rules on joinder and class actions provide the procedures pursuant to which the employees may ally to pursue shared legal claims. * * *

4

* * * Further attempting to sow doubt about § 7's scope, the Court asserts that class and collective procedures were "hardly known when the NLRA was adopted in 1935." *Ante,* at 11. In particular, the Court notes, the FLSA's collective-litigation procedure postdated § 7 "by years" and Rule 23 "didn't create the modern class action until 1966." *Ibid.*

First, one may ask, is there any reason to suppose that Congress intended to protect employees' right to act in concert using only those procedures and forums available in 1935? Congress framed § 7 in broad terms, "entrust[ing]" the Board with "responsibility to adapt the Act to changing patterns of industrial life." *NLRB v. J. Weingarten, Inc.*, 420 U.S. 251, 266 (1975); see *Pennsylvania Dept. of Corrections v. Yeskey*, 524 U.S. 206, 212 (1998) ("[T]he fact that a statute can be applied in situations not expressly anticipated by Congress does not demonstrate ambiguity. It demonstrates breadth." (internal quotation marks omitted)). * * *

Moreover, the Court paints an ahistorical picture. As Judge Wood, writing for the Seventh Circuit, cogently explained, the FLSA's collective-litigation procedure and the modern class action were "not written on a clean slate." 823 F. 3d 1147, 1154 (2016). By 1935, permissive joinder was scarcely uncommon in courts of equity. See 7 C. Wright, A. Miller, & M. Kane, Federal Practice and Procedure § 1651 (3d ed. 2001). Nor were representative and class suits novelties. Indeed, their origins trace back to medieval times. See S. Yeazell, From Medieval Group Litigation to the Modern Class Action 38 (1987). And beyond question, "[c]lass suits long have been a part of American jurisprudence." 7A Wright, *supra*, § 1751, at 12 (3d ed. 2005); see *Supreme Tribe of Ben-Hur v. Cauble*, 255 U.S. 356, 363 (1921). * * *

II

* * *

A

1

Prior to 1925, American courts routinely declined to order specific performance of arbitration agreements. See Cohen & Dayton, The New Federal Arbitration Law, 12 Va. L. Rev. 265, 270 (1926). Growing backlogs in the courts, which delayed the resolution of commercial disputes, prompted the business community to seek legislation enabling merchants to enter into binding arbitration agreements. See *id.*, at 265. The business community's aim was to secure to merchants an expeditious, economical means of resolving their disputes. See *ibid.* The American Bar Association's

Committee on Commerce, Trade and Commercial Law took up the reins in 1921, drafting the legislation Congress enacted, with relatively few changes, four years later. See Committee on Commerce, Trade & Commercial Law, The United States Arbitration Law and Its Application, 11 A. B. A. J. 153 (1925).

The legislative hearings and debate leading up to the FAA's passage evidence Congress' aim to enable merchants of roughly equal bargaining power to enter into binding agreements to arbitrate *commercial* disputes. See, *e.g.,* 65 Cong. Rec. 11080 (1924) (remarks of Rep. Mills) ("This bill provides that where there are commercial contracts and there is disagreement under the contract, the court can [en]force an arbitration agreement in the same way as other portions of the contract."); Joint Hearings on S. 1005 and H. R. 646 before the Subcommittees of the Committees on the Judiciary, 68th Cong., 1st Sess. (1924) (Joint Hearings) (consistently focusing on the need for binding arbitration of commercial disputes).

The FAA's legislative history also shows that Congress did not intend the statute to apply to arbitration provisions in employment contracts. In brief, when the legislation was introduced, organized labor voiced concern. See Hearing on S. 4213 and S. 4214 before the Subcommittee of the Senate Committee on the Judiciary, 67th Cong., 4th Sess., 9 (1923) (Hearing). Herbert Hoover, then Secretary of Commerce, suggested that if there were "objection[s]" to including "workers' contracts in the law's scheme," Congress could amend the legislation to say: "but nothing herein contained shall apply to contracts of employment of seamen, railroad employees, or any other class of workers engaged in interstate or foreign commerce." *Id.,* at 14. Congress adopted Secretary Hoover's suggestion virtually verbatim in § 1 of the Act, see Joint Hearings 2; 9 U.S.C. § 1, and labor expressed no further opposition, see H. R. Rep. No. 96, 68th Cong., 1st Sess., 1 (1924).

Congress, it bears repetition, envisioned application of the Arbitration Act to voluntary, negotiated agreements. See, *e.g.,* 65 Cong. Rec. 1931 (remarks of Rep. Graham) (the FAA provides an "opportunity to enforce . . . an agreement to arbitrate, when voluntarily placed in the document by the parties to it"). Congress never endorsed a policy favoring arbitration where one party sets the terms of an agreement while the other is left to "take it or leave it." * * *

2

In recent decades, this Court has veered away from Congress' intent simply to afford merchants a speedy and economical means of resolving commercial disputes. . . . In 1983, the Court declared, for the first time in the FAA's then 58-year history, that the FAA evinces a "liberal federal policy favoring arbitration." *Moses H. Cone Memorial Hospital v. Mercury Constr. Corp.*, 460 U.S. 1, 24 (1983) (involving an arbitration agreement between a hospital and a construction contractor). Soon thereafter, the Court ruled, in a series of cases, that the FAA requires enforcement of agreements to arbitrate not only contract claims, but statutory claims as well. *E.g., Mitsubishi Motors Corp. v. Soler Chrysler-Plymouth, Inc.*, 473 U.S. 614 (1985); *Shearson/American Express Inc. v. McMahon*, 482 U.S. 220 (1987). Further, in 1991, the Court concluded in *Gilmer v. Interstate/Johnson Lane Corp.*, 500 U.S. 20, 23 (1991), that the FAA requires enforcement of agreements to arbitrate claims arising under the Age Discrimination in Employment Act of 1967, a workplace antidiscrimination statute. Then, in 2001, the Court ruled in *Circuit City Stores, Inc. v. Adams*, 532 U.S. 105, 109 (2001), that the Arbitration Act's exemption for employment contracts should be construed narrowly, to exclude from the Act's scope only transportation workers' contracts.

Employers have availed themselves of the opportunity opened by court decisions expansively interpreting the Arbitration Act. * * * It is, therefore, this Court's exorbitant application of the FAA—stretching it far beyond contractual disputes between merchants—that led the NLRB to confront, for the first time in 2012, the precise question whether employers can use arbitration agreements to insulate themselves from collective employment litigation. * * *

NOTES ON EPIC

1. *The Court's Invitation to Congress in* Epic. Justice Gorsuch's opinion suggests many times that people might not agree with the balance Congress struck with a forceful FAA, but emphasizes that the balance is not the Court's to decide. Justice Ginsburg more directly invites Congress to act in the very first paragraph of the dissent, urging: "Congressional correction of the Court's elevation of the FAA over workers' rights to act in concert is urgently in order." Her words bring to mind an earlier dissent of hers. In 2007, Justice Ginsburg penned an important dissent in an equal-pay sex discrimination case brought under Title VII of the Civil Rights Act, in which she similarly chastised the majority for its "cramped" statutory interpretation and then took the rather unusual step in her opinion of urging Congress directly to change the law. She wrote: "Once again, the ball is in Congress' court. As in 1991, the Legislature may act to correct this Court's parsimonious reading of Title VII." *Ledbetter v. Goodyear Tire & Rubber Co.*, 550 U.S. 618, 661 (2007) (Ginsburg, J., dissenting). It worked. Less than two years later, the Lily Ledbetter Fair Pay Act was the first law President Obama signed in office. Four years later, in 2013, Justice Ginsburg used nearly identical language to ask Congress again to override the Court's restrictive reading of Title VII. See *Vance v. Ball State University*, 570 U.S. 421, 470–71 (Ginsburg, J., dissenting). She was not answered that time. You already know from earlier in this chapter of the Casebook that congressional overrides of Supreme Court decisions are not as frequent as they once were. See Matthew R. Christiansen & William N. Eskridge Jr., *Congressional Overrides of Supreme Court Statutory Decisions,*

1967–2011, 92 Tex. L. Rev. 1317 (2014). Fewer overrides mean dissenting judges may have to find more dramatic ways to get Congress's attention—like Justice Ginsburg's direct requests. Is there a better way?

2. *Canons in* Epic. There is a lot going on in this opinion. Canons—including harmonization of statutes, repeals by implication are not favored, *ejusdem generis*, elephants in mouseholes, the canon favoring broad application of the FAA; the fight over legislative history use; and some negative words about *Chevron* deference from the majority. Which of these tools is most effective or important here? Was there really only one way to harmonize the statutes? In one of the decisions below, Chief Judge Diane Wood of the Seventh Circuit criticized the Fifth Circuit for not trying harder to harmonize the statutes:

> "Epic must overcome a heavy presumption to show that the FAA clashes with the NLRA. '[W]hen two statutes are capable of co-existence . . . it is the duty of the courts, absent a clearly expressed congressional intention to the contrary, to regard each as effective.' *Vimar Seguros*, 515 U.S. at 533 (applying canon to find FAA compatible with other statute) (quoting *Morton v. Mancari*, 417 U.S. 535, 551 (1974)). Moreover, '[w]hen two statutes complement each other'—that is, 'each has its own scope and purpose' and imposes 'different requirements and protections'—finding that one precludes the other would flout the congressional design. *POM Wonderful LLC v. Coca-Cola Co.*, 134 S.Ct. 2228, 2238 (2014) (internal citations omitted). . . . [Epic] makes no effort to harmonize the FAA and NLRA. When addressing the interactions of federal statutes, courts are not supposed to go out *looking* for trouble: they may not 'pick and choose among congressional enactments.' *Morton*, 417 U.S. at 551. Rather, they must employ a strong presumption that the statutes may both be given effect. See *id.* The savings clause of the FAA ensures that, at least on these facts, there is no irreconcilable conflict between the NLRA and the FAA." *Lewis v. Epic Systems Corp.*, 823 F.3d 1147, 1157–58 (7th Cir. 2016).

3. *The* Chevron *Discussion.* Look more closely at the majority's sweeping aside of *Chevron* deference. One problem for the Board, in the majority's view, is that the employees sought deference for the Board's interpretation not just for the NLRA but also for the Fair Labor Standards Act and for the FAA—two statutes not within the Board's area of expertise and one it does not administer. One takeaway from *Epic* on the *Chevron* front, then, in addition to hammering home Justice Gorsuch's general distaste for the doctrine, is that *Chevron* deference is going to be very difficult to come by when multiple statutes from different areas are involved. Moreover, the majority seemed highly suspicious of the Board's motivations, in terms of deferring to any attempt by the agency to reconcile the statute it does administer (the NLRA) with one it doesn't (here, the FAA): "An agency eager to advance its statutory mission, but without any particular interest in or expertise with a second statute, might (as here) seek to diminish the second statute's scope in

favor of a more expansive interpretation of its own—effectively bootstrap[ping] itself into an area in which it has no jurisdiction." (internal quotation marks omitted). The Court also undercut deference to the agency on account of its alleged change in position. But is that really fair? It was the Obama-administration DOJ that stepped in to defend the Board and helped to persuade the Court to grant certiorari. The Trump administration then refused to defend the agency's view, and the agency lost credibility at the Court as a result.

4. *The Court's (Not So) Stealth Role in Expanding the Scope of the FAA.* The most important canon in this case is probably the presumption in favor of broad interpretation of the FAA. But where did that canon come from? As Justice Ginsburg points out, this was a Supreme Court created canon of construction. Beginning in the 1980s, with the *Moses H. Cone* case discussed in the opinion, the Court announced "a liberal federal policy favoring arbitration agreements." *Moses H. Cone Memorial Hospital v. Mercury Constr. Corp.*, 460 U.S. 1, 24 (1983), and embarked on a decades-long project expanding the preemptive reach of the FAA in case after case and area into area. Jean R. Sternlight, *Panacea or Corporate Tool—Debunking the Supreme Court's Preference for Binding Arbitration*, 74 Wash. U. L.Q. 637 (1996). This makes *Epic*, at bottom, a "substantive canon" case—a case that turns on the Court's application of its own subject-matter-specific, normative canons. (One of us believes we should recognize and acknowledge this kind of substantive canon creation by the Court as the making of federal common law, notwithstanding the Court's claims to be only a passive actor vis-à-vis Congress. See Abbe R. Gluck, *The Federal Common Law of Statutory Interpretation*, 54 Wm. & Mary L. Rev. 753 (2013).) Perhaps Justice Ginsburg is right that the Court has dramatically overreached in its interpretation of the FAA over time. But if so, why hasn't Congress stepped in to change the Court's course? Is Congress too lazy or too gridlocked? Or might Congress be happy to let the Court do its dirty work rather than face disgruntled consumers and employees who would undoubtedly protest any legislative strengthening of the FAA? It is also a little hard to take Justice Ginsburg's criticism of the Court's expansion of the FAA canon completely seriously, given that some of the recent arbitration cases have not divided the Court much at all. For example, one of the most recent cases, which was discussed in the opinion, *Kindred Nursing*, 581 U.S. ___, 137 S.Ct. 1421 (2017), was decided 8–1, with only Justice Thomas in dissent. Perhaps the *Epic* dissenters are now having canon-creators' remorse.